MAN POWER
GOD POWER

By Phillip Elton Collins

THE ANGEL NEWS NETWORK

MAN POWER GOD POWER

Copyright © 2013 Phillip Elton Collins

All rights reserved. No part of this book may be used or reproduced by any means, graphic, electronic, or mechanical, including photocopying, recording, taping, or by any information retrieval system without the written permission of the author except in the case of brief quotations embodied in critical articles and reviews.

Contact: info@theangelnewsnetwork.com.
ISBN: 0983143374
ISBN 13: 9780983143376

DEDICATION

"MAN POWER GOD POWER"

Written the day of Robert Baker's memorial service in New York City.

Dear Robert,

The spiritual and energetic training and personal counseling I received under your master teachership as a trance channel of divine spirits continues to be the foundation of my personal and professional lives.

Because of the Reiki and Light Ascension Therapist training I received from you, I was able to establish a private therapy practice that has continued my growth and expansion within a clinical setting. With you as a role model, I became a channel of spiritual entities from the higher realms and was chosen to lead sacred journeys of my own. Through your inspiration, I became a teacher, founded a metaphysical school, cofounded the Angel News Network, and have written three books of my own. I already had a high profile, successful film production career before meeting you, but you allowed me to soar fully into my divine soul plan to contribute to Earth's Golden Age future.

But the greatest gift to me was the profound love I developed for you, Robert, the man. When I saw you struggling with issues of your own, it was easy to show my unconditional love for you. I am deeply saddened and somewhat angry that we shall no longer have your presence in this dimension. You are one of the most gifted messengers and teachers the world has ever seen. I know you are now with Archangel Gabriel off on some amazing projects. How fortunate I am that our paths were destined to meet. I know they will meet again.

Keep us posted on your continued adventures. This MAN POWER GOD POWER is a small tribute to you from below and above...

I Love You Robert,

Phillip

QUOTE

TAKING OUR POWER BACK

Once upon a time through
The abuse of our power
We lost our power
In order to regain it in a new hour,
Now.

We were connected to
ALL THERE IS,
But that wasn't enough.
Through freedom of will and choice
We thought our minds
Could make a better choice.

For eons in our "mind field,"
We've learned a lot about,
What is, through what is not.

Now the mind is returning
To the heart,
And we are ready
To start a new start.

Let us reconnect,
And correct and connect,
To ALL THERE IS, in effect.

Only through a renewed true connect
Can we correct our forgetfulness,
And create heartfelt consciousness.

Once awake,
We shall remember,
Who we are,
Why we are here,
And take our power back,
And never throw it back,
As true divine beings,
Being ALL THERE IS.

>SACRED POETRY & MYSTICAL MESSAGES, To Change Your Life and The World by Phillip Elton Collins.
>NOTE: The Poetry introducing each chapter in this book is also from SACRED POETRY & MYSTICAL MESSAGES

PREFACE

There is nothing I enjoy more than talking with divine messengers such as Ascendant Masters, Archangels, and the Mary energies. In fact, I have written three books filled with my questions and their answers, and they are at times lovingly integrated into this endeavor.

But nothing I have done prepared me for the sheer volume and brilliance of the wisdom contained within the pages of Man Power God Power. It's true that I participated as a questioner during the Divine Discussions included here and perhaps in a few other chapters, but Phillip has gone way beyond my meager contributions to present an astonishing compendium of divine wisdom that he personally channeled. If there is a more comprehensive source of teachings available from the higher dimensions, I have not seen it.

I am not a channel, so it takes me a long time to write a book, which is usually the product of my work as a spiritual interviewer and reporter. I kid Phillip all the time that it takes him a week to produce what it takes me a year to write. And not only is he fast, he produces great stuff.

So if you are eager to discover spiritual answers to almost any question—from who are we, and why are we here, to how should I be living my life, plus hundreds of other questions relating to your spiritual growth and development—you have found the perfect resource.

Randomly sample any chapter. I predict you'll be amazed at how the perfect teaching will present itself to you. What a gift! Thank you, Phillip.
Joel Dennis Anastasi
Cofounder Angel News Network

CONTENTS

ACKNOWLEDEMENTS xv
INTRODUCTION xvii
USING DISCERNMENT AND RESONANCE
    WITHIN OUR SPIRITUAL GROWTH xxi

1. Chapter I: Man Power God Power 1
2. Chapter II: Sense Of Self 11
3. Chapter III: Alchemy: Changing Yourself
   Into Gold 19
4. Chapter IV: Do We Have Wisdom Or Just
   Knowledge? 27
5. Chapter V: What Has Love Got To Do
   with It? 35
6. Chapter VI: A Mystical America 41
7. Chapter VII: Two Wondrous Way Showers:
   Transmuting I Am Christed Light 55
8. Chapter VIII: Wonders To Come 63
9. Chapter IX: Divine Inner Essence (Die) 71
10. Chapter X: America, Land Of Light 79
11. Chapter XI: What Now? I Am Presence
    Activation 87
12. Chapter XII: Enlightenment From
    The Intergalactic Federation 91
13. Chapter XIII: Archangel Actions 95
14. Chapter XIV: The Second Coming Has Come. 103
15. Chapter XV: Christ Consciousness Season 107

16. Chapter XVI: Call Upon Higher Realms Regularly 111
17. Chapter XVII: Message From The Two Mary's 115
18. Chapter XVIII: 12/21/12 Celebration 117
19. Chapter XIX: New Year's Day Message, Six-Sided Merkaba 121
20. Chapter XX: Relationship Of Death and Consciousness 125
21. Chapter XXI: Why Is The World Changing? ... 129
22. Chapter XXII: How To Manifest 133
23. Chapter XXIII: America, The Final Golden Age 137
24. Chapter XXIV: Ascended Master Support 139
25. Chapter XXV: Rejoice, Rejoice, Rejoice 143
26. Chapter XXVI: Intergalactic Federation with Mother Earth 147
27. Chapter XXVII: A Christmas Message From Your Heart 155
28. Chapter XXVIII: Inner Mastery God Power ... 159
29. Chapter XXIX: Final Golden Age 165
30. Chapter XXX: Great White Brotherhood 167
31. Chapter XXXI: Mother Love Defined 171
32. Chapter XXXII: There Are No Accidents 173
33. Chapter XXXIII: Intergalactic Federation with Gaia 12/21/12 177
34. Chapter XXXIV: Another Christmas Story and Mysteries Revealed 183
35. Chapter XXXV : Divine Discussions 193
Divine Discussions #1: Mode of Expansion; Adama, the Council of Twelve, and the Archangelic Realm of Uriel 193

Divine Discussions #2: Final Golden Age:
Archangel Michael, Adama, Lord
Sananda, and Saint Germain 209
Divine Discussions #3: Ascension Process, Giving
and Receiving; Great White Brotherhood,
Saint Germain 221
Divine Discussions #4: Powering Up
New Chakras; Keepers of Creation 230
Divine Discussions #5: Connection to Higher
Realms; Saint Germain 240
Divine Discussions #6: Golden Age of
Gaia; Mother Gaia, Adama 250
Divine Discussions #7: Temple of Sun,
Goddess of Liberty, Christ Consciousness,
I Am Presence, Archangel Michael 261

36. Chapter Xxxvi: Conversations with Adama,
High Priest Of Lemuria, Father
Of Humanity 269

37. Chapter XXXVII: Uploading Archangel Uriel .. 297
Uriel Message #1: My First Invitation
to Channel via Trance Channel Jeff Fasano 297
Uriel Message #2: Uriel, Yes, We Are
Working Together 301
Uriel Message #3: Our Planet's Soul Plan 303
Uriel Message #4: Who Are You?
Why Are You Here? 306
Uriel Message #5: Truth and Hope 308
Uriel Message #6: Your Planet and Love 310
Uriel Message #7: Higher Realm Messages and
Support 312
Uriel Message #8: Children of the
Awakened Heart 314

    Uriel Message #9: Moment of Now 317
    Uriel Message #10: Ready and Prepared 319
    Uriel Message #11: Beloved Channel 321
    Uriel Message #12: If Not Now, When? 323
    Uriel Message #13: Commitment 325
    Uriel Message #14: Choice 328
    Uriel Message #15: Peace 330
    Uriel Message #16: Chose Truth 332
    Uriel Message #17: Where Did You
    Come From? 334
    Uriel Message #18: Seasonal Shift 338
    Uriel Message #19: Lack of Self-Love 340
    Uriel Message #20: You Are Limitless Light 341
    Uriel Message #21: Talk about Love 343
    Uriel Message #22: Truth 346
    Uriel Message #23: Self-Empowerment 347
    Uriel Message #24: Keepers of the Earth 351

38. Chapter XXXVIII: Anna, Grandmother
    of Jesus 355
39. Chapter XXXIX: Bountiful Blogs 365
    Bountiful Blogs #1: Understanding Oneness 365
    Bountiful Blogs #2: One with All There Is 365
    Bountiful Blogs #3: Mother Love 366
    Bountiful Blogs #4: Most Important
    Part of You 366
    Bountiful Blogs #5: True Alchemy Defined 366
    Bountiful Blogs #6: University of
    the Spirit (US) 367
    Bountiful Blogs #7: Master Teachers 367
    Bountiful Blogs #8: Ownership 367
    Bountiful Blogs #9: Source of All Life 368
    Bountiful Blogs #10: Divine Love 368
    Bountiful Blogs #11: Consciousness=Creation . 369

Bountiful Blogs #12: The Light of
Source Never Fails..369
Bountiful Blogs #13: Gratitude 370
Bountiful Blogs #14: Purpose of Life.................370
Bountiful Blogs #15: To Know...........................370
Bountiful Blogs #16: Life as Perfection.............371
Bountiful Blogs #17: Discernment.....................371
Bountiful Blogs #18: Harmony and Peace.........371
Bountiful Blogs #19: Permanent Perfection......372
Bountiful Blogs #20: Human Monsters 372
Bountiful Blogs #21: At This Time.....................372
Bountiful Blogs #22: Reincarnation...................373
Bountiful Blogs #23: I Am Presence 373
Bountiful Blogs #24: A Real Master 373
Bountiful Blogs #25: Desire to Commit.............374
Bountiful Blogs #26: Uncontrolled Feelings......374
Bountiful Blogs #27: Being God.........................374
Bountiful Blogs #28: The Time Has Come 375
Bountiful Blogs #29: Student of Life 375
Bountiful Blogs #30: Equality,
Harmony, Balance 376
Bountiful Blogs #31: Relationship of Death and
We Consciousness...376
Bountiful Blogs #32: University of Spirit...........377
Bountiful Blogs #33: 2013 Soul Plan.................378
Bountiful Blogs #34: This Year of We
Consciousness 378
Bountiful Blogs #35: Portal Opening.................379
Bountiful Blogs #36: Personal Oath...................379
Bountiful Blogs #37: We Oath............................379
Bountiful Blogs #38: 12/12/12 through
12/21/12 380
Bountiful Blogs #39: 12/12/12 380

Bountiful Blogs #40: Ascended
Master Defined 381
Bountiful Blogs #41: Love 381
Bountiful Blogs #42: Love toward Source 382
Bountiful Blogs #43: Importance of Love 382
Bountiful Blogs #44: Divine Truth 382
Bountiful Blogs #45: Cosmic/Universal Law 382
Bountiful Blogs #46: Cosmic Colonic 383
Bountiful Blogs #47: Spiritual Alchemy 383
Bountiful Blogs #48: Reincarnation 383
Bountiful Blogs #49: Christ Consciousness 384
Bountiful Blogs #50: Atmosphere of Earth 384
Bountiful Blogs #51: Man: The Divine
Alchemy 385
Bountiful Blogs #52: Heart of the World 385

RESOURCES 387
ABOUT THE AUTHOR 389

ACKNOWLEDGEMENTS

To the diversified higher realms that connect with us every day. This endeavor is a very small tribute to your magnificent love and all you give to humanity each day. I receive you gratefully.

Once again playwright, actor, metaphysician, and social media publicist, Omar Prince, has taken a large outpouring from me and organized it and made this publication possible. He is indeed my guardian angel.

To my Angel News Network brothers Joel Anastasi (who edited much here) and Jeff Fasano, who amaze and delight me in the ways they just show up and lovingly share their talents and gifts to support mine. Throughout this book I shall be referring and quoting aspects from my brothers' divinely inspired books: *The Second Coming: The Archangel Gabriel Proclaims A New Age* (trance channeled by Robert Baker, author Joel Anastasi) and *Life Mastery: A Guide For Creating The Life You Want And The Courage to Live It* (trance channeled by Jeff Fasano, author Joel Anastasi). A companion to *Life Mastery* is *Journey of the Awakened Heart*, trance channeled and authored by Jeff Fasano. I am in deep gratitude for your permission to refer to your divine endeavors that not surprisingly integrate into this one. All our unique, diversified paths are heading to the same destination. When I refer to *The Second Coming*, I shall use the letters "TSC" and when referring to *Life Mastery*, I shall use "LM."

To all the Light Workers and Way Showers of the world who preceded me and who join me now in this expression of our often simultaneous soul plan endeavors.

To my husband, James Gozon. Through his unconditional love, he makes all probabilities and possibilities possible. He is my gift from God, myself.

And to myself for just showing up when my physical, emotional, and mental bodies did not always agree.

INTRODUCTION

The word "humanity" means "God being man," hu (God), man, ity (being). The purpose in us being here is to remember and know this truth. Not knowing and remembering that we are God experiencing itself has caused us great suffering in the past and still in the present. We have given our power away to others and allowed them to control and separate us from our cosmic reality. Now, as we approach the creation of a final Golden Age, the time has come for MAN POWER to become GOD POWER. Are you ready?

All previous Golden Ages (Lemuria, Atlantis, Mayan, Aztec, early Egypt, Greece, etc.) were created and supported by their connection to higher realms. These all fell as a result of their disconnection from whence they came. We are being given an opportunity to create a permanent Golden Age where we never lose our connection to our creators. They are here to guide, love, and support us into eternity.

The purpose of this book is to reveal as much truth as possible and inspire you to new heights, allowing this new truth to finally set us free. It appears humanity is ready in our consciousness to enhance the reality of truth rather than the illusion of non-truth. We no longer have to give our power away to a god to take care of us. As God, we can take responsibility for ourselves, as we continue to receive and accept wisdoms beyond the human mind...we simply cannot be/do it alone any more...we never could.

The teachings and messages in *Man Power, God Power* are intended to assist us in our personal and collective processes of ascension, moving into a higher frequency of existence. In this book, you can see yourself as your role as God (power). By being God, you are God's messenger. God gets to experience you in the beingness of you. Please know if you resonate with what is being said here, you will receive an energetic download. Many throughout the world are receiving these wisdoms. I salute you and humbly ask that I join all those who have preceded me, as you continue to inspire others and me.

What is contained throughout these pages is a collection of higher-realm wisdoms others and I have received and I am called upon to share, to balance giving and receiving. Again, I am one of many sharing and receiving such communications. There is nothing special about my or others' receiving these; we are simply showing the way for others who soon will be doing the same. We are all moving into telepathic equality, harmony, and balance.

If it resonates, randomly go through these teachings and allow your resonance and discernment to select the message/teachings for you in that divine moment of now. For those who decide to read all that is here, you will have the glorious gift that affected me greatly. We are all teaching what we need to learn.

Welcome to the creation of a new you and world of We Consciousness and wonder. You are here to transform from Man Power to God Power, which has always been inside of you. This will be done through the mastery of self, to be able to love you, others, your planet, and the entire cosmos. This is actually the activation of your divine soul plan!

My birthday is August 16th, the birth of The Harmonic Convergence, which gave humanity a chance to achieve a quantum catch-up in consciousness. This was the greatest birthday I could possibly receive and now join many in giving...

GOD POWER IS EVER PRESENT, ALL POWER, ALL LIFE, TRUTH AND LOVE OVER ALL AND ALL. "You are always in communication with God, because you are God and God is you," Archangel Gabriel, *The Second Coming* (TSC).

USING DISCERNMENT AND RESONANCE WITHIN OUR SPIRITUAL GROWTH

Many of us are now aware that our planet and species are involved within a shift like never before within our recorded history. This shift has happened before in past Golden Ages. Now the old paradigm of our governments, religions, corporations, and educational and medical institutions (which control us) are once again not meeting the needs of the people. And we are now waking up to this reality and becoming ready to commit to creating a new, true reality of equality and balance.

Many of the tools and teachings to effect change are coming from higher realms, not the human mind. This is a challenge for some and not so for many. The truth is that these higher forces have been supporting humanity for eons in moving us into a divine destination of unity and oneness for all. Are we ready to fully embody the truth that forces outside ourselves can and will assist us in creating a world that reflects a "universal wisdom" allowing us to move into an evolved reality? Through our discernment and resonance (how we feel about something, an internal gyro system) we can employ this higher support or not.

There are many human teachers and messengers receiving guidance from higher realms and bringing them to us. How do you know who is true and who to trust? Let's create some guidelines that can help us:

BEING THE MESSAGE: Pay attention if the one bringing higher truths to us appears to have a private and public persona that is not the same. There are those teaching one thing and being another. This deceit will no longer work in our world of faster cyber communication and transportation. Do they seem intent on selling you something, a remedy or workshop, at an inflated price that reflects their wounded ego? Then they just may be involved in their endeavor to be validated and gratified, not truly caring about helping. Being the message is essential.

BEING IN A PERSONAL PROCESS: It is essential that we be involved in a deep examination of the self through a process that supports your highest good. You can do this individually or with others. There are many metaphysical therapists trained to support this process.

But use your discernment and resonance and find the one that feels right for you. Our advancement is a process of inside out, not outside in. If someone tells you otherwise, use your discernment. If someone is attempting to fix you from the outside in—"take this, do that"—beware. You will apply what resonates on your own timetable and throw the rest out the window. Knowing who you are and why you are here within your talents and gifts and what brings you joy are fundamental to this process. We are all in an eternal process of growth and expansion. (See Chapter 8, WONDERS TO COME, and the twelve life lessons).

YOUR DIVINE BIRTHRIGHT: Know in your heart that whatever is happening within you and the world is a divine process within you taking place. No one else is "making" anything happen except you being supported by higher realms (whoever you chose to call them).

If someone else's names for these higher realms resonate, apply them. If not, don't. Our ability to grow and expand is a natural part of who we are. Awakening/remembering your divinity (not necessarily associated with any religion) is key. You are divinity expressing itself within each and every moment. Look at the world around you; "we the people" are demanding our divinity and equality.

SPIRITUALITY IN THE WAY: Let us be careful that "thinking" we are spiritual is special or makes us better than anyone else. As in many matters in humanity, spirituality can also be used to say we are special and know the true path to enlightenment. There are many paths to the same destination. We are all going to get "there"; it's just a matter of when and how we chose to learn. It's your divine right to be/to do so. Each unique one of us is on a specific point on our path. Let us accept this with compassion for self and others.

IT'S ALL ABOUT LOVE: We are all on this planet of "LOVERVERSITY" to learn to love self, which allows love of others. If we so chose, we are creating communities of equality, harmony, and balance that support a universal cosmic love. And if we so chose, we can and will create a new Golden Age of Oneness. What do you chose?

Chapter 1

*Twelve-Star Systems "seeded" plant Earth
Through these systems we gained great girth.*

MAN POWER GOD POWER

Inspired by Archangels Gabriel and Michael, and Ascended Master Saint Germain

In a world where a small percentage of the population continues to control the majority, perhaps it would be helpful to begin a discussion about power. We sense and know the 1 percent cannot and will not continue to control the 99 percent if we are to advance as a species and support the survival of our planet. There are many awakenings throughout the planet demonstrating self-em-power-ment. We all have experienced ourselves abusing power or being abused by it. Our incarnational cycles seem to be a good mix of both. This is how we learn what we came here to learn.

What is this thing called power? From whence did it come? What is the real purpose of power? Why do we often give our power away? How can we make better uses of God Power that has always lived inside us?

Now is the time to stop our inequality, separation, and confrontation forever by an improved understanding of power and making new choices concerning the constructive use of power and to stop giving it away to others.

"You have displaced your power and greatness. You have given yourself away and put yourself in the hands of others. It is time to go inside to find your authentic self, so that you may discover and be whom you are. You can deactivate the old conditioning of the nervous system and retrain it into the beingness of the self" (Archangel Michael, *Life Mastery*, LM).

The word "power" can excite or frighten us at the same time depending on which aspect of it you are experiencing. "A soon as you choose a figure to be your intervention between you and God to tell you who God is and to act as the intervener between you and God, you're in trouble" (Archangel Gabriel, TSC). A controlling, untruthful government or religion attempting to control its people scares us and we wish to move away from it.

"The earliest forms of religion were the earliest forms of government, the earliest ways of governing people so that you didn't have chaos. You could control people if you could make them fear God, or fear the king" (Archangel Gabriel, TSC). Does someone else have the power or do you? Man has remained in an infantile state of wanting that unconditional love of someone else to take care of him. Are you giving your power away (a core issue with humanity) to beliefs or morals?

Most religions and governments are based upon a system of morality or moralism. "Moralism is a system that is based upon reward and punishment, right and wrong, good and bad. It's a system based upon duality; it's not a system based upon conscience. When you develop a conscience, all individuals are responsible for themselves. They are responsible for their acts. They are responsible for their development through trial and error. They are responsible for their development through their ability to experience remorse and to correct their mistakes and grow and discover from them and move on. They are able to take responsibility for their actions and the consequences of their actions. The consequences of their actions are not punishable, they are responded to. And through the education provided by the trial and error of their mistakes, they learn and grow. They cease to make those mistakes and they become more" (Archangel Gabriel, TSC). And they have not given their power away.

"In a system of right and wrong, a system of moralism, you control people in a system that has only one choice available at any time. And that is the right choice. If you make the wrong choice, you are damned, bad, punishable" (Archangel Gabriel). And your power is taken away.

"Do not give your power to beliefs. Beliefs are not truth. A belief is a doctrine. Belief is dogma. It creates a limited frozen frame that can never grow. The truth is infinite. It is ever expanding. Do you not think that God, the Creator, is in a process of discovery and expansion all of the time in His infinite knowledge of His being just as you are in a constant process of expansion and discovery of the knowledge of the truth of your being?" (Archangel Gabriel, TSC).

Perhaps power is best defined depending on how it is used. As stated above, power can take many forms. Abuses of power are the destructive uses of power and ultimately destroy, while constructive uses of power create, connecting to its true purpose.

As within the structure of human beings, the primary types of power are emotional, mental, physical, and spiritual. These types of power can be electromagnetic, nuclear, chemical, and cosmic/universal. Humanity is not ready to use and be able to control most of these types of power. And we are experiencing the consequences of that lack of knowledge within our current events. Past Golden Ages, particularly Atlantis saw the demise of their civilizations through the misuse of these powers through their separation from where these powers came. The human mind came to believe it was separate from the universe, from God.

As we are beginning to learn with all things, all power is interrelated. Some is dynamic and can release itself, some can be stored and used later, and some is simply static. The two universal types of power are divine, God Power, and human, Man Power.

"In the beginning there was the word," has resounded throughout our religious/spiritual history. The power of a godly-intended word or our spoken or unspoken "thought-words" has proven to be the most powerful force in the universe. We think, we feel, we speak and an action is creation. The power of the word has always changed the course of our lives and history.

"You are ready to be the creators. You are ready to be the administrators. You are ready to exercise the power of the God within, but first you must realize that that is so. And the only way you can realize that is coming to peace with the inner workings of your own being and being able to know that reality is so, within your own heart and with the experience of that heartfelt knowing" (Archangel Gabriel, TSC).

Whether constructive use or destructive abuse, we are once again remembering how powerful are our words. We are knowing once again we are creators through our self-em-POWER-ment.

It is easy for us to complicate something that is simple. We do it all the time through our attachments/addictions to drama and glamour. It is more difficult for us to simplify something that is truly complicated. In a further attempt to simplify the understanding of the true nature of power, it is important to know that the components of humanity (emotional, mental, physical, and spiritual) are the cause and effect of power. How we "give and receive" power depends on our consciousness. The intention of these teachings is to achieve enough awareness in order to not give your power away to a representative to decide your reality.

Depending upon our ego-defended wounds, our emotional, mental, physical, and spiritual bodies become the etheric "networkers of consciousness" as receivers of the charge of power released through an electronic-magnetic network. "We are living in a period of consciousness that breaks down all old forms that are not based upon equality, equanimity, and balance where the highest spiritual good is concerned. Therefore it breaks down all that is in duality. You must first let go and make space before you can build a new house" (Archangel Gabriel, TSC). The further study of alchemy and sacred geometrics can assist in better understanding this network.

Our ability to be conscious (aware) and perceive is the activation point of power's release/use. Few of us are aware of the degree of power that God has gifted humanity merely through our very consciousness. We actually know we are here, something we take for granted each and every moment. We can ask, "Who am I? Why am I here? What is the purpose of my life?" Other life forms on our planet do not appear to be able to ask these questions. But perhaps they can?

This allows us to reach a deeper understanding of power; to allow the purpose of our life to unfold in order to focus on the activation of our divine soul plans (our purpose in being here).

It is the intent of the God Powers that created us that we maintain and sustain as much sovereignty over our individual, unique self, as possible. When this happens, and it is our divine birthright that it does, you know the value, meaning, and purpose of the power of self-mastery. "Know thy self" and "to thy own self be true" may be two of the most powerful phrases ever uttered. Although we surely live in a 3-D human consciousness, let us not be victims of it by being "in" it rather than "of" it. You alone can govern your own world through the right use of power through transmuting into self-em-POWER-ment: to be the power to love you and mirror that out into the world; that is the mission of this world.

Throughout the universe, there is a constant exchange/coexistence where the energies of the macrocosm and microcosm do a divine dance as one. We truly are one. Through humanity's freedom of choice and will, we often find an abuse of this daring dance within humanity. Some individuals watch the abusers of others and then respond with an equal or greater abuse of power. Others often, consciously or not, create destructive thoughts and actions.

"There are extremes of duality acting out in the physical objectification of the world. They are simply mirroring what is going on inside the wounded child inside each and every one of you. What happens is the collective is mirrored in the microcosm. As between matter and spirit, between the inner child and the adult, between the divine feminine and the divine masculine, until soul and spirit are joined together in the physical, you will see duality (the abuse of power) acted out in the world" (Archangel Gabriel, TSC).

Let us now list some of the causes and abuses of power (effect) that actually become discharged and stored into our earthly atmosphere and affect our weather, geological activities, and historical events. Humanity like advanced civilizations, will soon become aware of this and better be able to control such events.

People can actually become unknowing agents, in their ignorance, fear, and doubt, of negative qualities and amplify them and discharge them. At first glance, these causes of the abuses of power may seem quite unimportant, but look deeper...

Let's begin with simply being bored; this is a detached state of being where everything seems somewhat hopeless and the individual cannot see beyond his or her own "narcissistic me" into higher realms of existence. In this state of giving your power away (a core issue for humanity), the life force weakens and other forces can enter and control you. When humanity knows that life is governed by the order of the universe or governed by higher realms, we are going to be capable of using our God Power.

Secondly, there is unhappiness through a lack of ownership and self-deceit and denial of the deceit. Thus, an individual's dissatisfaction is created. These people wish to blame and shame and judge others rather than taking responsibility/ownership for their own lack and limitation.

This often occurs on an unconscious level and creates future imbalances of positive energy/power. Taking ownership of what we create in our lives, thus recognizing our power will set us free from the imbalance and abuse of power.

And do not forget to include the many experiences of fear (an absence of love). The individual is not seeing himself or herself good enough or worthy enough to receive the bounty of life. Some simply withdraw from the world in depression, sometimes becoming anxious. Others may tend toward aggressive behavior and react; terrorism is an extreme expression of this behavior that we are seeing in our world today. "The terrorist is at home in our backyard. He is the inner child who is wounded. That is the terrorist. It is coming closer and closer until you cannot ignore it. It is showing you there is not separation that you are your brother's keeper. Do unto others, as you would have them do unto you. Love one another as yourself" (Archangel Gabriel, TSC).

The vibration of doubt originates from fear and a lack of self-knowledge/self-mastery that can reflect out to others in one's life. FEAR, DOUBT, AND IGNORANCE of self and others have been called the "monsters of mankind" and will diminish and corrupt power absolutely.

Needless to say, there are many other reasons for the abuse of power. These stated here are some of the core issues. Simply put, humanity's abuse of power is usually a result of our ignorance and lack of understanding ourselves and the cosmic laws governing the flow and use of energy. This wisdom will soon be given to us again from higher realms in order to improve our lives and rebalance our use of power. Then through the conscious constructive use of energy, we shall begin to build communities of equality, harmony, and balance, which is our divine destiny as we now enter a final Golden Age. Through Man Power becoming God Power, we shall become free in our final epoch.

Please note the science of karma is intentionally being minimized in this brief discussion of power. It would take another book to explain the cycles of reincarnation that affect the return of abused power to those who misuse it. When humanity further awakens, the interrelationships of karma will be fully understood and applied. The sooner we awake, the better.

But please know, dear ones, that karma is a vital element, and as someone once said, "karma can be a bitch (tough way to learn)." Trust and know the universe knows exactly how to balance itself. Someday we shall know this and not need Man Power laws.

During this final two-thousand-year epoch, we shall once again know that all life is one and an abuse or right use of power by all affects all. This final two-thousand-year cycle is the ascension evolution that every solar system and every planet in matter goes through at one point in its evolution. Look up in the night sky; all those stars were once planets like us that have returned to the light. And so shall we...

Beloved Souls, God Power is encoded within the hearts of each of us. The right use of God Power will ensure our freedom from the misuse of Man Power, which has kept us prisoner long enough. Are we ready for not an increase in Man Power but a better understanding of how to use our God Power in order to finally become the immortal beings of light we are?

Place your hand upon your heart, dear ones. With each beat of your heart that you feel, you are experiencing the essence/presence of your God Power flowing throughout you, the solar system, the galaxy, and the universe...the power of your divine soul plan developing...Man Power is ready for its God Power awakening and it has surely begun...

Chapter II

*To commit to a PERSONAL PROCESS
Of an in-depth examination of self
To know how self relations
Effects all relations and nations.*

SENSE OF SELF

Inspired by Archangels Gabriel and Michael, and Ascended Master Saint Germain

"Know thy self" and "To thy own self be true" may be some of the wisest words ever thought, felt, and spoken. Many teachings from the higher realms are reminding us that the greatest need within humanity is to have the awareness and loving support of a SENSE OF SELF. This will allow the individual to know he or she is an aspect of the universal whole. In effect, the Self and Universe belong to each other, as One. We have been asleep a long time. It's all about becoming conscious. Time to wake up...

As students of truth, there is nothing more important than understanding and accepting Oneness. All of our separations and duality and confrontation have been a result of absorbing "me" into the "we." It is time for our belief systems within our religions, corporations, and governments to support We Consciousness coming forward. And no longer bringing the unhealed me into the conscious, we. Or we will not be happy with the consequences.

Once we move from Man Power to God Power, we can reveal ourselves anew, open to give and receive love in balance, feel our feelings, no longer shame, blame, and judge and make new choices to change everything. "In effect we are moving from childhood to adulthood within our evolutionary process from Man to God power. All the words here are about your relationship with self and moving that newness out into your world, solar system, galaxy and universe" (Archangel Michael, LM).

Few have realized or accepted that God is consciousness (and consciousness is energy and energy knows no distance nor time) and as consciousness he or she is life, intelligence, intention, and love manifested in a diversity of multi-dimensions—this 3-D form being one of many.

In effect, God is an impersonal personality integrating the consciousness of being through his or her Divine Self being you and I. We are all in the process of connecting with multi-dimensions and our God Power-selves; thus, eternally connecting and expressing with the universal consciousness of God. Are we ready to clear and cleanse the separation of the past and present and move into the highest aspects of our divine selves, our true sense of self?

"God is undifferentiated consciousness until it connects with a soul like you. As has been said many times and will be many more until you know it, the purpose of all physical evolution is for the purpose of learning how to love. Your individual part of God is learning to become experiential" (Archangel Gabriel, TSC).

Our thoughts and feelings make up much of our sense of self and our created reality and can both disconnect or connect us with our divine self. Mastering the energies of our thoughts and feelings through We Consciousness is a sure pathway to self-mastery and freedom from self. Our misuse of energies through our thoughts and emotions and their consequences are legendary. We have kept ourselves and our world in prison to the point of near destruction. Are you ready for something else? I am.

"Emotion is the expression of the feeling. The emotion is how the feeling moves. Each feeling, if you accept it, will allow another feeling underneath it to unfold. As a matter of fact all of your feelings are going on simultaneously. When you resist one, you block all of them" (Archangel Gabriel, TSC).

As we transcend from the human to the divine in the graduated levels of our consciousness, it is time to take personal responsibility/ownership for changing the imbalanced situations/conditions within our sense of self-moving into our God Power-selves. This requires shifting our wounds and ego defenses in the mental body and the unhealed emotions in the emotional body into the heart space that allows the transmuting of anything less than love.

Through a higher sense of self, it is time to release any belief systems acquired through family, environment, attachment/addiction to persons, places, things in our race, sexuality, religion, and national or family origin that do not serve our highest good and that of others. This includes

13

equality, harmony, and balance for all, thus reflecting humanity's true sense of self, our God Power-Self.

When this is in place, we shall have the foundation of building our final Golden Age within ourselves first and then the world. We shall be conscious and present. "Enlightenment is being in the now, fully present" (Archangel Gabriel, TSC).

This new world of equality, harmony, and balance is mirroring the truth: it is a loving and truthful universe, thus God is always loving and truthful. All non-truths have risen from humanity's misinterpretation and misunderstanding of true love and equality. This reflects the relationship with self, the sense of self.

Are we ready to release false teachers that have controlled us far too long? Each person must decide this for himself or herself, through his or her sense of self and freedom of will and choice. Your resonance (how you feel about it), your internal gyro system, and discernment will direct you.

In strengthening our desire to be free of self throughout the world, a new humanity and new paradigm of Oneness is being created: a golden human for the Golden Age. This is the reason we are here to create a new spiritual humanity reborn through a new sense of self-love.

Then through the death of the weary, wounded old, we shall create a new world becoming the daughters and sons of Creation/God Power.

The new spiritual humanity, connected to higher self and consciousness, is the transmuting- being, transformed by the intention of change, through the science of the sense of self. Then each day we shall have an opportunity to live free of self. Then, the planetary/God self, the transformed sense of self, will network throughout the rebooting portals and vortices of the world reviving Mother Earth and humanity alike. From the breakdown of the old will come the breakthrough of the new. We shall no longer be separated, but all of and in the oneness of creation.

God has only been separate because we have been separate: "You've created separation; therefore, God couldn't possibly be a part of you. Now as you come into this age, you begin to awaken body consciousness as the vibration rises in the body (moving from carbon to crystalline). And now the possibility arises that you can detect and awaken God Power within yourself. You can begin to realize yourself as God, as God beings" (Archangel Gabriel, TSC).

The meaning, value, and purpose of our planet's divine soul plan is to understand and transcend all the wounds of human emotions, intelligence, and memory of the past and present. Then we shall be in world service to creation and life. And if we so choose, we shall be filled with wonder and the expectancy of constant growth and expansion in joining the sheer bliss of being God Power during this two-thousand-year cycle into our final Golden Age.

It is the love of the consciousness of God to give freely. Are we ready to receive it? Only we have been standing in the way for eons. We shall create a higher way of life where competition, deceit, denial of deceit, inequality, war, and disease are wounds of the past.

We shall know we are never alone in the constant presence of Creation/God Power. We shall know we came forth from Creation through cosmic love, and will return to that love by becoming it through our God Power Oneness/ We Consciousness. We cannot do this alone.

Through our divine evolutionary process of spirit to matter and matter to spirit, density to crystalline, it is our divine destiny to become consciousness and be self-mastered, as long as we do not forget from whence we came. It was this forgetting that caused the demise of all past Golden Ages. We cannot evolve alone. Spirit is not matter, and we in matter need spirit.

Cosmic Law states ascension is freedom: that which descends into density must and will manifest its freedom, thus ascending back to that Source from whence it came. This is the reason there are more of us on the planet than ever before. The billions of us aren't here because conditions are better. We all chose to be here to fulfill our original reason for being on this planet in accordance to cosmic law and our soul plans...to move into a higher realm of existence.

"Ascension is giving up the separated self. That's all it is. All you're talking about in awakening the soul is giving up the separated self, giving up your fight for separation and acknowledging your unity within" (Archangel Gabriel, TSC).

Much of humanity is waking up to the truth that we are not here just to work, reproduce, and die. We are part of a universal plan with a higher purpose.

The supreme purpose of Creation is for each of us to know that we are eternal divine beings of light intended to be and explore the universe and Creation through our God Power. This is our true sense of self.

The ascension process, moving to a higher realm of existence, will come when the majority of humanity's energy and sense of self have been transmuted into conscious purpose and our hearts join with Creation/God Power; then what descended will ascend back into the Light, as the god-sense of self.

"God is all there is. God is ever present in everything that lives. God is the very force of life itself. How can you divorce yourself from God unless you divorce yourself from the force of life? You can distort the force of life. You can separate your consciousness from it to some degree through fear and through the machinations of your personality and your belief in separation and isolation, but you still cannot divorce yourself from God" (Archangel Gabriel, TSC). Because you ARE God.

Chapter III

*Cast out all doubts and fear,
Just know in your heart
Your creation is near.*

ALCHEMY: CHANGING YOURSELF INTO GOLD

Inspired by Archangel Gabriel and Michael and Saint Germain

"You are starting the process of the fire, the burning away of the dross, the alchemical moment of the transformation of lead into gold. The lead is the old reality of duality. And that is being transformed. The gold is the new you. That changes and shifts you into the next millennia, the millennia of quantum shift and transformation from the destruction of the old. This process now is taking place" (Archangel Gabriel, TSC).

From the unknowing and nothing comes everything. This is so difficult for the human mind to comprehend and accept. But your heart knows this already. The alchemist needs to develop a 'heart-trust' of this truth in order to create out of what appears no-thing, for, in reality, there is nothing. There is only everything! And God, you, is ALL THERE IS.

True alchemy—mastery of self and ALL THERE IS—can only come as a result of your divine connection to Source/God Power, the original Creator of All who dwells in no-thing. For in nothing, the void, lies all probabilities and possibilities. It's difficult for the human mind to wrap itself around this truth. "You're remembering through one fragment of your being when, in truth, you are the wholeness of being. You are God. The container you've chosen has chosen one fragmentary aspect of God to experience, one speck in the cosmos, one cell in the universe" (Archangel Gabriel, TSC).

If you are merely interested in changing a base metal into gold, what is about to be said is not for you. But if you are interested in transforming yourself into gold, well that's another matter that will allow you to truly transform matter, for it only matters in matter.

The ascended masters of alchemy call alchemy the "true science of spirit." When you know yourself and achieve self-mastery, you can master creation. For alchemy is simply the law of the transfer of energy, which you are. It is the impersonal law that nothing can create something.

It's the way God Power created everything. This law is fueled by a "constructive consciousness" that only serves the highest good of all. Just one iota of negativity or intention to harm will prevent alchemy, thus creation. Ignorance, fear, and doubt will prevent alchemy. Attempts to abuse the laws of creation only prevent creation. Since true alchemy begins with self, let's now factor in the individual and his or her role in the use of alchemy.

Alchemy is the science of the enlightened individual who has come to know himself, to master self and to see himself as a reflection and an aspect of God Power, someone willing to activate his soul plan and to manifest his reason to be here. (Google *Life Mastery: A Guide For Creating The Life You Want And The Courage to Live It* and *Journey of the Awakened Heart*). This is an ever-evolving process that does not develop overnight. It requires consistent commitment and support by your higher God Power-Self, higher realms, your I AM Presence, and the Christ Consciousness. This commitment and support will in time produce a real spiritual alchemist.

"The Christ Consciousness is the awareness and it is the job, so to speak, of the Christ to awaken the awareness of the soul. The Christ (soul awakening) Consciousness is the ascendant master who awakens the awareness of the soul in physical matter" (Archangel Gabriel, TSC). "All matter is held in place by the vibration frequency of consciousness."

Some wonderful examples of successful alchemists are Jesus, the Christ, and the many ascended masters (including Saint Germain, who is also guiding this teaching) who all walked this Earth perfecting their alchemy prior to ascending to higher realms. Studying *The Seven Sacred Flames* will give you the history of these marvelous masters of alchemy and their many incarnations and contributions to humanity.

The concept and reality that nothing becomes something is challenging. Let us express it another way to allow us to integrate this cosmic truth. Can you see nothing as simply unexpressed energy, since everything is energy, expressed or not? The void is filled with electromagnetic energy ready to be converted. True alchemy—employing universal laws and spiritual science—cannot yet be measured with the "natural" scientific tools we now have. We shall have these tools someday, but, for now, the true alchemist relies on the relationship with self in order to connect with the awesome laws and energy of creation.

"God is complete within itself. But by the very nature of its creation and the exploration and evolution of that creation, it gets to experience all parts of itself by default. The fact that God is all that is and by each and every aspect of creation fulfilling the task of being its individual expression of that being, being you knowing itself as God" (Archangel Gabriel, TSC).

As humanity raises their consciousness, more and more of these laws of creation will be revealed. If we all knew these laws now, that could be a dangerous thing for our planet and for humanity with our present state of awareness. Atlantis learned this the hard way when its civilization was destroyed because it was not able to use these laws for the good of all.

"God gets to experience all parts of itself and each creation of God gets to experience the whole. So one serves the other serves the other. This is the force of love. That is learning how to love. By learning about all the different infinite aspects of possibilities of creative expression of being of which God is made up, man (power) gets to experience himself as God (power), and God gets to experience all that He or She is made up of. And that is why God is love. For the purpose of creation is to love" (Archangel Gabriel, TSC).

It would be good for the aspiring alchemist to realize that this true spiritual science is gifted to the individual who knows from where the wisdom came. The meaning, value, and purpose of alchemy are to teach humanity a way back home to where we came. We are all working our way back home. (Google *Coming Home To Lemuria: An Ascension Adventure Story*.)

So many teachings coming to humanity now are arriving at the same destination: our Source, our home. Once back home, the fulfillment of our immortal destiny can really begin in service to Source through divine alchemy.

On our way home "one third will leave the planet. One third will carry on as they were before, struggling and resisting and fighting because they love war so much and they basically have little wisdom. But they have the capacity to make world-changing decisions and the capacity to fight. Then the third group are those who are bringing about that golden light of the soul"(Archangel Gabriel, TSC). Which third are you?

Earlier alchemy was originally intended to be a way of enriching individual abundance by teaching the techniques of changing base metals into gold, thereby freeing many under the control of the few. Even though the few continue to control the many today, a new sense of freedom is at play now during these unique opportunities of ascension (moving into higher realms of existence that was not available in the past).

Today, the transformation into gold is represented by your self-knowledge and self-mastery connecting you with your divine soul plan—knowing who you are, why you are here, and moving through your talents and gifts into joyful unity/oneness/we consciousness. That's the real gold! You will then know you are the alchemist who will determine the design of your manifestation.

The only way the alchemist can be successful is to know it is your God Power-given freedom to create through your freedom of choice and will (which no force can take away). As Beings of Creation—and being creators—we must create with no restrictions or restraints by anyone or anything. Once you know this, you are ready for further studies in alchemy that will allow you to manifest for God and humanity (world service) that which serves the highest good of all. When the student is ready, the teacher will appear. The intention of this book is to be part of your process.

"As a spiritual alchemist you will be in charge making conscious choices whenever you have awareness on all levels. You will choose consciously to move toward life to move toward the expansion of life, toward the awareness of life, toward acceptance of life rather than resistance to it. Then you will be choosing life. You are the truth, the light. And the truth shall set you free" (Archangel Gabriel, TSC).

This process will begin by creating communities of equality, harmony, and balance for all (human, animal, plant, and mineral) and knowing your planet is a living, conscious being who will not accept any further abuse of her body. You, the alchemist, will begin to remove the imbalances imposed upon your planet and humanity by yourselves. The most insidious type of bondage occurs when the slave knows not his or her bondage. It is time to wake up world. The true science of alchemy can set us free on Earth. Are you ready to receive it? And create a new paradigm? Have you noticed the old one is dying?

Amazing alchemical advances (as we continue to awaken) can and will be achieved by all who are able to apply universal teachings.

Remember and know, dear ones, the purpose of the true science of alchemy is to increase joy and happiness and to free humanity from every outer imbalance that does not serve the whole so you can be the God Powers you are.

"The universe is a unified whole. Nothing is separate" (Archangel Gabriel, TSC).

Chapter IV

*Beliefs change,
But truth remains the same,
Is the game.*

DO WE HAVE WISDOM OR JUST KNOWLEDGE?

Inspired by Archangels Gabriel, Michael, and Saint Germain

For a long time, the world has been "ruled" by the human mind. Where has that gotten us? In spite of the amazing advances humanity has made, the world still does not allow equality for all. Many are fighting for their right to be equal and free. Much of the world lives under oppressive governments, religions, and cultural values, a few controlling the many.

All teachings within this book are from higher-realm messengers. They are messengers of truth of the relationship of humanity to the divine and the divine to humanity. The beings here act as interpreters of a specific portion of the universal divine plan, which is an aspect of our divine soul plan.

At present, we still believe war and killing each other is acceptable behavior. Our way of thinking and being really isn't working very well. In fact, if things stay the same, we most likely will not survive as a planet or species. It is time to wake up, or else...

No wonder the planet has now activated an aspect of its divine soul plan that allows an ascension process to move into a more advanced, higher-frequency existence where the behavior of the past is simply not allowed. The divine destination is that we live forever to serve the forces that created and love us eternally.

This new way of being is the result of the human mind, at long last, returning in service to our all-wise God Powered heart. This is our divine destiny. Our heart holds all the wisdom that we need to grow and expand that is not contained in the intelligent/knowledgeable human mind. This heart wisdom is the result of all past and present wisdom being stored in the DNA/RNA of the etheric heart and passed on from reincarnation to reincarnation. The collection of knowledge becomes wisdom as it accumulates.

Maybe we need to know the important difference between wisdom and intelligence/ knowledge. To know something does not make us wise. Our history proves this. Data needs to be stored and used over time. Welcome to the terrific thinking heart and the value of immortality.

The word wisdom comes from the phrase "wise dominion." The dominion is dominion over self—to understand and accept and forgive the human self (as a learning tool) and choose to rise above and beyond it to the divine/higher self. This is "divine" wisdom. There are many messages, tools, and teachings coming from higher realms to assist humanity in this process. This is one of many.

Let's take a closer look at the difference between wisdom and knowledge. We all know a lot of things through memory. Most of us memorized our way through school and soon forgot most of what we knew. Our schools are set up for testing, which encourages knowledge, not wisdom. But students' hearts are hungering for a new paradigm in education that includes wisdom. Memory alone cannot assure us the proper use or release of stored knowledge at the moment it is needed nor does it fully allow timely discernment.

Wisdom does allow discernment since it accumulates over time, many lifetimes. When we study the ascended masters and their many incarnations, it becomes clear how they have accumulated knowledge into wisdom. Remember to apply your discernment and resonance in all being said here as well.

"Discernment involves consciously connecting with your senses to discern what is true for you...what resonates for you as it relates to your choices and decisions and what does not" (Archangel Michael, LM).

So an essential pathway to wisdom is the knowledge (the heart knows, the mind believes) of repeated lifetimes, incarnational cycles. It is truly unfortunate that there are large components of humanity who still do not accept the universal truth of reincarnation. For only through the acceptance of this cosmic fact can humanity achieve the wisdom of eternity and truly know who they are and why they are here.

Our planet now combines twelve archetypes of evolution from the twelve-star systems that began us. We are a grand, unique cosmic experiment. We are now to create a unity of the twelve archetypes through all their diversities into oneness. This is our mission and purpose and one example of wisdom gained from incarnational wisdom.

Western religions have taught eternal souls but have left out the part about repeated lifetimes. It's easier to control people with only part of the information/truth being given.

By knowing, accepting, and understanding our own incarnational reality, we know the "cosmic continuity" of self, and the true love of the forces by which we were created. We are a reflection of that force, and as surely as God is eternal, so are you.

You just do it through many embodiments as God just keeps expanding. Once we have the wisdom of the centuries at our disposal, this becomes a game changer.

Just because we cannot remember previous lives does not mean they did not exist. The minds of many individuals will never accept this statement. The knowing must come from the heart, where all those past lives are stored.

Metaphysics explains that the reason for not always remembering our past lives is so that we can more fully experience and learn what we came here to learn in this lifetime. The heart remembers through experiences such as déjà vu (flashbacks from previous lives) and past life regressions and channeling, such as in this book. It simply does not make cosmic sense that we are eternal souls with only one chance at being human.

Eastern religions have supported the idea of repeated lifetimes for millennia. Incarnational reality is the universal science of eternal being. Many people have accepted sometimes misguided religions without incarnational truth with their dogma that says what we see is all we get. By withholding the truth, church and state have gained greater control over the people.

Dear ones, stop and take a breath and connect with your heart and ask for the Wisdom of Your Heart to be imparted to you. There has been so much suffering in our world by denying incarnational reality as an essential component in our being. The truth will now set us free.

The same principles that make a university or library a great place of learning apply to our lives. It is the accumulated and stored information/knowledge that allows us to ascend into our soul plans and destiny. Stored knowledge such as: each planet in our solar system went through an evolution as Earth is now...from a primitive phase through an advanced phase. Each planet is in the process of becoming a star. We cannot see life on other planets in our solar system because they have advanced to a higher-frequency existence we can't see. It doesn't mean they are not there!

The encoded wisdom stored in our spiritual DNA from many lifetimes (now awakening) allows us to truly know who we are and have access to all the knowledge beyond our planet, connecting us with the God Power Source that created us. Then a unified relationship of world service to creation begins. Through becoming a master of self, we master the universe.

For our planet Earth (the Lover-versity, on which we learn to love self and ALL THERE IS) is a reflection of the universe of learning. And all of us shall soon know there can be no such thing as so-called death.

If death were permanent, as we are often taught, we could not clear and cleanse ourselves in order to become the master of our destiny as the divine beings we are. This is the great gift of God: to behold God Power and gain true wisdom. "Eventually all members of mankind will be able to transcend the physical altogether.

There will be no need for it because the physical world is simply a state of consciousness used for the purpose of growth experience—how the soul grows, expands, and deepens its awareness of self. This is the purpose of the physical plan. No other purpose" (Archangel Gabriel, TSC).

As the ascended masters continually teach, the first contribution of God to humanity is a continuous life stream, followed by our freedom of choice and will, which allows us to gain spiritual wisdom, freedom, and blessing eternally.

Once we break free of the confines of the one-life concept, we can break free from the planet itself, revealing other dimensions, worlds and civilizations, and true wisdom. When the universal laws of frequencies and dimensions are opened, we enter etheric octaves within the "garden of God Power," where Oneness reigns supreme and everything becomes possible as we master the tools of creation. All chains of the past controlling and imprisoning humanity (even karma) are broken and are replaced by glorious guidance from our Higher Self, allowing the full birth of the immortal/eternal God Power-giving beings we are.

We are then able to access all the wisdoms of Earth's past Golden Ages, to know what created them and why they failed through the disconnect to the higher realms. This creates a vortex of opportunity for world service and we now have the wisdom and knowledge through our God Power to facilitate the final Golden Age of Mother Earth, Gaia. We fully know now who we are and why we are here.

We shall soon have full access to the cosmic crystal universities, the universal wisdom and direct connection to realms that join our mission of world service. All barriers in our being and consciousness are cleansed/cleared and the right use of wisdom comes pouring forth. We see that love is fueled through true service to wisdom. The ascension of the planet, solar system, galaxy, and universe is now at hand...it is your divine birthright.

We are coming to know all this is a process from inside out, not outside in. We are on a path of connecting with the light, the God Power that's always been inside us. Through our freedom of choice, we shall discern what we chose. We shall come to know our truth, needs, and boundaries. Through our talents and gifts, we shall simply levitate into the new me, life, world, solar system, galaxy, and universe.

Chapter V

*There is only One Law of Life,
And that is Love.*

WHAT HAS LOVE GOT TO DO WITH IT?

Inspired by Archangels Gabriel, Michael, and Saint Germain

Love is one of the most used words and supposedly experienced emotions in human existence. Do we really know or understand what love is? Do we know the true purpose of love? What is the understanding of love beyond what we think we feel or have experienced? Through the connection and support of higher realms beyond humanity, let us see if we can gain a new insight and truth about this thing called love...

"Love is a force, a force of God, a force of creation, a force of being. Therefore, learning to love means learning to awaken, realize, accept, express, and experience in the fullest way possible the experience, expression and potential of your being as an individual. That is the divine plan embodied. That is the force of love embodied. That is the soul awakened. So your purpose in the divine plan is to learn to love" (Archangel Gabriel, TSC).

The energy/vibration that is love is the manifesting power within creation, the building block, the power behind and within ALL THERE IS. It is almost impossible for the human mind to comprehend this thing called true love or to know exactly what it means. The human experience of love is a mere reflection/shadow of the true essence of love. The mystery of love is an essential part of its power and glory. True love is the attraction of the magnification of the eternal divine wisdom and God Power of Creator/Source or whatever you chose to call the most loving and powerful force in the many universes. Since we are all unique, perhaps our definition and experience of the most extraordinary force in the universe is meant to be unique to each one. True love always understands, yet not necessarily always understood nor needs to be.

But let's see what we can piece together about love. The ascended masters who once were human and walked our Earth and experienced love in a similar fashion as we human mortals may give us some clues. Their Law of Oneness and Unity seems to be an offspring of love. "Love one another as you love yourself," is the blueprint of knowing who we are and why we are here. "Love one another as you love yourself.

Imagine God saying to itself love one another as you love yourself. God would be speaking to all parts of itself that are in fragmented experiential array in the universe" (Archangel Gabriel, TSC). But we still appear to learn "what is" through "what is not," most often.

"God brings together the fusion of the Consciousness of God in physical form. No more duality, instead there is oneness, unity, wholeness, completeness, merging, connecting"(Archangel Gabriel, TSC).

The separations of alpha and omega, light and dark, masculine and feminine, right and wrong can only become one, whole and healed by healing our illusions through love of self and others.

Love is composed of itself, wisdom, and power in order to create the Oneness. But its wholeness can never be divided by its parts. For the foundation of reality is WE ARE ONE. Humanity has chosen to experience the separate parts of oneness and divide them, but that has never been truth. This is our not-so-simple way we have chosen to learn what we need to learn. The separating is now coming back together in oneness...duality is in the process of ending.

Love is accepting through understanding (compassion) that allows forgiveness, which frees the one forgiving. We need forgiveness since humanity has the capacity to be other than love. This capacity is the reason for human life's drama (the divine can never be so). Divine love, unlike human love, is not giving to get, but simply giving with no expectation. The substance of divine love is the power within creation, as well as the sustenance of such creation. Without faith and trust that love actually exists, it is impossible for us to know that it exists. At present, human love is an aspect of divine love not the whole yet...but we are working on it...

"The core of what love is, is the expression of your being, the revelation of your being, showing and sharing all of who you are with life, with the world, every other human being, with one individual being. All of that is love" (Archangel Gabriel, TSC).

The quest for the true meaning of love is often found with so-called metaphysicians and spiritual seekers. They hunger for mastery of self and the universe, while not satisfying the "grand requirement" to honor before all else a meaningful and committed love toward God that created them, and self and others (selfish love is not self-love). True self-love is the foundation of all other relationships. You cannot love another without loving you first. This has kept humanity in separation and duality, and has been the downfall of all past Golden Ages. The applied requirement is the pathway to the final Golden Age. True Love is the God Power of the universe.

There are many types of feelings and emotions that we call love but in truth are not. Love is neither an emotion nor a feeling but an action of God Power manifesting. Love is penetrating and forever expansive and growing and enfolding and transforming and transmuting. Love is all the Beingness of God combined with many mysteries that humanity is not yet ready to neither understand nor receive. Love is the foundation of life, and you refined and defined.

True love is changeless and always. It is the one element in the universe into which all others meet. Love is the highest expression of you and God in and beyond time and distance. True love is a natural expression of you and God Power, while most human love is an aspect of truth aspiring to be true. True love is filled with an "attitude of gratitude" that becomes a magnet for love radiating out all around you. True love is God Power beating your heart and being manifestation at the same time.

One day soon, our scientist will develop "love instruments" that will be able to measure the love energies that radiate out, but they will never be able to measure the all-encompassing God Power of true divine love. Only you and God can do that, as Man Power becomes God Power...

"The most critical thing is to become still within, to still the mind, to still the feelings, so that you can begin to experience the guidance. So you can begin to notice how your soul through love is guiding you this way or that way... how it is connecting you with this person or that group or situation. What is it teaching you? What learning experience is it introducing you to? How to love." (Archangel Gabriel, TSC).

Love is God being YOU.

Chapter VI

All nations are divine expressions
Of creation's diversified revelations.
But America for most of her people
Is much more than they ever dreamed, it seems.

A MYSTICAL AMERICA

Inspired by Archangels Gabriel, Michael, and Saint Germain

Most of us are aware by now that our world and selves are changing like never before. That we are living within a unique opportunity of creating something new and leaving the old behind. A country called the United States of America appears to have a key role in the creation of this transitioning new world. But most do not understand why or how. Maybe a way of better understanding what is happening is to connect with the God Powers of the United States and dialogue with them as to what happened in the past and how that is effecting our present and future. This United States appears to have been "divinely" inspired with God Power higher-realms support and it has not completely activated its "soul plan" quite yet. "The divine plan for physical matter on Earth is to learn to love. That is the divine plan" (Archangel Gabriel, TSC).

"Basically, America has been put in place by the Freemasons. All you have to do is look at your dollar bill. Look how Washington DC is laid out according to the pentagram of the Masons. Look at the Pentagon. Look at the fact that all the main buildings are interrelated as to the number of blocks according to the sacred numbers of the Masons. The head of the Masonry is exactly thirteen blocks from the White House, the sacred number of the Masons, etc., etc." (Archangel Gabriel, TSC).

Many scholars and metaphysicians have examined the visual clues within the Great Seal of the United States (a powerful eagle, an unfinished pyramid, and various mottoes and numerological symbols) that point to esoteric and mystical support. The eagle is an ancient symbol of spiritual vision and God Powers and protection. The olive branch in the right (assertive, Man Power, masculine) talon means the "Priestess of Peace" of God Powers who transcends time and space, as I AM THAT I AM.

The unfinished pyramid is symbolic of the mission of perfecting one's soul through Christ/We Consciousness and manifesting a nation into a final Golden Age. The motto "annuity coeptis" means "He has smiled on our creation," and the motto "e pluribus unum" means "Oneness." These mottoes have thirteen letters each and the pyramid has thirteen steps.

The often repetition of the number thirteen appears to reflect the founding fathers' revealing we are twelve tribes (representing the twelve-star systems that seeded the planet) and a thirteenth yet to be within the final Golden Age. "The foundation of America goes back to secret societies, secret orders. They were originally mystery schools that got distorted, such as the Illuminati, the Left Eye and Right Eye of Horus from Egypt" (Archangel Gabriel, TSC).

Today, during this seemingly cynical (if I can't see it, I won't believe it) and often chaotic times (out of chaos comes creation), it may be challenging for many to believe that the United States could have ever been founded with the unseen hands of Man and God Powers. But it appears that George Washington was quite aware of the unseen support he received when he said in his first inaugural address, "No people can be bound to acknowledge and adore the Unseen Hand which conducts the affairs of men more than those of the United States."

"The original intention of the planet Earth is for the success of a democracy, a communion of twelve-star systems together as one. A system of democracy is simply a system where the equality of the individuality is embraced, where equal importance of all expression is held sacred, where all beings live for the good and the wholeness of one another. What a concept!" (Archangel Gabriel, TSC).

Many early Americans appeared to believe that God Powers directed the outcome of the American Revolution when John Adams spoke, "America was designed by Providence for the theatre on which man was to make his true figure," and Patrick Henry agreed, "There is a just God who presides over the destinies of nations."

When you stop and think about it, doesn't it seem impossible that a loosely united group of "states" clinging to the eastern coast of a huge continent, under the control of the mightiest Man Power on the planet, the British, with limited resources and organizational ability, could create what would become the most powerful country in the world? By anyone's standard, the swift ascension of the American Republic was nothing less than a miracle! Unless we come to realize they did not do it alone. Perhaps we've never been alone. That's, it's all been a preparation for the second coming of God, YOU.

Early Americans often felt a mystical connection to their situation and those of the ancient people of Israel, and their God Power. George Washington and John Adams were often referred to as Moses and Joshua in their aim to "set their people free." Even the desert sands of the Sinai were later found out West. The blueprint for political and governmental structure was religion, and the Bible laid the foundation for laws (Man Powers) and ways of being in the early colonies and established a pattern of behavior for our country today.

We are still attempting to sort out truth and Universal Law within the translations and intentions of the many versions of the Bible. "The Bible was written and conceived during an age of duality. If you look at the commandments, they're all about what you can't do. They're the beginning of the age of duality" (Archangel Gabriel, TSC). We are in the process of connecting with cosmic truth that can set us free from any Man Power creations/translations.

Much is being revealed now as we once again reconnect with God Powers and unseen hands assisting in "setting us free." Ancient texts are being discovered often, allowing the old truths to become new again.

Even before the forefathers existed, there seems to be some divine intervention in the "discovery" of America. Although many came before Christopher Columbus (Vikings, Druids, Egyptians, Phoenicians, Chinese, Arabians), he chose and was chosen as the man destined to recreate the New Jerusalem (notice the USA is in the middle of Jerusalem) and the New Atlantis (the East coast of America is the remaining west coast of Atlantis), so the unfinished energetic intentions that advanced civilization may complete today. "Neither my mind, mathematics nor maps were any use to me" Columbus wrote in his diary. Today, as back then, we are once again speaking of the rising of Atlantis and finding physical evidence.

There's not a lot actually known about Columbus. He seems to have appeared from cyberspace. His exact date and place of birth are not known. Some think he was Greek, others Italian. History tells us he was professed in ancient astrology and his names foretold his divine soul plan: Cristobal Colon means "Christ bearer," and "colonizer." This mysterious man was initiated in the secret societies of his fifteenth century, such as Knight Templars, the Rosicrucians, and the Masons. These ancient secret societies handed down the mystery teachings throughout the centuries, and often became corrupted in their desire to control the world.

It was Columbus's sponsorship by these mystical societies that made his voyage to the New World possible and Man Powered. While America had been discovered many times before, it was an idea whose time had now come. The divine soul plan of America and Columbus was upon the world. The time had come. As a result of the Man and God

Power sponsorships, the "Christ-bearer colonizer" soul plan was firmly in place. Of course none of this took into consideration the spiritual connections and ways of life of the existing native cultures. While these native cultures influenced language and geography, we are only now accepting our destruction of them and realizing their impact and contributions to the living diversified planet as a whole.

Thus a new nation, superimposed upon existing native cultures, was to be brought into life. While there was much to be done in the receiving and giving of the founding fathers' papers/instructions from God Power realms (the Declaration of Independence, the Bill of Rights, the Constitution, etc.), few knew or understood the karma connection of ancient people, past and present, and what effect that would have upon the New World.

Atlantis was the last Golden Age in this hemisphere that ended due to corruption and disconnection from God Power realms that caused that continent to sink. Proof that Atlantis existed beyond myth is now coming forth. Only now are we knowing that America today is birthing a final Golden Age upon this planet and beginning to see the revelations of past and present higher-realm connections.

The concept of repeated Earth lives is widely accepted in the Far East, and while it's not universally accepted in the West, this is shifting and it's beginning to make common sense to most and through shared near-death experiences. How can an eternal soul only have one physical chance?

So if we accept an individual may reincarnate more than once seeking to perfect the soul (to learn what we came here to learn), it makes sense that entire civilizations can do the same to work out their collective destiny/soul plan. With the aim of keeping things as simple as possible, we won't discuss all the civilizations that preceded Atlantis, and the Old World, and the names lost in time. But rest assured there's a lot more to this story than any of our history presently shares. This will all be revealed soon...this author intends to be involved with our true, complete history...

As we discussed earlier, the eastern seaboard of North America was the part of Atlantis that did not sink. Another initiate of the secret societies, whose soul plan was also to reestablish the final Golden age beyond Atlantis, was the amazing man Francis Bacon. These types of men (a balance of Man and God Powers) rarely exist today.

Francis Bacon was the Lord Chancellor of England, statesman, humorist, orator, author, scientist, and philosopher. For those astute in esoteric studies, Bacon is credited to be the author of all Shakespeare's works.

In his *Instauratio Magna*, Bacon presented a plan for the reconstruction of sciences, arts, and all human knowledge. He founded the first lodge of Freemasons, where almost every founding father was a member.

Through the Masons' beliefs, Bacon laid the blueprint for the establishment of the United States. Masonry offered "a doctrine of the spiritual life of man and a diagram of the process of regeneration." The mission and training of Masonry is "to be God Power reborn, authentic and allow the death of our lower nature, our Man Power." The Masons' "great science of soul building" is built into many of America's founding fathers' papers. Applied to America, this meant the resurrection of our final Golden Age, the New Atlantis, the New Jerusalem. A word of caution. Like all human endeavors (corrupted Man Powers), not all compartments of the Masons were pure of heart. The high top was often corrupted while the middle and below knew nothing of the truth and corrupted dealings. We are speaking the high ideal here.

Few know of Bacon's contributions to America, since he worked "behind the scenes" and left few traces of his work. Most of the knowledge of Bacon comes directly from higher-realm connections. (Please use your discernment and resonance regarding all being said here.) With the foundation and manifestation of Masonry in America, the blueprint was formed for a new country. There was just one big problem. America was still under British Man Power!

As the world knows, during the mid 1770s, the "spirit," the goddess of Liberty, swept the American colonies. The unrest grew out of reaction to British tyranny and greed and the "great awakening" that gave rise to the knowledge that God (Power) had founded a New Atlantis, a New Jerusalem in America. American liberty became God's cause. British tyranny was the anti-Christ. And to not fight the British was to burn in hell.

It is safe to say the American Revolution could have never happened without the Masons with their organization and ancient God Power wisdom/connections. There was hardly a town or city where some mason was not preaching fraternity and unity.

Through the famous Boston Tea Party, we remember that that city was the initial center of American motivation for change. And it was the Masons who could manifest that motivation and did. And a major Mason in the manifestation of America was George Washington.

Washington maintained and sustained colonial armies, and when Congress would not support him, he used his own money to make sure America could fight. Through his soul plan, Washington put his sacred honor on the line for the cause of freedom. The majority of the signers of the Declaration of Independence were Masons; even Paul Revere was a Mason. The major generals in the Continental Army were Masons. You get the picture. The states were unlikely to form a union without Washington and other Masons. Through Washington's insights and conscious actions, the office of president was formed and he seemed the only person the people could imagine to assume that office...it all appeared by divine God Power appointment.

The Man and God Power marriage of Bacon and Washington's soul plans came into integration with the creation and adoption of the Constitution. The Constitution embraced the Mason principles of brotherhood that each human would be abundant based on his own free efforts, the initiate path of the Mason. Never before had a country factored free speech, religion, press, and assembly into one mighty document (a true combination of Man and God Power). Humans would be given the chance to activate their divine soul plan, their destiny. These written principles still exist and we are still working on the equal, balanced, and harmonious reality of them. The foundation is in place for the next Golden Age. We just need to heal any and all elements standing in the way of the full expression of these divinely inspired principles so they can spread throughout the world...

The Goddess of Liberty is the patroness of the Masons' "sacred cause," and their motto "novus ordo seclorum" (new order of the ages) supports America leading the planet into its final Golden Age of WE THE PEOPLE CONSCIOUSNESS.

The art and literature of early America is filled with angelic beings, gods, and goddesses, reflecting the higher realms supporting all efforts of freedom and equality. Of course, we are still working on these! And we shall not be free until all are equal.

It is the opinion of this writer that the basis for most of our duality and separation is the imbalance of the masculine and feminine energies reflecting out into racial, religious, cultural, and sexual divides in our world today. When will we accept that we are all a diversified version of the same Source/God Power?

Literature of the colonial period reveals that the Goddess of Liberty came to George Washington several times within his lifetime, giving him a vision of the three tests that America would endure: (1) The Revolutionary War, (2) the Civil War, and (3) surrendering to the unknown destiny of the country through the support of higher realms. It was clear to Washington no mere mortal could solve all these tests. That without the support of higher God Power realms all would be lost.

Scholars and philosophers of the past have noted throughout our history that during periods of transitions/shifts/ascension, the process of spiritualization (not to be confused with religion), through God Power creates a resolve of higher consciousness connections, allowing a balance of Man and God Power.

The human mind is simply incapable of resolving planetary and humanity transformations by ourselves! The sooner we know and accept this truth, the better. We have never been alone.

Let us resolve to call upon ALL THERE IS (God Power) as "we the people" through our I AM THAT I AM presence and know it is our divine destiny to create together a new paradigm of Oneness, a final Golden Age servicing Source. As students of truth, let us heal our thoughts and emotions to create loving thought/emotion forms on both Man and God planes; knowing these have the ability to transform the course of events in the 3D world... Knowing God Power being the most powerful force and tool in the Universe.

"In becoming a homogenous society, it is a fight for separation because it alienates you from yourself by trying to fit in with others. Fitting in with others is not communion, is not unity, is not oneness and wholeness with yourself. Individuality is. Standing alone within yourself and having ownership of this whole self then enables you to be able to reveal it, to share that whole self with others. So it's an ironic paradox that in order to be unified (United States of America) you need to be alone with yourself" (Archangel Gabriel, TSC).

Now that we've entered the last two-thousand-year epoch of planet Earth foretold by Archangels Gabriel and Michael, leading to our final glorious Golden Age, let us also focus on the "spiritual sponsor" of America, the Ascended Master guiding the Aquarian Age, the beloved Saint Germain.

It's truly amazing that so few Americans know who Saint Germain is. Sweet people, it was Saint Germain who embodied the "Christ-bearer colonizer" Christopher Columbus and the founder of Free Masonry, Francis Bacon. And all along it has been Saint Germain who held in his heart the vision of the New JerUSAlem and New Atlantis solely based upon the principles of spiritual freedom and equality for all! Man Power becoming God Power.

Government today is controlled by economic forces. It's largely about the product and money, not the people. "The energy of the people is largely sacrificed to the corporate. What truly works is a system of equity where people operate as independent individuals taking responsibility for their own reality and for the reality of their fellow man. I do unto others, as I would have them do unto me. The good old Golden Rule" (Archangel Gabriel, TSC).

"The fact your government (reflecting the people) has run away with much of your true freedom is simply mirroring back to you how easily and effortlessly you have given up on holding sacred your individuality and being able to contain your space in reality. That's all being mirrored back to you now" (Archangel Gabriel, TSC). Would we like to make another choice now?

Saint Germain now again invites us to rise to our God Powers and connections of WE CONSCIOUSNESS, in order to manifest our freedom and immortality. As Archangel Gabriel reminds us, "the original intention of the planet Earth is for the success of a democracy, a communion of twelve-star systems together as one." And that is what Mystical America is all about!

Chapter VII

Probabilities and possibilities
Live in the unknown
And when we can surrender to them
They become our own.

TWO WONDROUS WAY SHOWERS: TRANSMUTING I AM CHRISTED LIGHT

Inspired by The Christ Consciousness, and Ascended Master Saint Germain

OATH OF THE LIGHT WORKER AND WAY SHOWER,
Adapted from Archangel Michael via trance channel Jeff Fasano,
Sacred Poetry & Mystical Messages, To Change Your Life & The World,
By Phillip Elton Collins.

We are all light workers
To a greater or lesser extent,
It merely depends on your bent.

MAN POWER GOD POWER

You have a mission and purpose
In this lifetime.

And if you so choose,
It is time to release the conceal and reveal
The various healing modalities that are your true realities.
You may partake in these modalities,
Any way you choose,
There is no way to lose.

Some may work with individuals or groups
In certain techniques
And that remains your mission and purpose,
Feeling quite complete.

Way Showers are Light Workers
Who bring their gifts and talents
Out into the world in a larger way,
That is their pay.

A Way Shower shows the way
For others to move onto their path,
With no wrath,
To create communities,
Of equality, harmony and balance,
So there is no malice.

You may ask, at last:
Am I a Light Worker?
Am I a Way Shower?
How can I know?
Am I both, not to boast?

Some will know their total purpose now,
Others need time for it to reveal,
And that's no crime to let it be real.
Not to worry,
It will all be defined and refined
As you continue your journey,
For life is a continuous refinery.

If and when you are steady
And ready to take the oath of both,
The Light Worker and Way Shower,
The heavens will shower their Light on you,
No matter what the hour.

Many of us are aware we are moving from the worn-out old to an unknown new. Our planet and ourselves are now being given a most divine gift to awaken to our true selves and purpose in Being (here). To let go of duality and confrontation that have kept us separate far too long. To now join in Oneness and We Consciousness to fully activate our divine soul plans, planet and people alike.

A precious pair of Ascended Masters, who once walked this Earth as we, are vital links to this process of moving from the mercurial me to the wondrous we: Jesus Christ and Saint Germain. As we further awaken, more and more is being revealed, beyond our religions and past metaphysical studies as to who these devoted God Power "Sons of Source" truly were and are.

What are the meanings, value, and purpose of these divine duos' actions? Within their soul plans and service to Source that ushered in the Christ Consciousness (Jesus) and the I AM THAT I AM higher self-presence (Saint Germain) from the Piscean into the Aquarian Ages. This transition thus activated what has been called the Ascension process of the planet and humanity moving into a higher frequency of existence (moving from Man Power to God Power). In effect, this allowed the integration of the I AM presence with the Christ Consciousness. Neither man nor any other being can now shut this unified portal. This is a balancing of personal and planetary karma. It is our divine birthright for this event to take place now. Man Power is truly becoming God Power.

"The Piscean Age is represented by two fish swimming in opposite directions. These represent the lower and the higher self that are in opposition to one another that are evolving through duality. So the higher and the lower selves in the last 2000 year cycle have been evolving in duality. Now you have evolved to a state where in this age the two can join together in the Age of Aquarius, which is represented by the water bearer, balancing the emotional body to bring about unity. The Aquarian Age is the age of unity, with the water bearer carrying the two buckets of water in balance. The balance of the emotional body will bring about the awakening of the soul, which is the experimental aspect of spirit or God that now awakens in the Aquarian Age" (Archangel Gabriel, TSC).

Let us fill our hearts with gratitude that we have all chosen to be here for this glorious event of Creation.

Saint Germain has had many extraordinary incarnations/ embodiments on this planet, always assisting humanity in ascending onward. Please see the studies within *The Seven Sacred Flames* for a complete understanding of them all. In the eleventh century BC, he was the prophet-priest Samuel in Israel, and as the "sponsor" in creating the United States of America, he is belovedly known as "Uncle Sam, where he brought forth the twelve (tribes) star systems that seeded Earth revealing each one's true mission as light bearers in service to Source.

"Your planet now combines twelve archetypes of evolution from the twelve-star systems that began your planet to now create a unity of twelve archetypes into oneness. This is your mission and purpose" (Archangel Gabriel, TSC). This is a unique divine experiment in the universe, reflected in our diversified races, languages, cultures, sexual preferences, and gender...all becoming united.

The recreation of paradise (Oneness) on Earth through the Word (Consciousness) becoming density was/ is the mission of Earth, the Lover-versity of the Universe.

Through the integrated teachings of Jesus, The Christ Consciousness, and Saint Germain we can know our higher Christ self as our Divine Self as we heal our wounds and ego defenses, and negative karma from past and present lives.

Through the Law of Transformation utilizing the Christ Consciousness and I AM presence, humanity worldwide is being given the opportunity to become free of false prophets, false pastors, false gurus, and false Christ's in our religions, governments, and corporations. Thus, through the intentions and energies of Ascended Mastership, and The Christ Consciousness, the TRUTH SHALL SET US FREE by the spoken Word. The Word that can be expressed through prayer, meditation, and mantra (breath, sound, and motion). Even the sacred frequency AUM (OM), the universal sound and syllable of the Divine Mother, which represents and balances all chakras, can employ light workers and way showers to assist our Ascension.

"Breath, sound and motion is the source. Without breathing you cannot think, you cannot feel, because breathing awakens the consciousness in the physical body. When you breathe into the body you stimulate awareness. You stimulate life. You stimulate consciousness. So the physical body, the emotional body, and the mental body are dependent upon the breath. Everything in life is dependent on three things: the breath, movement and sound. Life is movement. Resistance is non-movement, which is death, destruction" (Archangel Gabriel, TSC).

Saint Germain and Jesus, The Christ Consciousness, are quite simply and clearly teaching and reminding us the SECOND COMING is within each one of us, as our Man Power is becoming God Power. If all the ways that separate us could know and accept this truth, peace and oneness will come to this world!

Let us reveal and stop the often hidden forces that keep humanity pitted against itself for profit and greed. The solution lies within ourselves, not outside. This is a personal process of inside out, not outside in. A process of you being God...

Two Wondrous Way Showers: Transmuting I Am Christed Light

"Creation is God, universal mind, universal consciousness. It is made up of all that is and all that is not. It is all that is and was and ever will be and is yet to come. It is you. Can you wrap your brain around that one?!" (Archangel Gabriel, TSC).

It's now forever present through our Christ Consciousness and our I AM Presence. No one, and nothing can take this away from us. Are we ready to wake up and claim our divine God Power? And know I AM God in me is the truth and I am in the process of accepting this now.

Your Christ Consciousness and I AM Presence is God being undifferentiated consciousness until it connects with a soul like you. As has been said many times and will be many more, "the purpose of all physical evolution is to learn to love. Your individual part of God is learning to become experiential" (Archangel Gabriel, TSC).

We would like to leave you with this visualization and powerful tool... always see yourselves holding your right hand in the hand of The Christ Consciousness and holding your left hand in the hand of Saint Germain. Call upon these wondrous Way Showers of Truth and Love any time, day or night, holding each other's hands. These miraculous masters will never leave you as long as you remain true to the reality YOU ARE GOD EXPERIENCING ITSELF.

"You have been frozen in a state of childhood now graduating to adulthood, accepting your god-hood" (Archangel Gabriel, TSC).

Chapter VIII

*The Creator wishes to remind you,
All things are possible
Through knowing your divinity
Which is, by the way,
Always within your vicinity.*

WONDERS TO COME

Inspired by Archangel Gabriel, Michael, and Saint Germain

As humanity reconnects more and more with higher God Power realms and moves further into "We Consciousness," wonderful gifts will be revealed to us when we are ready. This is how it has always been during the creation of Golden Ages. These ages were never created alone but with the love and support from higher dimensions/frequencies. Let us know the separation from higher sources was the demise of past Golden Ages and the assurance of this permanent one we are creating now.

"Everything in nature takes total responsibility for its place in nature and its effect. Man is the only creature that does not" (Archangel Gabriel, TSC). So after previewing some of the proposed wonders to come again, we shall study some advancement necessary in our lives to ensure the receivership of these powerful technologies.

After we have further advanced in our consciousness (the purpose of this endeavor), here are some technologies we used in the past and can now again change the way we live forever, thus fulfill creating a world filled with freedom, equality, balance, harmony, and oneness; Man Power truly employing God Power. Since we have a limited experience with God being a physical experience, we must be ready to receive God Powers that can destroy or create ourselves and the planet.

USING BODY-CONSCIOUS ENERGY: This will enable humanity to power electronic/digital apparatus through brain waves by the use and mastery of the energy currents flowing through the heart and the mind. Our thoughts and emotions have always created our reality.

Now we shall understand the brain and heart more through higher-realms scientific use. We are beginning to see body-conscious energy use in computer phonetic usage and artificial limbs. As we move further into unity consciousness, this will grow and expand, "You are as a human being live in a body. That body appears a self -contained vehicle. The consciousness of God is flowing through it all the time through the life force here called God Power" (Archangel Gabriel). We shall now harness this power for the good of all.

PHOTOGRAPHING THE UNSEEN WORLD: Cameras will become so sensitized they will photograph the human aura, our etheric, unseen, nonphysical body just outside our physical body. This is the portion of us that maintains and sustains the physical.

This will allow medical physicians the ability to see the causes of many physical and mental and emotional imbalances caused by emotions and thoughts from past and present lives known or unknown to the patient. This will begin healing the true cause and effect of imbalances. This is a preamble of our becoming telepathic and knowing the truth at all times. Our world is filled with deceit and denial of the deceit at the moment.

MAGNETISM POWER SOURCE: With the greater understanding of magnetism, it will become possible to suspend objects in midair without any form of visible support. This will explain how many ancient structures were built through levitation, magnetism, and sacred geometry that cannot be built today. This is the constructive wisdom of the Ascended Masters revealed. There is enough unseen free energy in the world today to power the entire planet. This will be a game changer in the governmental and economic structures of the planet.

EXPANDED FORMS OF TRANSPORTATION: New forms of air/water/land navigation and transportation/teleportation will be made possible by utilizing inner and outer Earth electro-magnetic energies. Thus objects will rise in complete resistance to gravity and we shall be free to explore the cosmos without further consuming the Earth's resources. These vehicles will be God-Powered by safe magnetic-electronic frequencies.

CONTROLLING WEATHER: Through our raised consciousness, we shall know that our thoughts and emotions create weather. Once we become aware/awake to the true power of our minds and emotions, we shall create perfect weather. Think of the time and resources that are lost presently due to weather.

The above wonders will soon be dwarfed by still greater wonders to come from higher realms as we maintain and sustain a state of growth and expansion of self, leading into our final Golden Age.

In order to prevent humanity from repeating the past and destroying itself again from advanced technologies such as the above, we shall discuss some suggestions to change and initiate in our lives to ensure our divine destiny.

These twelve suggestions reflect the twelve-star systems that seeded our planet and come from *The Second Coming: The Archangel Gabriel Proclaims A New Age*, trance channeled by Robert Baker and authored by Joel Anastasi.

1. Humans must grow up and take responsibility for their reality, for themselves and for others. They are acting as though life is happening to them as opposed to their acting on life.

2. Give up duality. Give up a system of right and wrong, good and bad, reward and punishment that produces fighting against one another. Allow space for all that is. Don't judge one side as good and the other as bad. Embrace both and create a state of neutrality.

3. Give up the herd consciousness. By embracing the herd, you give up the self. Understand the celebration of

the middle road. Embrace neither one side nor the other. Allow both to be included. That is how you let go duality.

4. Embrace the nurturing of life, all forms of life. Nurturing all forms of life develops intimacy, sharing, and communication, particularly with families.

5. Give up judgment, which creates shame and condemnation.

6. Exercise forgiveness for yourself and others.

7. Develop a conscience. Recognize there are many choices in all situations. Choose, and if you make a mistake, forgive yourself and others. Developing a conscience allows for your mistakes and the mistakes of others. It allows you to explore many possibilities. The possibilities of choice become endless and that allows the creative force to be expressed.

8. Do unto others, as you would have them do unto you. Look at each choice that you make and know that choice has an effect not just on you, but resonates endlessly into the universe. So always ask yourself, if I were to be affected by this choice, would I want that? If the answer is no, then reevaluate your choice. If the answer is yes, then by all means make that choice.

9. To thy own self be true. This involves connecting to the soul self, to the truth of being. It contains three lessons:

A. The first is your life lesson that involves your talents, abilities, and qualities of being that bring about the realization and fulfillment of self. By honoring that which is inherent within you, those talents, abilities, and qualities are uniquely expressed through you. Even though they may be similar to those of others, it is important to express them because they carry within them the unique signature of the soul sound that is you. From this comes fulfillment because you are honoring the truth of who you are. So look at whether you are indeed honoring the truth of who you are by honoring your talents, abilities, and qualities of being because that is what you have to give and to share with your fellow souls that contributes to all creation or the God body.

Who you are is absolutely unique and must be honored as such. Who you are is of value in its uniqueness.

B. The second lesson is the soul lesson, which is the ability to experience everything that life has to offer with acceptance—acceptance of your feelings, allowing those feelings to be felt, experienced, and completed in each moment. This brings about a depth of meaning to life that reveals your unique needs. If you are not able to experience life through your feelings, then your needs cannot be revealed because it is what you need. And those needs are unique to you, even though you share some common needs with every human, such as the basic needs of health, well being, shelter, food, etc. But from the unique perspective of your creative self, your needs are honored that bring about the fulfillment of the third lesson, which is your purpose.

C. Your life purpose cannot be fulfilled without your knowing your needs and understanding the meaning those needs have for you. The conscious direction of your purpose involves the choices that you make and your ability to choose freely. Freedom of choice only becomes freedom of choice when you know your value and you are able to fulfill your meaning by being in touch with your feelings and your needs so that you may act upon your talents and abilities and exercise you qualities. Then you are able to direct your choices and your actions with a purpose that fulfills the truth of who you are.

10. Heal the emotional body. Accept all your feelings without shame and realize the highest aspects of yourself. This has to do with releasing yourself from living out the myth of the past and being present in the moment of now—being able to respond to what is rather than what is not without projection of the past as the past has been completed because you allow all feelings. You allow each moment of experience to be completed by allowing the feelings.

11. Heal the mental body. Free the mind of all thoughts so that you have the direct pathway to the soul's knowing, so the soul can take charge of directing the personality, the ego self. Through that knowing, there is a connection between spirit, soul, and matter. The soul is the joining point. That is the Christ Consciousness. That is the resurrection. That is the life. The soul is always present in the here and now. The personality, which is confined by the mental body and the emotional body's business and noise, is not able to be present with the soul because of all the noise. The soul is ever present whether you are or not, and the soul operates through the love force. Therefore, when the emotional and the mental bodies are healed, when you are present in

reality, you are present in the experience and the expression of the creative force of love.

12. Love one another as you love yourself. This involves realizing that you are your brother's keeper that your choices are not separate, and the choices of others are not separate from you. Everything is connected. Look at nature to realize this. But have humans looked to see the divine plan and its teaching in nature? No. Instead, they have tried to conquer nature, conquer and divide as they do everything else. Therefore, they have created themselves separate from nature and sought to destroy nature—thus the problems of the ecosystem.

We can learn these twelve lessons now and move into a new advanced world paradigm or take the next final two thousand-year-cycle to do so. What do you choose?

Chapter IX

Within every Divine Desire
Is the power if its inspire...

DIVINE INNER ESSENCE (DIE)

As we continue to evolve through and beyond Man Power into God Power, let us now focus on the inner powers we possess that can and will support our ascension process into a higher frequency of existence—one of equality, harmony, and balance. Having been human, the ascended masters are a precious source of support within our personal process, which can lead to our ascension. Today, we shall call upon the Christ Conscious energies of beloved Saint Germain and Lord Sananda, a.k.a. Jesus.

Phillip: Thank you for being with us again at this crucial time in our evolution. We are just beginning to comprehend your eternal love and support within our process. What exactly is happening with the energies we are receiving now? And we've been told in the past that America has a "heart of the planet" role in all this...leading us to our next golden age...

Saint Germain and Sananda: Sacred, cosmic energies are being intensified throughout the planet through what is called ascension dispensation. You are receiving these daily, and they affect everything that is happening in your world now. This is Man Power becoming God Power in action.

Phillip: How exactly does this work, and why is it happening?

Saint Germain and Sananda: There is a cosmic light that is entering the atmosphere of Earth. It is your destiny that this happens now. It is dissolving and consuming all the destructive activities created by man-not-so-kind Man Power.

This light will create some pleasant and not-so-pleasant results as the planet clears and cleanses herself from your abuses.

This will appear in natural and weather events, as well as the activities of humanity. You have recently seen some, and more can come if awareness does not shift.

Phillip: How does this affect individuals?

Saint Germain and Sananda: The planetary process taking place can also take place within the individual as you clear and cleanse what caused the external events (cause and effect) of the past and present. It's all about awakening your consciousness of self and knowing how it affects others, dear ones.

Phillip: This has also been called personal processing.

Saint Germain and Sananda: Yes, as individuals take more responsibility for self, accept with compassion how they choose to learn, and make new choices, a greater connection to their I Am presence can be gained and reflect out...We call this aspect of self *divine inner essence*, the name of this teaching.

Phillip: Please further explain this new term for many... *inner essence.*

Saint Germain and Sananda: The inner essence is a connection of your higher self light to the higher mental body to the physical nervous system, allowing being to become doing. This inner essence pulls power all around the person, a shield, creating an "atmosphere." This allows a limitless creation of good for self and all.

Phillip: This sounds like a super Man/God Power that can do anything?

Saint Germain and Sananda: There can be no failure with those accepting this "light tool"; only doubt can stop it You merely have to call it forth and know and trust you are worthy for it to work. This is a major part of your self-mastery you are in the process of learning. When you fully know it, you can and will ascend as we.

Phillip: How does this "tool" affect destructive people doing destructive things?

Saint Germain and Sananda: If a person seems to be not doing the constructive thing, be not concerned, dear ones. We know this is difficult for you. The doing of constructive things requires the constructive use of the inner essence light. If a person chooses not to do constructive things, cosmic law dictates that a stronger someone else will be created to be and do good for all. There are universal and cosmic laws that you will soon come to know that require none of your present punishment and Man Power laws. The universe works in perfect balance for a reason, and these laws are why. More and more, you will learn these universal laws and how to apply them.

Phillip: Please further explain what seems like a cosmic balancing.

Saint Germain and Sananda: When someone affects *we the people* of the planet, trust and know there is always an inner essence created to fulfill the need.

Phillip: I don't quite understand how this happens. It seems like magic.

Saint Germain and Sananda: It all comes from your sacred I Am presence (the divine eternal portion of you that always knows what to do), and we ascended beings support you. Divine inner essence guides the healed me consciousness into the we consciousness of world service. This has never failed you, dear ones.

Phillip: Please go on. I think I am beginning to get it...

Saint Germain and Sananda: If humanity only fully understood the power of their I Am presence and divine inner essence that can assist them in loving and supporting themselves and one another. It allows a mighty self-mastery of the wounded self that finally frees you, dear ones. Wait till you see more of it fully in action! Then you will know your God Power.

Phillip: How does this self-mastery work?

Saint Germain and Sananda: Healed consciousness enters the emotional, mental, and physical bodies of humanity to shift the actions of self out into the world.

Phillip: From your point of view, how does all this look?

Saint Germain and Sananda: You cannot imagine right now or realize what God Power lies within you when you work within the we. It has been asleep a long time, but it is awakening now. When you work within the we, you allow yourself to be free of the me faster. When you are in world service, we see you being the glorious God-within beings you are!

Phillip: Why are the Americas important right now?

Saint Germain and Sananda: The Americas (North and South) contain one-quarter of the planet's crust. Within these geographic areas are wondrous powers and gifts from the past that are going to become part of your heritage soon. These are being protected from the negative forces in 3-D. As your consciousness continues to shift, through the ascended realms, these blessings will be shared with your world and change it forever. This will involve new, abundant sources of energy and financial supply.

Phillip: What has to happen to release these past American powers?

Saint Germain and Sananda: Humanity must further awaken and embrace and receive the I Am presence and divine inner essence in order to receive the past God Powers secured in the mantle of the Earth.

The disconnection from these is what caused the destruction of past golden ages. Remember, you are destined to create the final golden age. So lessons must be learned, for there will be no going back, dear ones.

Phillip: How does this affect the entire world?

Saint Germain and Sananda: As your divine inner essence begins to grow and expand through the Americas, it will reflect out into the rest of the world through resonance, not force. When people take full responsibility for themselves, the light will grow and become brighter and brighter as the world becomes a being of light.

Phillip: So all the people are important?

Saint Germain and Sananda: All the people of the world are essential and destined to come to the light. It's just a matter of how and when. The universe would be incomplete without each and every one of you. People are being healed in greater numbers, for it is your destiny to do so. Many tools from many higher realms, such as the God Power, are assisting.

Phillip: Is there anything that can prevent all this from happening? I know you say it is our destiny.

Saint Germain and Sananda: Many people feel helpless and hopeless and believe there is nothing they can do. The feeling within them is not strong enough to demand and command God's Power. This reflects their relationship with self not being good or worthy enough. It's one thing to want change, another in the midst of danger to demand it. This God Power comes from your divine inner essence, dear ones. So until this ability is fully awakened in people, they may remain in lack and limitation.

Phillip: It seems people are awakening.

Saint Germain and Sananda: Yes, consciousness is coming to the American continent and to humanity through how you feel and think about yourself. Through this, humans can become further aware of their divine inner essence, their God Power presence. And through knowing more of the self, you will know how to use it in the world around you.

Phillip: At the risk of sounding greedy, how else are you helping us?

Saint Germain and Sananda: There are many transforming and transmuting energies constantly being sent to you to further awaken the divine inner essence within you that will quicken your self and world mastery. This will allow the creation of a new paradigm world order that will amaze and delight you...all through the expansion and intensification of your divine inner essence, which will truly set you free. It's all under the umbrella of God Power.

Phillip: For those who think this is impossible and unbelievable and do not understand what you say, what can you tell them now?

Saint Germain and Sananda: Surrender to not knowing. Stop trying to figure it out. Hand it over to a higher power, whatever you want to call it. Whether you believe it or know it or not, there are cosmic laws that run this universe, bigger than Man Power. How do you think it all stays together, dear ones? It requires trust that there is something within you and outside you that is more powerful than you ever realized. And little by little, you will begin to accept, understand, and know by really looking at the world and universe around you. You cannot call cosmic action into force without it happening. But you must trust and surrender. The lack of this is what caused every past golden age to die.

Phillip: Please continue...we need your words...

Saint Germain and Sananda: The time has come for your freedom. It is expanding daily all around you. You will find the answers within your divine inner essence calling for equality and justice for all...Thousands of tools and teachings are coming through again. Can you receive them?

Through your divine inner essence and service to *all* and our continued assistance, your freedom through your ascension is assured. Your self-mastery will then mirror/reflect in the physical world around you and beyond...You are being prepared to be the ascended master teachings of the universe, utilizing your God Power.

Phillip: Thank you, beloved Ascended Brothers and Sisters. I am forever merging my Man and God Power.

Chapter X

America was once a land of great light,
And might, eons ago.
And nothing now
Can prevent her spiritual awakening
To rise again, no how.

AMERICA, LAND OF LIGHT

A Dialogue with the Combined Saint Germain and Lord Sananda Christ Consciousness Energies

After the 2012 (a year of increased vibratory frequencies) American presidential elections, there was a quantum shift in human consciousness, which allowed a dispensation from source that allowed truths to once again come forward. This is a dialogue between two ascended realms that are very involved in the creation, destiny, and evolution of America, the heart of the world. It matters not if you do not recognize or believe the source of this conversation. Can you hear the content and, if it resonates, apply it?

Phillip: Beloved Saint Germain and Sananda, what is the most important thing you wish to say at this time?

Saint Germain and Sananda: America "belongs" to the higher realms of light that created it, not you. America belongs to God Power. We feel the same way about the nation as you do. We are one in the same; we are one.

Phillip: What exactly does this mean?

Saint Germain and Sananda: Unknown to most of you, we beloved forces have been working for mankind for eons, especially in the creation of America.

Who do you think inspired your founding fathers and those enlightened papers they wrote? Through our love and support, America is a gift to those who wish to be free. And even though things are not yet perfect, you are the freest people in the world. And this is about to shift even more...

Phillip: What do you mean "a gift to those who wish to be free"?

Saint Germain and Sananda: You see, dear ones, America belongs to the we conscious people of the light, not to any dark forces that have attempted to control you for so long. The gift is your awakening into freedom, at last.

Phillip: How did all this start? Why is America so important to the rest of the world?

Saint Germain and Sananda: Most of you do not know that America is where humanity first took human form in the original land of light, called Lemuria. Only a brief part of that physical world still exists in your Western United States. It was in Lemuria that your soul blueprint as a nation began through the direct connection and service to *all there is*. This was millions of years ago, not hundreds or thousands. That unconditional loving energetic blueprint still exists within each of you through the central Sun core of Mother Earth. As many of you are choosing to complete your ascension, along with Mother Earth, into higher realms now, many chose to do the same in the time of Lemuria.

Phillip: So you are saying that our American origin came from the light and still belongs to it and our genetic coding connection to previous light people still exists with us? And you and they are guiding and supporting us in our ascension process now?

Saint Germain and Sananda: Yes, dear one. You have more love and support from us than what exists within most of you. Can you receive now what we have to give?
Phillip: Can you further explain exactly what happened during and after our presidential election?

Saint Germain and Sananda: Through your ascension process, what has been most importantly revealed (again) is the necessity for a "God-Powered government," an authentic, transparent government filled with justice and equality for the people of the light, you. So far, you have had manmade (Man Power) governments reflecting all your wounds and ego defenses. This must end, dear ones.

Phillip: Why are you doing all this?

Saint Germain and Sananda: Because we came from the people (we were once just like you). We are now returned to the light, and our mission is to guard it and never again allow the darkness to prevail, for America belongs to the higher realms of light, where the light and we came. And our destiny is to unite in oneness.

Phillip: So how can we make sure this return to the light happens?

Saint Germain and Sananda: You must be careful to no longer give your power away to those who think they are the rulers of the land. You must now move away from any and all concept or belief in giving your power away. America, the Land of Light, must be ruled by the people, for the people, we the people through Man Power becoming God Power.

Phillip: Is that where "we the people" came from?

Saint Germain and Sananda: Yes, dear one, where else? We the people came from the beings of light. America belongs to that light. America, you can and will now set yourself free by the light within you. Can you now demand and command that the light rule the land (God Power), not the man-not-so-kind Man Power?

Phillip: How else will this transformation take place?

Saint Germain and Sananda: Through the love of self, others, and nation, the destruction of negative forces can appear near.

Let the light hourly grow and expand through the American hand throughout the land and the entire Earth. This process has greatly begun, and you felt it during your past elections.

Phillip: It seems you are ever present?

Saint Germain and Sananda: The higher beings of light from which we came are waiting and watching for every possible opportunity to bring into your 3-D reality an awakened people ready to return to the way of the light, oneness, we consciousness. This is the true feeling within most of you, isn't it?...In spite of your dualistic and confrontational ways.

Phillip: Please further explain the cause and effect.

Saint Germain and Sananda: Stop accepting "wounded," unhealed authority outside yourselves, which has kept you in bondage so long. Command and demand the light authority, the I Am presence, to God-govern and lead you. The lengthy wait of humanity is over, if you can only receive and accept this God Power within yourselves. Remember, Earth and you and we are one.

Phillip: Please continue...

Saint Germain and Sananda: So much of your struggle and energy has not helped your ascension process and only created more lack and limitation. Examine how you use your time and energy. Does it always serve your highest good? Now embrace your inner light and power forevermore...and finally, shut off the separation of human creation!

Phillip: It seems now is the time for us to demand that our world be free of man-made authority (Man Power) and embrace our freedom that can only come from the light within.

Saint Germain and Sananda: When you finally embrace this light, almost instantly, the barriers will fall like the Berlin Wall. Any other way can only cause more delay. Aren't you ready?

Phillip: So we have got to break the destructive cycle that has controlled our nation and the world too long.

We need to set America and the world free from all authority that is not rightfully from the light within each of us.

Saint Germain and Sananda: This will allow a God Power to be used on your ascension process that will create great joy.

Phillip: What further prevents ascension?

Saint Germain and Sananda: You cannot take separation and duality and confrontation into the ascension frequency. This density is what is keeping you where you are now. Your present frequency simply is not allowed within higher realms.

Phillip: But it is our destiny to ascend?

Saint Germain and Sananda: Once you fully connect to the light within, the mass (we) consciousness of humanity can and will shift. Can you accept with compassion and forgive the past and the present? It's merely how you choose to learn. Then you will be truly free, forever, dear ones. Remember, there is no law in the universe that can ever enslave humanity by the light within; God Power is always good.

Phillip: So let's briefly recap your teaching...

Saint Germain and Sananda: Human Man Power authority is what has enslaved you; the light within authority (God Power) is the freeing power that has always been available and with you. It is time for you to be free from the many things you struggle against within yourself and others. The higher realms are pouring their love and light into you every day to assist in freeing you from your human authority. We can only do so much not to interfere with your freedom of choice and will.

Are you willing to do the work and join our efforts moving Man Power into God Power?

If you so choose, you can serve the light within you and radiate it out in world service. And be totally free, at last.

Phillip: Thank you, beloved beings of truth and the light.

Chapter XI

What is this thing, this force called the I Am?
What exactly is present in this name?
A force, a presence that has no shame nor blame.

WHAT NOW? I AM PRESENCE ACTIVATION

The time has come when we humans will have more connection and recognition of the higher realms that constantly pour love and light our way, maintaining and sustaining our very existence, in spite of ourselves. It is time for Man Power to become God Power...

Now we are creating a more conscious cooperation between our 3-D life and 5-D beings who are our protectors and teachers. We are joining through our multidimensional ability with star systems that seeded us, ascended masters who walked our Earth, angel realms, inner-Earth frequencies, and the Intergalactic Federation. These higher realms may be new to many, but we are not new to them. In fact, we would have destroyed ourselves eons ago without their support.

It is our destiny to join in a mass-consciousness with each other and these higher realms to move into our next and final golden age on this planet, a new age of oneness, called we consciousness.

These higher realms are pouring great amounts of energy of light at certain vortices/portals on our Earth to be received by the consciousness of light workers and way showers who can accept with compassion these energies as part of their divine soul plan. Once received and integrated, these energies focus upon the I Am presence within each individual. Only through the I Am presence can we reestablish equality, harmony, and balance on Earth. The I Am presence is your direct reconnection to the forces that created you and support you now.

The separation/veils between where humanity is now and the higher realms is as thin as it's ever been. Man Power and God Power are at long last meeting.

Many of us will feel, hear, and see our connections with frequencies above and below us (as above, so below). It is essential within our freedom of will and choice to acknowledge these higher realms within the hearts and minds of humanity. These higher beings have, from the beginning of our existence, loved and supported us more than we were/are capable of loving ourselves. They can give aid without limit to those who trust and surrender to their existence. Now, with the more integrated connection and activation of our I Am presence, we are manifesting our final golden age within the last cycle of this planet before it and we ascend into beings of light (our true, eternal state of God Power- beingness).

We have learned all we need to learn from the isolation within what is not, the time line of what is now. The tool of the I Am presence can reestablish the original balance and oneness upon Earth. It can consume all imbalances through unconditional love of self while dissolving the fear in our emotional bodies that has caused so much pain.

Through the connection and combination of Man and God Power with our I Am presence, we can reawaken our divinity, clearing and cleansing all that is not love and light. Unlike past golden ages, this final one will allow a permanent connection to source / God Power that will ensure our ascended mastery of self. This will allow a transition into world and then universal service.

Higher beings, some in human embodiments and other forms, will now walk and talk face-to-face with mankind on Earth. It is time we know we are not alone and know what loving forces really are in divine control of our world and the universe. The original divine way of life will be explained once again, the human and planetary imbalances revealed and cleared. Human lack, limitations, and fear will be washed away, and we shall recreate communities of equality, harmony, and balance. The light and love of these higher realms never fails. And you chose to be here now for this glorious event.

Stay steady in your trust, and surrender to what is said here no matter how things appear now. Much more is about to be revealed...Man and God Power are becoming one!

Chapter XII

*To learn to love,
Is the sacred mission of Mother Earth.
First love of self,
Allows all the rest.*

ENLIGHTENMENT FROM THE INTERGALACTIC FEDERATION

We come to you from the Intergalactic Federation in concert with the Five-Pointed Star System portal opening that you are learning of now. We join the energies of the Pleiadians and the Arcturians (balancing the masculine and feminine energy) with the Orion energy from the inner-Earth—demonstrating, if you will, as above, so below.

Dear beloved humans, you have learned so much over the last few weeks about yourself through the combined energies, unprecedented in your frequency, coming together to bring to you a mighty teaching of oneness through knowingness of self.

We wish to add an addendum to your teaching to give you an even deeper understanding of what is happening, why it is happening, and where it is happening. These frequencies have come together on 12/12/12, 12/21/12, and most recently on 12/25/12. Because these portal openings, these vortex openings, these energetic connects are to activate a force within the core of your planet, which has always been there and was transported from your beloved sister planet, Venus, so many millennia ago.

This force is called unconditional love; you are in the process of reactivating it through the process of self, as you have discussed tonight in the teachings of your Twelve Life Lessons classes. You have gone as far from self, from source, from one another, from your home planet, as you could possibly go through the gift and the hardship of your freedom of will. It was a dispensation that was given to you through a veiling of yourselves and through the abuse of wisdom and power that you once knew.

You were gifted with this freedom of choice and freedom of will in order to get as far from yourselves, one another, and source as possible to work your way back through hundreds and thousands of incarnations in this frequency to get to the end of time, to get to the time line ending, if you will, where you are now, which simply reflects where your planet is and where she has chosen to be in her ascension process. Thus, including everything within and upon her body, your planet, your mother Earth, will ascend with the divine beings of light that you are.

So why has this entirety taken place? Why have you chosen this journey, dear ones? What is this all about, and how does your divine plan mirror this divine universal cosmic process?

The purpose of this planet was to learn and to teach love, dear ones. So now through the process of learning to love yourself, you are preparing yourselves for the grandest service of them all. You are returning to world service through love of self as your foundation, connecting in your so-called we consciousness, in your oneness, in your equality, with harmony and balance, to now go out throughout this solar system, throughout this galaxy, beyond universes known and unknown, to become part of the ever-expanding and growing universe that knows no limit and knows no end, dear ones.

There are worlds behind you. There are worlds where you presently are. There are worlds, as you know, much more advanced than you are. All these worlds are waiting for you. Can you feel it in your heart? You've always known there was more than what appeared to be, have you not?

The dispensation of so many frequencies coming together is a revelation, a transformation of what is taking place. So many of you, more than ever before, consciously and unconsciously, have chosen to be here at this divine moment. So as you have discussed, heed now what happens to be transpiring in your outer world, as you have discussed through the channel we are coming through now. It is simply the final clearing and cleansing of yourselves, of your planet, to activate this final golden age, which is activated by this unconditional love in the core of your planet, reflecting the core of not only Venus but also so many ascended and advanced worlds that no longer participate in freedom of choice and freedom of will through a veil.

They are in full service to source and all that there is, which allows the manifestation of all things in your ascended mastership.

You are in the process of not only moving from your carbon to your crystalline existence, but you are also being empowered to control electrons and atoms and to create through your thoughts and your feelings every single thing that is needed to serve and service *all that there* is, dear ones.

There are millions and billions of beings in service to all that there is. You are joining this divine cosmic community. It is your time to do this. It is time for Man Power to become God Power. It is your final cleansing and clearing of self. So now, fill your hearts with gratitude that you have chosen to show up and to learn from something other than the human mind, to know that there are other sources of wisdom, that there are other sources of tools and teachings to propel you into the frequency of oneness, and to finally expel you from this dense frequency of 3-D.

You have learned all there is to learn from cause and effect and karmic disposition. Be compassionate. Be accepting. Be forgiving of how you have chosen to learn and know that way of learning has ended if you so choose. Now, dear ones, your real learning, the true magnificence of you, shall come into full manifestation and fruition on this grand planet of love. Your Man Power and God Power will become one.

Chapter XIII

Beautiful beings who love and support
The ever-evolving human space
Can be called higher beings,
Of love, light, and grace.

ARCHANGEL ACTIONS

During these extraordinary times of change on our planet and within humanity, many higher realms are "weighing in" to support our personal and planetary shifts. Such higher beings include ascended masters, who were once human; star beings, who "seeded" our world; inner-Earth civilizations, who once lived upon the surface of the planet; and archangel angels, hovering above, to name a few. At this precious time, all these forces and more are joining together in love and support to assist us in creating a new reality of unity and we consciousness, as Man and God Power become one. The world cannot and will not continue as the past, or we shall not survive as a species. But there is a grand plan that we do survive and move into heights of beings beyond our imagination at this time.

We shall now focus on one of these divine beings, Archangel Michael, with his mighty God Power sword teaching us to move from our mind, which believes, to our heart, which knows.

Phillip: Dearest Michael, there are so many archangels, what exactly is your focus and role?

Archangel Michael: Certain endeavors and intentions are assigned to various frequencies of consciousness. We within the Michael angelic realm largely guard and stand present to repel any and all who intend to destroy self, others, or the planet. We vibrate at a frequency of love and perfection for your use. Michael means, "Who is like God Power"; we embody the word for truth, moving from the mind to the heart, allowing you to know who you are and why you are here through a process of your choosing.

This will allow you to take responsibility for yourselves and the activation of your soul plan.

Phillip: Exactly how does your frequency achieve this?

Archangel Michael: You do, dear ones, through the integration of your I Am presence, your divine essence, and your God Power as you anchor more fully into your divine soul plan, the reason you are here. Then you can learn the things that are preventing this in yourself and your world. Once you know and apply this wisdom, it will be a game-changer.

Phillip: It seems you are a sort of "preventing presence."

Archangel Michael: The veil between our worlds is thinner than ever before, dear ones. This will further allow you to move more deeply in your understanding of what service the angelic realm plays in your world, especially in relationship to yourself (the basis of all).

Phillip: Most people perceive you as a protector-power with your sword.

Archangel Michael: Humanity's awareness of most angels is through the concept of a guardian angel mission. So that's how most angels are in the consciousness of humanity to a lesser or greater degree. How this expresses itself within each angelic realm has to do with the mission of each frequency. We are discussing Michael at the moment.

Phillip: So how does what you do really work?

Archangel Michael: Be careful when you call upon us, dear ones. We shall assist you in fulfilling your personal and world soul plans. Are you truly ready to do that?

Phillip: Please further explain...

Archangel Michael: It's really about the revelation of what exists within you. The "protection" comes from the God Power within you, dear ones.

We merely teach you how to awaken this truth through a loving relationship with self and others.

Phillip: You're like ever-ready men...

Archangel Michael: We are ever ready to respond to your slightest call by your focusing on us. It makes no difference if you see or feel us or believe in us. When you connect with our frequency through your emotions and thoughts or incarnational evolution, we automatically stand ready to protect and support that which is of God Power, the good of all, within you. And to assist you in healing what is preventing this.

Phillip: So we just need to focus on you?

Archangel Michael: If mankind only knew how simple this is. It's just a matter of you getting yourself out of the way, trusting and surrendering to our existence, and knowing we are here to assist in maintaining and sustaining all soul plans. We are not a figment of anyone's imagination, dear ones. Whenever we are given the slightest opening or recognition, we appear.

Phillip: Have you always been present in mankind's history?

Archangel Michael: Mankind, through Man Power, would have destroyed itself long ago without our constant presence. We are greater than humanity's intellect, ceaseless in our service, dear ones. Fasten your seat belts; our greatest efforts are yet to come during your dispensation of ascension!

Phillip: What does that mean?

Archangel Michael: There is much change in process within yourselves and your world where only higher-realm support can be fully effective. We are here to protect all that is good. There are many shifts in your emotional, mental, and physical bodies that will affect your world. You are moving into a new age (the seventh and final golden age) with new inner God Powers you do not fully understand or know how to use. But when you are ready, all will be revealed...

Phillip: You will show us how to use these God Powers?

Archangel Michael: Yes, through the fulfillment of your divine soul plans, as you learn how to master self and existence.

Phillip: Please further explain...

Archangel Michael: You will learn the powers of self and nature and the cosmos as you ascend into a higher frequency of existence, You will be creating, growing, and expanding beyond your awareness now.

Phillip: As if this isn't enough, what else?

Archangel Michael: Much of our assistance will come through your healing, by love and the further activation of your I Am presence. We are the ways and means to your I Am presence and all higher realms through the healing of self and awakening of your divine essence.

Phillip: Please continue...

Archangel Michael: Humanity has no idea of the inner God Power within itself. The angelic realm is connected to this ability and power within each of you. Together, there is no limit to what can be achieved...no limit to the balance of giving and receiving, dear ones.

Phillip: There is nothing in the physical world as strong as this I Am presence, is there?

Archangel Michael: Can you show us anything as strong? Can you compare anywhere what we can accomplish together without limit?

Phillip: It seems like it is time for mankind to better understand the angelic realm and how we work together.

Archangel Michael: There are legions of us to support your fulfillment of your divine soul plans and your attainment into ascension, dear ones. You are not alone, never have been, never will be.

Phillip: Wow!

Archangel Michael: We are here to assist in the balancing of any negative forces inside and outside you that are preventing your divine destiny to ascend back into the light. We've been doing this for eons. The time is now for blast-off.

Phillip: All we have to do is call upon you?

Archangel Michael: Yes, dear ones. Trust and surrender; we are here to assist in presenting nothing less than the perfect coming forth. Our sword of truth will cut through this. Any doubt will prevent this.

Phillip: What is the biggest prevention now?

Archangel Michael: Mankind must become conscious and desire to receive the God Power within itself. War does not work and cannot continue; honor yourself, others, and your planet. You need to reconnect with the higher realms from which you came, all lack and limitation and suffering you have created will end. Can you simply trust and surrender and come to us?...We are all-powerful and wish only to spread our blessings upon you. Can you receive them now?

We shall answer every heartfelt call and fulfillment of each soul plan. This is how much we love you. Now love yourselves enough to receive our giving.

Phillip: Thank you with all my heart.

Chapter XIV

*The Christ called forth a compassionate cosmic blueprint
For people to be treated equal, and love one another,
No matter what the imprint.*

THE SECOND COMING HAS COME

Mother Earth Speaking

Dearest Children, this is your Earth Mother. As you continue to live upon my body, your planet Earth, I wish to remind you of my beingness as a conscious, feeling, God-parent power and force, whom, in your recent history, you have not learned to honor or obey. As a consequence of this, a clearing and cleansing of both of us is having to take place so we both survive. This survival represents a great Second Coming of your higher self, planet, solar system, galaxy, and universe.

New structures of energy are being built in your human energy/nervous systems that reflect what is taking place outside you. You are now uniting with the twelve new chakra systems, which reflect the twelve star systems that seeded humanity. Divine love is awakening and encoding/downloading a rebirth of unity / we consciousness in your beingness.

You were born for this now moment, dear children. You have chosen to be here now for this great shift. It is also time to accept with compassion all the wounds and ego defenses you created to learn what is through what is not. That end time has come. You don't have to learn that way anymore!

Through divine love, a divine alchemy process is transpiring where portals/vortices in time on 12/12/12, 12/21/12, and 12/25/12 now allow you to move and expand into your divine blueprint, soul plans, and God Power.

You will create new communities of equality, harmony, and balance reflecting the divine beings you are. The primary tool in all this comes through your higher selves: I Am presence, Christ Consciousness connections.

This will be a time of introspection and possible disruption of the old patterns that no longer serve your higher good or that of your mother, planet Earth. Old, destructive patterns of the past will pass...

This clearing and cleansing of planet and person are essential, dear children. Be forgiving of the chaos that just might occur. Fill your hearts with gratitude for what we must be and do together.

In effect, a divine alchemy process through your I Am presence, Christ Consciousness is transforming your structure from carbon based to crystalline light. You are an eternal being of light; it is time to be and know this. This transformation process allows the highest frequencies of Christ Light to be experienced and encoded as you move from the old to the newness of oneness, dear children.

The laws of karma and cause and effect are ending. You don't need to learn this way anymore. If you are reading this, you are aligned to the Christ energy that God-empowers new life. This process will continue for several years. This is a beginning, not an ending, of the new you and world and our survival to achieve our divine destiny: to be ascended masters in service to *all there is.*

It only takes a small percentage of you to effect the necessary changes to create the new world that awaits you. What do you choose?

This so-called ascension process of which we speak is a natural evolution and cycle of all planets. Look up into the night sky, dear children; all those stars went through a process not unlike your own. Your ascension process was reactivated a generation ago during the harmonic convergence on the birth date of the channel through whom we speak now.

What will take place will be unique for each of you since each of you is unique. Some may not choose ascension, but all will eventually reach the same destination whatever you choose through your freedom of will. Much that has been kept hidden for various reasons is yet to be revealed; this will be a game-changer in your world. You will fully awaken as to who you are and why you are here.

This will be largely achieved through your reconnections to higher realms, through your I Am presence, the connector.

See this ascension process as a divine intervention by those forces that love you more than you are capable of loving yourself right now. Trust and surrender to the process of divine perfect order; your heart knows and your mind may doubt. All that has ever stood in your way was your disconnect to the divine in you and outside you. Now, all that is not of the divine will be transformed/transmuted by the light of your I Am presence and the love forces that created you. Dear children, are you ready to accept and receive this truth now?

Soon, your world will be governed by God Power reflections of your higher self through councils connected to higher-dimensional beings; this mirrors all advanced civilizations in the universe.

Dear children, the Second Coming is your coming to the realization of all we speak of here. Heed your mother now once and for *all*.

Chapter XV

Now we are awakening in the all-seeing,
The Christ Light within every human being.

CHRIST CONSCIOUSNESS SEASON

As we approach the final weeks of this year with still so much energetically happening within/on our planet and throughout humanity, our thoughts and emotions turn to the Christ Consciousness this spiritual Christ season. This short conversation is with the combined energies of the collective ascended masters' realms and myself.

Phillip: What exactly is the Christ Consciousness, and how does it assist us?

Ascended Masters: The Christ Consciousness is a dispensation from your creator to alleviate humanity from the massive levels of lack and limitation you have created for eons through your emotions and thoughts. This teaching/energy has been brought to humanity by many teachers, many times throughout your evolution, most recently through Master Jesus.

Phillip: How can it best be used?

Ascended Masters: It is suggested that you use your free will and time to focus regularly on this Christ Consciousness energy. This will overcome and transcend your negative emotions and thoughts that create your reality. The Christ Consciousness energy will consume anything less than itself by transmuting it into pure, divine light. This requires self-discipline and self-realization. The tools to achieve these have been given to you many times and are present in your world again now. The channel we are coming through now and his brethren (the Angel News Network) can direct you to many of the needed wisdoms.

Phillip: What about those who do not believe in Christ Consciousness, especially the young, who may see it as some corrupted religion?

Ascended Masters: We are acutely aware of the nonbelievers and the destructive cultural trends in government, religion, and corporations that especially affect the youth. Many youth actually believe through their rebellious egos; they are convinced that their free form of thinking, without any awareness of higher realms, achieves self-realization and truth. Nothing could be further from the truth. Self-mastery and discipline are essential to freeing you from yourself. This needs the support and love of higher-realm energies of contacting your God Power.

Phillip: So are you saying we cannot advance without the Christ Consciousness?

Ascended Masters: The highest awakening is through the Christ Consciousness energy. And each generation is advised to pass this truth on to the next generation. Me consciousness of greed, immorality, selfishness, and non-truth have never advanced humanity. All past golden ages have died because of their lack of connection to their source / God Power. Only light can advance humanity. And light will ultimately consume anything less than itself. This is the process you are involved in now, dear ones, what you call ascension.

Phillip: What else does the Christ Consciousness do?

Ascended Masters: Most important, it allows you to know you are God experiencing yourself. And once you know this, you come to know you are in service to this truth. God is the great *who* and *why*, and you are the mirror of that truth. Now transmute your Man Power into God Power. Are you ready?

Phillip: And then what happens?

Ascended Masters: When a human's Man Power becomes one with God Power, through love of self, he or she realizes he or she is truly God. The Christ Consciousness is the journey/pathway to this reality. This force has lived within you always. Are you finally ready to apply it and free yourself from yourself?

And continue your service to the ever-expanding universe as the master teacher you came here to be?

Phillip: Does the spiritual holiday season affect this?

Ascended Masters: Humanity is more sensitive to the energies that are transmitting from above and below the Earth; your heart opens more widely. In fact, your heart is designed to house and dispense the Christ Consciousness energy at will. Call upon it anytime.

Merry Christ Consciousness, dear ones.

Chapter XVI

These higher beings
Truly have freed themselves
From human limitations,
And all evaluations
Through blazing outpouring of light
That constantly brightens the night.

CALL UPON HIGHER REALMS REGULARLY

As the elements continue to shift and change in our relationship with self, others, and the outer world, let us continue to call upon higher God-Power realms for love and support. These realms include archangels, ascended masters, star beings, inner-Earth civilizations, etc. Their goal is for us to master self / Man Power and have that mirror out into the outer world.

Humanity has largely lost contact with these ancient, God-powerful and protecting forces, which have always been with us. We have never been alone. These energies can and will infuse self and the environment with support/wisdom much stronger than anything in our frequency. Their aim is to eliminate any imbalances in the human self in order to create a new world of equality, harmony, and balance.

More than ever before, let us call upon these higher realms to allow them to offer support in our building of a new civilization reflecting a permanent "we consciousness" of unity and oneness. The time has come to move from the "me" to the "we" and man to move into God.

The shocking realization is that if mankind continues to be left to its own devices, our destructive desires within us are capable of destroying the planet and ourselves. It has happened before.

These Man Power forces are insane, and the support of the higher God Power realms is essential and can and will assist us in awakening our inner divine essence and save us from ourselves.

It is time to establish a new pattern reconnecting us to our innate goodness through these higher realms and have it mirror out to the many, Then we can become the custodians of boundless oneness, God Power, abundance, cosmic intelligence...boundless everything. Are you ready?

The balance and action of our emotions and thoughts will allow a new world to unfold. Through the higher-realm teachings, we can become fully conscious of any imbalances in our emotions and thoughts that do not support the highest good of self and others. The Angel News Network and many, many other outlets are dedicated to such teachings.

There is much mischief in our emotions and thoughts and it has caused us to give our God Power away to others in religion, government, corporations, etc. We can set ourselves free from what we have housed within us by calling upon the invincible higher realms' ever-present support. Mankind has held itself prisoner far too long, these mighty forces can teach us how to process ourselves into freedom.

Remember, when we call upon higher realms:
1. Negative Man Power forces cannot affect higher realms,
2. Negative forces are consumed by the positive, and
3. Negative forces know the higher realms mean their annihilation.

Energy always entrains to the highest frequency; every positive has an electronic force field that attracts like kind. Higher realms have the ability to control any amount of energy and keep it from lower/denser energy.

When, through our freedom of will and choice, will we have the courage to choose a higher frequency of existence? These higher God-Power-realm energies are greater than the humanity of this world. It is our destiny to embody them and annihilate anything other than the highest good of self and all.

Let us maintain and sustain the inner God Power within each of us ever growing and expanding into the mission of creating the seventh and final golden age of oneness / we consciousness.

Allow our destiny now to clear and cleanse all the negative emotions and thoughts of the past and present.

If not now, when, dear brothers and sisters, are we going to demand and command ourselves, our world into our birthright of God Power oneness? This can only be done with the unconditionally loving support of higher realms, which are ever ready and ever present.

Then we shall be victorious in embracing and embodying the divine soul plan of self and planet to become the higher realms that guide and support us. Let us go forward and feel the presence of these divine beings who love us more than we can ourselves right now to free ourselves from further suffering through becoming our higher selves and joining the higher realms in oneness. Now is the crucial time.

Chapter XVII

Beloved weary, wonderful world,
It is time to take the I's from thee,
And replace I and me,
So then you can really see,
The we.

MESSAGE FROM THE TWO MARY'S

Beloved children of our collective receptive and assertive mother energies, whom you call Mary, meaning enlightened feminine energy appearing within every spiritual truth upon your planet, we come to you at this time with a message of motherly love, authenticity, and transparency and support. Call us whatever proper name resonates within your heart. You know who we are, dear children.

During these necessary and sacred times of planetary and human ascension processes, many are currently "connecting" with "higher realms" through an astral projection via fourth-dimensional frequencies. There is wisdom there, but it is veiled with the wounds of the illusion of the third dimension. Most important, the process we describe reflects the "filter" of the receiver. So we ask you to use your discernment and resonance and the guardianship of your mothers. As we fill our hearts with compassion and forgiveness for those of whom we speak, please know it is simply their way and your way to learn and for all of you to eventually arrive at the same destination of oneness by seeing the mirror, dear children. True wisdom, free of humanity's Man Power, comes purely from fifth-dimensional connection and beyond. This is where we truly reside.

It is essential not to use connections with us as a device against or toward another. We rarely respond through specific individuated soul plans; rather, we speak to humanity as a collective whole. Thus, proper names and specific forecasts are reflections of the receiver's filter and can violate your freedom of choice and will.

This is a grand and momentous moment, for you have all chosen to be here at the most crucial event in your history... to permanently return to your connection to *all there is* and fall into full service to the God Power within each of you through the creation of the Golden Age of Gaia. There are many unseen and seen events assisting this process...balancing of energies, emotions, and thoughts; further openings of portals; revelations of ancient truths and wisdoms; and most important, the opening of your divine hearts through cosmic love. You cannot do it alone. It will come through your returned connection to we who maintain and sustain you and the forces that created us all. We shall consume all that is not constructive and destroy any destructive intention like a mother protecting her child. What you are experiencing is the death spiral of your altered ego, which has kept you in duality and separation far too long. Have compassion for how you have chosen to learn; the completion of your learning is upon you.

Call upon us. We are unconditional love through the motherhood of *all*.

Chapter XVIII

Planet Earth has entered
A most sacred cycle now,
Through ascension's
Outpouring of great light,
Somehow.

12/21/12 CELEBRATION

Dear Beloved Children of Humanity,

We of the Intergalactic Federation (IGF) in concert with your mother Earth and other multi-fifth-dimensional energies come to you now at this auspicious time to further enlighten you regarding your events/celebrations of 12/21/21. We of the IGF are acting as stewards of a process that last took place some twenty-six thousand years ago on your planet, a process that allows you, if you so choose, to reawaken to the truth of who you are and why you are here as you reconnect/recalibrate to the forces that maintain and sustain your existence.

This is a process that begins with portals of fifth-dimensional energies opening and interacting with Mother Earth and humanity. Your major time lines on these portal openings were 12/12/12 and 12/21/12. This is a process that will extend for many years with other star-realm participations and us.

You will receive additional guidance and support at that time....

This is a process of releasing the old paradigms that have kept you in duality and lack and limitation while reconnecting with your source and now moving into a consciousness of oneness, moving from the me to the we, if you will...moving from Man Power to God Power.

Through resonance with one another, you will create various gatherings of celebration to acknowledge this extraordinary gift/happening in your world. You have drifted as far from your source as possible through your freedom of will and choice, and the time line has come to reconnect to self, one another, and source.

The divine soul plans of your planet and yourselves are in full activation as a result of the energetic portal openings that took place 12/12/12 and 12/21/12. This was a cosmic event of your solar system, galaxy, and the entire universe; you are all connected, dear ones. It is time you know and apply this wisdom.

Within your various celebrations/gatherings of this shift of self and world, you will participate in various guided exercises and restatements of light worker / way shower oaths that will serve as a Communion of Souls in communities of oneness. In these communities of equality, harmony, and balance, you will be asked to release the old and open and embrace the unknowing of the new you and world.

Beginning noon 12/21/12 and lasting until midnight, a twenty-four-hour period, was a unique opportunity to integrate these multidimensional energies (portal openings) to facilitate your transition/transformation into the new.

Dear ones, this is a mass convergence of higher realms, Earth, and human energies to create your new age of moving from the "me" to the "we" consciousness. There are many billions of you present now to experience this event consciously or not. Whether you are aware of this or not, it is taking place.

Have acceptance and compassion for all the lifetimes you have had to bring you to this glorious moment.

We are here to assist and guide you as your time-space continuum shifts, changes, and transpires. This is the ending of the old you and world and the beginning of the new you and world. Rejoice and fill your hearts with joy!

Chapter XIX

This is the grandest event
Earth and humanity have ever known
To redefine and refine
All love and light, with all our might.

NEW YEAR'S DAY MESSAGE, SIX-SIDED MERKABA

Greetings, beloved brethren of your Angel News Network. We of the Intergalactic Federation (IGF) with Adama, High Priest of Lemuria, bring you tidings of great joy and support on this your first day of your new golden age of we consciousness. You have waited many millennia for this moment.

We have been granted dispensation to give you further clarity of your mission and karmic connections, dear souls. All of you have had various and many lifetimes together on this planet with similar missions as present, some deeper than others but all with the same purpose to bring truth and light into this world.

Now, in this incarnational cycle, it is your destiny, desire, and direction to heal all aspects of self that have impeded you in the past and present, to be your message, your purpose in being here.

You are, in fact, continuing to be proxies of humanity who shall clear and cleanse all 3-D unhealed aspects of self in order to raise your vibrations and to be the beingness of your soul plans. This is why you chose and were chosen for your past sacred journeys, dear brethren. This now is a continuation of your soul plans within the endeavor you call the Angel News Network.

Dear brethren, if you so choose, it is time to accept with compassion and forgive any and all wounds and ego defenses created around those wounds that stand in your path.

This has not so simply been the way you chose to learn what you needed to learn.
You are to become a mighty beacon reflecting the mighty I Am presence within each of you that cannot and will not house wounds and defenses. Are you ready to receive and give this to yourself and your waiting, weary world? Are you ready for your Man Power to become your God Power?

This year, as has been foretold, you will receive guidance from the IGF, various star realms, and inner-Earth forces, including Gaia. Your relationship with your conscious, living planet is crucial, for her forces and love maintain and sustain you.

Being what you receive from higher realms is now essential to your individuated and collective endeavors, dear brethren. This necessitates utilizing all the tools and teachings given you in the past and present. These can no longer remain locked in your mental bodies. Your awakening of your knowing heart will empower your I Am presence into the oneness of we consciousness.

You are all to become conduits of higher realms, not just one or two of you. This is the way to show others.

As you know, our five-pointed star portal will be accessible for years to come to further assist you in any needed healing and processing that you will achieve among yourselves. You have already begun this final process. This internal work is essential to your external work, dear brethren.

The right and fight of separation and confrontation is over, if you choose to move into we consciousness. Remember, this is what prevented your success in the past. Realize you have chosen one another time and time again to learn what is needed to heal self and ascend from dense duality.

Awake, dear brethren, now, and replace your wounds and defenses with healing gratitude in order to fully move into being your mission. Your entire galaxy, various star realms, and inner-Earth beings are beside you.

You can now join all these God Powers in your world and be the divine beings of light you truly are.

Fill your hearts with joy that this glorious moment has come!

Your brethren of the Intergalactic Federation with Adama, High Priest of Lemuria

Chapter XX

Death is feared,
And yet ever so near.
Let us retrain ourselves
Through another view
And review a new view
Of what we call death.

RELATIONSHIP OF DEATH AND CONSCIOUSNESS

We humans are beginning to understand the relationship between our imbalances, unhealed ego defenses, negative thoughts and emotions, and our physical deaths. This "discord" within us actually results in our disintegration, which is another name for death.

We are in the process of learning to love self and others and have this reflect out in all aspects of our life in order to reclaim our immortal state of being. In effect, Man Power is learning to live its life by the eternal law of love. We are beginning to fully understand the God Power and essence of this thing called love. And when we learn how to fully integrate this love law into civilization and ourselves, we can and will be released from the cosmic wheel of birth and rebirth. Repeated Earth lives will no longer be necessary, and the imbalances/problems we experience now will disappear. We simply will no longer need to learn the way we have in the past (often through what is not).

Rather than lack and limitation, duality, separation, and confrontation, in their place will come joy and abundance in ever-expanding perfection, which forever manifests within love. Then our most powerful enemy, our old selves, and death will simply vanish into the new world.

When our human wounds, defenses, and discord dissolves, not by so-called death but by constantly raising our consciousness by the activity of the I Am presence (your connection to source), its power will be released into the outer world service through the individual first and foremost by complete life / self-mastery. This consciousness embracing the I Am aspects is being called we consciousness. And the relationship between consciousness and the I Am energies is vital in order for humanity to move into its final golden age.

Through we consciousness, every human being can release the limitless God Power of the mighty I Am presence within each of us and each of us as an equal, God-given supply that can be embodied to build communities of equality, harmony, and balance worldwide.

We can use these terrific tools of we consciousness and the I Am presence just like the all-powerful ascended masters who once walked this Earth and continue to support us now. This is the cosmic Christ/God Power within us all!

Throughout the universe, we consciousness is the only consciousness that can say I Am. And when we choose to say I Am, we are being and using the divine power of the God-Power, *you*.

Chapter XXI

When mankind, truly being kind
Has fully awakened and gained further wisdom,
We may join in perfect cooperation
With the magnificent force of Mother Earth,
Creating heaven on Earth
Being one again.

WHY IS THE WORLD CHANGING?

Have you noticed that our world is shifting into something new? Man Power is shifting into God Power.

The old doesn't seem to be working anymore.

All of the leading forces that have controlled our world for a long time are changing: governments, religions, corporations, and financial systems. All are under change. What used to work just doesn't seem to anymore.

Why?

We are now living within an era of transformation. Our planet and the civilizations upon it shift every few thousand years (check history). But this one feels and seems different from anything ever before. It is essential to now understand what is going on (and why) physically and energetically within and upon our planet as it and we evolve at this time.

My theory—and that of many others—is that it is the destiny and plan of our Earth, a living, conscious being, to move to a higher frequency of existence and consciousness. Thus Man Power becomes God Power; everything within and upon our planet will join the shift forward.

It will be forever forward from this point on...What we have experienced in the past is past. More than ever before, there is a need, a desire, to reach outside the "standard" learning and realize, understand, and embrace the change. It is the blueprint of all worlds to move forward in their evolution...our time has come.

It is time to better understand who we are and why we are here (our purpose). What do you think our purpose is? Who are you? Why are you here? Today, we have an opportunity to heal and grow in wisdom (if we choose) to accept and embrace the new world being created: a world that reflects "Unity Consciousness (US)," not the continuation of every person and nation for him- her- or itself.

In effect, we've all been asleep for a long time, and this has brought us much pain throughout our history. But we can change that now...

For a long time, humanity has not always been told the entire truth of what's happening and our true history. Thus, much of what we think is true about our world and ourselves is not. Many of our belief systems are based upon these untruths. Now is the time, an opportunity to tell the truth through the truth. Are you ready? Can you handle it? Can the world handle it?

The truth is we are not children being controlled by unseen forces anymore. Nor is this shift a process in which the few can continue to control the many.

If each of us can discern the truth of our reason to be here, not to judge it or shame it, but to accept it...we can dissolve the illusion of separation and confrontation within us to know we are a kind race of human beings moving more clearly to see the beauty and common energy that runs through everyone and connects us to Earth (our home).

The time has come for us to shed our many erroneous beliefs about ourselves, our planet, governments, religions, corporations, and the universe itself that have kept most of our kind in varying degrees of lack and limitation far too long.

We alone can do this through connecting with our true being, our God Power.

The times ahead will be challenging for many and exciting for others, as we now shift from an old, divided world into a new one of oneness.

And more of you (many billions) than ever before chose to be here for this change...

Chapter XXII

No form can come into creation
Without a thought as a picture
For every thought contains an idea
That is the criteria of expression.

HOW TO MANIFEST

A Teaching and Tool from Saint Germain

The ancients knew how to manifest and create at will. We see remaining examples of this ability in pyramids and temples we could not create today. It is time for us humans to rediscover our ancient birthright and to know how to use it within the service to ALL THERE IS. Any abuse of these wisdoms will simply not be allowed within Universal Law (the oneness of all). Many past advanced civilizations abused Man and God Power and soon discovered another force other than themselves was in control. Let us learn from the past, as this powerful tool is taught to us again.

Basic Truth: Nothing can come into existence in the universe unless we consciously hold a picture of that in our thought, for every thought (and emotion around it) contains a picture of that idea within it.

In order to assure manifestation, there are several steps to bring visible, tangible results:

HOW TO MANIFEST
From Sacred Poetry & Mystical Messages

No form can come into creation,
Without a thought as a picture.

For every thought contains an idea
That is the criteria of expression.

Let us look at the process
That brings access
To creation...

What is it you wish to create?
Is it worthy of your time and energy?
What is your reason to bring this into existence?
Is it to satisfy an addiction or comfort zone
Or get you arrested on the way home?

Make sure what you wish to create
Has no motive or need to do harm to another,
But has an intention of a loving brother.

Write down your plan in your own words,
As clearly and consciously as you can,
Then you have a starting plan.

Know you have the ability to create,
See it like a picture on a plate.

The seeing and the power to create
Are the gifts of God Power within.

Seeing and feeling within yourself
Allows you to lift creation off the shelf.

The heart already knows,
But keep reminding the mind
Creation is the ability
To see the God within all the time.

For God is the doer, the doing, and the deed,
And you through Him can create and proceed with,
Whatever you need.

Read your written plan again and again
At the beginning and end of each day.

This was your creation downloaded in your heart
That is the best part and start.

Keep your intention to yourself,
Hold your intention to yourself,
Hold its power inside you,
So only you know its view.

When you are ready,
Steady yourself and allow
Your inner vision to come through,
Consciously connecting to the Law of Making
And the God Power within you.

MAN POWER GOD POWER

Cast out all doubts and fear
And know in your heart
Your creation is near.

Have no set moment for results,
Just know you and God are issuing
The picturing of results,
With no wishing.

Allow yourself to be surprised and delighted,
And filled with gratitude
When your multitude comes near.

Chapter XXIII

Saint Germain, most folks in America
Know you not,
That you are the great loving force behind our area.

AMERICA, THE FINAL GOLDEN AGE

The time has come for America and the world to know the meaning, value, and purpose of America in relationship to our planet's final golden age and to create "a more perfect union." That "union" will be with *all there is*, source, God Power, whatever you choose to call your creator. Long ago, higher realms infused our geographical location (the United States) with powerful unconditionally loving forces to ensure equality, harmony, and balance for all.

Portals/vortices are being activated at this time to assist once again in the creation of a golden age of oneness. All past golden ages died as a result of their lost "union" with source. Now is the time to create a more perfect permanent true union with God Power. Resonance created through this new golden age process will allow other countries to create the same. America's founding fathers' papers (inspired by Saint Germain) are still the "blueprint" to lead the way now. They have never actually been realized. It is our destiny that our world joins in oneness now. All the chaos you see in the world now is just the final clearing and cleansing of the old. Saint Germain is still working hard for us for his divine intention of America to come true. Will you join him now as we transform Man Power into God Power?

Chapter XXIV

Ascended masters are always among us,
Guardians and gifts of humanity.
Who have worked many millennia
From the unseen and seen, a plenty.

ASCENDED MASTER SUPPORT

We simply cannot create a new world paradigm by ourselves without the support of higher God Power realms. We never could. Let us now share some of the ascended masters' basic wisdom, which is intended to offer love and support. Which ones do you resonate with and are ready to apply daily in creating a new reality?

1. Life is the one thing that produces manifestation; all energy is some form of life. How are you using your energy?

2. When your awareness/consciousness connects with something, your life integrates to that part of life and you become one with it, thus, we and all things are one when we are conscious.

3. Our lack of control of our attention prevents manifestation. Maintain your focus.

4. Energy flows wherever your attention focuses it. Where is your focus now?

5. When we master the proper use of energy, it will be through the mastery of our emotional and mental selves. Our thoughts and emotions create our reality.

6. Ascended beings, once human, have chosen to be more evolved conscious beings than we. Are you ready to become an ascended master?

7. War-makers of the world do so through their deliberate misuse of energy. War simply does not work.

8. When we finally understand the abuse and right use of power, we shall evolve.

9. We are just beginning to understand the mastery of self that is ours through our healed emotions and thoughts and connection to we consciousness / God Power.

10. What cosmic shock is necessary to shake mankind from its creations? Do we need to be destroyed again to learn?

11. Are we ready to accept and know there is life greater than the one in this world and we need its support? We need God Power.

12. Cosmic assistance (God Power) can and will be the greatest help in attaining our ascension.

13. Overcoming so-called Man-Powered death is the greatest and last limitation for us to achieve as a species.

14. When we overcome so-called death through our God Power, our ascension will joyfully take place.

15. The destiny of America, the Heart of the World, is the future of Man Power becoming God Power.

16. We cannot rise out of our Man Power creation without the support of higher God Power realms.

17. Oneness with your divine essence / I Am presence / God Power becomes the ever-lasting condition of our future lives.

Chapter XXV

For divine love contains
Wonder-filled wisdom and perfect power,
It is composed of wondrous joy
And all-ready power of the God hour.

REJOICE, REJOICE, REJOICE

Inspired by Ascended Master Saint Germain

Beloved Brothers and Sisters of America,

What you witnessed during your past presidential election was the people's I Am presence at work with the support of our God-Power realm and many others. We cannot and will not interfere with your freedom of will and choice, but where we see eternal harm to others or the planet at play, we do exert certain forces to ensure the good of the whole.

We the people, through we consciousness / God Power, stepped in last night and further supported your mission to create the next and final golden age on our planet.

Remember, dear ones, all that does not support the good of all will be consumed in the light, as you experienced in your presidential and congressional elections. It was a shift as Archangel Michael's sword cut through injustice, allowing equality and harmony.

Now the principles of your founders' papers, inspired by us, shall go forward. America is the divine experience of all diversities uniting your world, coming together in their unique oneness.

You are awakening your individual and planetary souls' plans, dear ones.

Rejoice! Rejoice! Rejoice!

Extremes of duality and confrontation are beginning to end, as you join in oneness. But there is much work to be done in this area. Let this now begin a time of further healing and choice for those who have in the past opposed we consciousness. Know, dear ones, now is your invitation to come into the light, stay here, and see your mighty I Am presence, your God Power, create a new kingdom of love and light. For if you choose not to heed this divine invitation, you will not be part of the most glorious divine plan your world has ever seen.

As America, the Heart of the World, beats, you shall now resume your role and example for the entire planet. Stay focused on your internal affairs and needs, as you send love and light to the rest of the world. Attempt not to get involved in the destinies of other nations, as you embrace your own...Lead by example and resonance from inside out...Continue to clear and cleanse your harmful influences.

To reiterate, now many principles of the original creation of your nation shall go forward. This is a game-changer through a quantum shift that allows certain dispensations that can and will support your moving more into your divine essence, soul plan, and the light.

If you choose to continue on the path you have chosen, soon marvelous new technologies and God Power wisdom will be revealed that will support your golden age plan. These will delight and free you from the bondage of the past.

We are beside you and have been for eons. Call upon us...

Your co-creator in your golden age through love and light and your God Power.

Chapter XXVI

*All nature is self-purifying and protecting.
Let us now stop
Mankind's endless capacity for destruction,
So new construction can begin.*

INTERGALACTIC FEDERATION WITH MOTHER EARTH

Greetings, beloved humanity. We come to you from the Intergalactic Federation in concert with your mother, Gaia, Mother Earth.

Dear ones, at long last, you're awakening, you're awakening to your God Power divinity, to truly knowing who you are, truly knowing why you are here, truly knowing where you came from and what this journey through your hundreds, perhaps thousands of lifetimes on this particular planet has been.

It has been an arduous journey, a journey of learning what is through what is not by your freedom of choice and freedom of will, a gift that has been given to you (freedom of choice and will) that does not exist for everyone in all worlds, all galaxies, and all portions of the universe. And through the choices you have made, you have learned what you needed to learn to come to this moment in your time continuum as your beloved Archangel Michael has shared with you tonight, through the beloved soul chosen to channel for him, to teach you here 12/21/12 to, if you so choose to move into *we consciousness*.

As you have learned and been taught and told over the past months and most recently in the past couple of weeks, there have been portals opening upon this planet, vortices of energy that are connecting those of us of the Galactic Federation, if you will. Call us stewards of the frequencies of the inner-Earth, the archangelic and star realms all supporting your process of moving into a higher consciousness of existence, dear ones. That the time line, that the end time, of your three-dimensional experiences of cause and effect and karma, dear ones, is ending, at long last!

You have learned that that separation from yourself and others all you need to learn to be and do so. Pay attention to the current events that are taking place on your planet that you have discussed tonight. These will increase in intensity as the clearing and cleansing of yourselves through the processes you are teaching yourselves tonight and beyond reflect the clearing and cleansing that must take place upon your home planet Earth, Mother Gaia. She and you must clear yourselves now in order to go into your full divinity, your immortal divinity, your ascended mastership, if you will, to begin to know and understand and accept with compassion your purpose and your mission and your cosmic blueprint, dear ones.

Dear ones, you are divine, immortal beings of light who are here to be in service to *all there is*, source. You have lost your connection to source through your freedom of choice and will, which has been the demise of every past golden age on your planet. You are now evolving, as an essential part of your destiny into your final golden age, which will assure your immortality, your divinity, your service to self, your service to others, thus, dear ones, your service to the universe and service to *all there is.*

Dear ones, your work is really just beginning. This is not an end time; this is a beginning time, a time you have waited for, for hundreds and thousands of lifetimes. And, dear ones, this is the divine reason there are so many of you upon the surface of my body, so many billions of you. Some of you are conscious of these events. Some of you are not. So we ask you, as we receive this dispensation for all of these higher God-Power energies, which are part of your creation, the inner-Earth frequencies, the archangelic frequencies, the star realms that seeded your planet. All of us are coming together at this time simply to remind you, awaken you, if you will, to who you really are, dear ones, and to why you are truly here.

And as you have been taught by your beloved Michael tonight, it is a process of inside out, is it not, dear ones? Not outside in. You are downloading all of the frequencies in this dimension that you need to move into your divinity, to move into your individuated, thus collective, soul plans, dear ones.

We want you to imagine yourselves holding hands in an energetic circle. See yourselves circumstancing the entire planet Earth. All of humanity is receiving this 12/21 portal opening that will close at midnight tonight. Understand the preciousness of this moment that last happened some twenty-six thousand of your Earth years ago. This is a way, dear ones, that your mother, whom you have subjugated in many ways, clears and cleanses herself from your abuse and gives you the unique opportunity to join her in divinity, dear ones. For you are indeed source expressing/experiencing itself. Are you not, dear ones? This has been withheld from you. This has been hidden from you. You have been dumbed down.

There has been a veil created between you and us and your God Power. But that veil between us is very thin now, dear ones, the thinnest it's ever been. Many of you can hear, feel, and see the dimensions beyond you. The inner-Earth, the angelic and star realms that seeded you, they are all speaking and teaching you in unison now, dear ones, in preparation for us to join in oneness.

So, see us joining hands, hand and hand in this circumstance around the planet, this consciousness, this vibration of we consciousness and oneness, dear ones. As you hold this connection and energy within your heart, this energy comes up from the inner core of the Earth, as it comes from above to the inner core of your heart...as below, so above, dear ones. And you hold this frequency of above and below within your heart space for one divine moment and allow it, dear one, to move down your right arm, into your right hand, and pass it to the one on your right. And see this energy encircling, moving, vibrating, and pulsating around the entire planet ever so quickly at the speed of light. It flashes around the world from right hand to right hand, to the next hand, to the next hand to the next. And now, dear ones, allow yourself to receive in your left hand what has come full circle around the globe; feel it, hold it in that left hand for one divine moment, dear ones, and now return it to within your heart, your heart that knows all of which we speak. Now, allow the mind that believes to move back into service to the knowing heart that propels you to the being/beating of your heart. Connect with the pulse of your heart, which now connects with the central sun within the center of the pulse and electromagnetic force of the inner-Earth. These forces maintain and sustain one another, dear ones. Allow these God Powers to awaken you to your divinity. For it is time, dear ones, for you to awaken. Your sleeping, your slumber, is over.

Very soon, much of what we speak to you tonight will be physically, emotionally, and mentally revealed. There are God Powers joining through various dispensations that are allowing meetings with your world leaders and allowing them to know the time of your separation and duality and confrontation is over. We counsel you, no matter how your world may appear now, all that is taking place is the final clearing and cleansing of your world to move it into its oneness, its we consciousness, its divinity of self, dear ones. For you are to become, the mission of this lover-versity, learning to love self first and foremost...to now apply all that you have experienced...as far away from source and truth as you could go...and now to come back on this pathway back home. You will now go out from this planet, out into this solar system, out into this galaxy and universes unknown to you and become the master teachers you are destined to be, dear ones.

For all of this has simply been a way you have chosen to learn and a preparation for you to be the divine spiritual being that you are. We would also like to say in closing, later this month, particularly on 12/25, you will receive an additional portal opening to further prepare you for your new year. The group you are gathered with tonight has been chosen as well as many others to guide and support themselves and you for future messages and guidance they will receive. They are here to guide, support, and love you through this next momentous year, as additional vortices and energetic connections continue to open. Se we ask you to surrender to not knowing how, where, and when things will take place.

Through the surrendering, trust that all the possibilities and probabilities of these plans will be revealed to you. For it is your divine right to know at the right moment. But, dear ones, your trusting and your surrendering are essential. It was the lack of trust in source and higher realms that created all you have experienced, dear ones. Doubting can prevent manifestation and hold you in density and duality.

We honor all you who have gathered all over this continent. This continent (North America) is the divine heart center of your planet, which will lead your world into its final golden age. It is your divine destiny to do so. There were previous golden ages that laid the seeds for this to take place, such as Lemuria and Atlantis and ones lost in your time and language.

But these seeds are growing again. Look at the United States' founding fathers' papers and see the downloaded God Power wisdom, the cosmic consciousness, and the universal truth within these documents. Now allow the wisdom within these papers to come forth. They are the blueprints of the new paradigm of oneness, dear ones. Through your resonance and example of these sacred sources, you will lead the world into we consciousness.

We take our leave of you now. Know we are ever close at hand in love and support in oneness, and your God Power.

Chapter XXVII

As soon as we can realize
We're a collection of soul connections,
Then duality and separation
Will be simply sent, away...

A CHRISTMAS MESSAGE FROM YOUR HEART

From Ascended Master Saint Germain

Dear Beloved Children of the Human Heart,

At this special spiritual time of year for all humankind, let us speak of your heart, a subject you have heard much of throughout your many lifetimes on this Earth. And while this is a time of giving and receiving for many, we shall speak of the greatest gift of God: your heart. Are you ready to receive it? We shall now speak of aspects of your heart you may have never known, but the time has come for you to know and apply, if you so choose...

Within the interior of your heart, there is a spiritual central chamber surrounded by a powerful God Power field of sacred light and protection. This, we call the "cosmic cause." This chamber is not just of your present dimension/

frequency; no current medical doctor can find it. But you can. It occupies both your third dimension and fourth dimension and beyond (connecting to the higher God-Power frequency of its birth). This, what we call the "cosmic cause" central chamber, is also known as the altar of the heart (AH). The AH is actually the connecting point of your sacred silver cord (you've heard about that), which descends from your God-Power presence to maintain and sustain your physical beating heart, giving your life meaning, value, and purpose: a divine soul plan that integrates with the Earth's and God's divine soul plans: Man Power and God Power merging.

We urge all humanity to heed these teachings and to value and treasure this chamber of contact that you have with life by regularly giving your (Christ) consciousness to it.

Your awareness of this knowledge will create an invincible strength and power to manifest the sacred self-mastery / God Power within you.

It is not necessary to focus on the scientific how and why of which we speak. There is little understanding in the human mind of this, but your heart already knows. Rest your weary, war-torn souls, and be content to know that your God Power is ever present within you and you have this point of contact with the divine at all times, dear ones. It is a spark of light from your creator's own heart to you! That's how much this God Power of creation loves you. For you are truly one and your essence is divine, filled with love, wisdom, and power.

Each time you pay attention to this union within your heart, your love and power will grow within you, and it will mirror out into your world service. This is who you truly are; this is why you are here. Now you know the truth about you. You are God Power!

As your mind (which believes) moves back into full service to your heart (which knows), never lose contact with your heart again as your Man Power is doctored by your God Power. Then your God Power manifests all the power of love and extends and sends it out into the darkness of the world and becomes the being of light / God Power you truly are.

Chapter XXVIII

Someday, when I am an ascended master,
I Am, to graduate out of humanity,
Into the full expression of my divinity.

INNER MASTERY GOD POWER

As we draw ever closer to a new year, more powerful portals are opening; thus ancient tools await our application into ascension. There is much clearing and cleansing taking place, leading us into the new. This is the end of the old paradigm of me consciousness and the beginning of the new paradigm of we consciousness.

Let us again call upon the once human combined ascended master energies and wisdom to further support our entering the final golden age, a lengthy process at best, but our destination nonetheless.

Phillip: You have told us America is important in the creation of the final golden age. Why is this?

Ascended Masters: America is the remaining intention and manifestation for humanity to create a "God government" that honors higher realms (free of any control) and can maintain and sustain a country/nation reflecting the laws and wisdom from these higher frequencies. Then other countries can resonate or not with this.

Phillip: It seems "favoritism" is being played toward America?

Ascended Masters: It is not favoritism, but the saving of that which we have created and loved so long. It is the soul plan of America to be and create the planet's final golden age. Our love has supported this plan for eons, and there is no more time for manifestation; it is now.

Phillip: And how exactly is the final golden age to be accomplished?

Ascended Masters: That which is in imbalance is temporary, dear ones. We are eternal and are of the greater God Power of Love. Your America was created by us and now must expand upon a "God Power within the country" nation foundation, which will be permanent. Your founding fathers' papers express all this. It is time for you to become as we, the ascended master country / nation of planet Earth. Are you ready? Most of you are not yet being in process. We are here to support you.

Phillip: Wow, that sounds like a tall order!

Ascended Masters: As you strengthen, protect, grow, and expand everything divine and good within your physical boundaries, you will expel all that is not good from your perimeters through resonance and the use of your I Am Presence / God Power; along with our continued support.

For those not familiar with what your I Am presence is, we ask that you refer to previous conversations, or discuss it among yourselves.

Phillip: We must truly come to know and embrace this God Power presence?

Ascended Masters: When you fully understand and accept the full inner mastery power, I Am presence that you have, as individuals and as a nation, you can more easily manifest this in your 3-D world. You will have equality and balance flooding in rather than separation and confrontation. What you resist, persists, dear ones. Stop the fighting now. It does not work.

Phillip: Why has it been so difficult?

Ascended Masters: Because you have not seen yourselves as good/worthy enough to embrace your great inner master God Power...to pull it out from within and reflect it out. This will set you free and create the new world paradigm of oneness.

Phillip: This is what we truly need.
Ascended Masters: Yes, dear ones, to fully embrace the resolve within, the sacred being within. This will vanish all that prevents the final golden age.

Phillip: What has been preventing our resolve?

Ascended Masters: The emotional and mental bodies that you created...let them go now. Then you can be as we.

Phillip: What would you recommend we do daily now to support our process?

Ascended Masters: Connect daily with your inner divine God Power, your true essence, and accept with compassion the essential nature of this. See your invincible power and abilities, skills, and talents...Allow the lack and limitation and struggle to end. There are many teachings available to assist and support you in this process. This endeavor is one of them.

Phillip: So this will really work?

Ascended Masters: It allows you to be a magnet of good. It is the "remote control" of the universe. The old patterns, behaviors, and rituals won't seem so addictive and can be released.

Phillip: Is there a mantra that can support this intention?

Ascended Masters: "I Am, I breathe, and I know my God Power is within the invincible intention and love of my sacred inner God presence in me always." Say this throughout the day when your emotions and thoughts say otherwise. And see what happens!

Phillip: This should be applied to a person and the nation?

Ascended Masters: Yes, dear ones. Apply it to all aspects of oneness, and allow an empowerment of protection, love, and support to manifest. This will expel all that is not good for the all. There can be no failure when humanity desires and applies its inner God Power.

Phillip: When we talk about oneness and unity, what does that mean?

Ascended Masters: Unity of humanity with Mother Earth and all higher realms creates oneness, connection to God Power. And this oneness is eternal, dear ones.

Phillip: Where does the I Am presence come from?

Ascended Masters: It comes from the heart of creation and is the only God presence acting in the universe. All else is an absence of it. It contains more energy than any human activity. And it is time you know your I Am presence / God Power more fully and use and create your freedom at last.

Phillip: Thank you, beloved beings who love us more than we are able ourselves.

Chapter XXIX

Now focus on creating your next golden age,
And remember,
You are destined to be
The master teachers and senders
Of liquid white light and love,
Throughout the universe.
In oneness for ages more...

FINAL GOLDEN AGE

Connected with my God Power

The we consciousness is now in full process of manifesting. The activation will continue to come from within each of you, loving you and others. The time of duality, separation, and confrontation is over, if you so choose. You have learned all you need to learn from hating and killing one another. Haven't you?

You are united and one through your diversified selves. Your planet has activated her soul plan to move fully into the light; thus all within and upon her body will also (or not be here).

This is an exciting and challenging time for humanity and the world, and you have been preparing for this event for many eons. That's why there are so many billions of you here now: to be a part of the Great Awakening of Unconditional Love. Your planet and humanity are destined to evolve into ascended beings and allow this world to become a beacon of love and light throughout the entire universe.

Let us now join hands and set aside all that has separated us: male, female, religion, government, corporations; anything and everything taught that can cause duality and move into the light as one united in serving *all there is*.

Once this God Power reconnection is in place, together, we shall create the next, final golden age and never hate or separate again. And our real work begins...Can you see yourself worthy and good enough to finally be God Power?

Chapter XXX

The Great Brotherhood wishes
You to know
Discordant feelings and thoughts produce
Disintegrations, disease, old age
And every other failure in the world,
Throughout all the age.

GREAT WHITE BROTHERHOOD

Greetings from the White Brotherhood from the halls of Amenti in what you call the advanced 5-D civilization of Atlantis.

We come to you at this time to recognize the healing of the assertive masculine energy. A lesson we learned all too painfully ourselves in Atlantis when we were a divine ten-island civilization in the Atlantic Ocean many millennia ago.

The task at hand is working with the balancing of the masculine and feminine energy with the endeavors and journeys that you have been participating in with our beloved Lemuria and their home upon Mount Shasta. We come to you at this time because your work also includes the balancing of the masculine energy with the feminine, directly working in concert with us.

The gateway to us lies underneath the Great Pyramid in Giza. It is no coincidence that all of you have taken your initiation in the temple above this gateway. It is your connection to this mission at this time. The Great Pyramid was built by the Great White Brotherhood. It was not built by the Egyptians, nor was it built when your histories are telling you it was.

This telecommunication center you call the Great Pyramid is part of a global inter-solar and inter-galactic telecommunication system, which was activated by the statue of what you call the Sphinx in front of this great pyramid.

The Sphinx had been deactivated because of the density of the veil put upon humanity through the misuse of Man Power. Its misuse being directed to *all there is.*

The time has come for the reactivation and the rebooting of the Sphinx, which was originally built for a goddess whose name (Sakamaba) has been lost in your Earth time. She was in charge and still is in charge of all the pyramids throughout your planet and all of the pyramids throughout your solar system.

All of the pyramids and the crystalline information that lies within them are being activated at this time. And you are aware through many ancient scrolls—the Dead Sea Scrolls, the Emerald Tablets, and other texts that are being activated. The resonant information that will come out of these will be downloaded into each of you directly.

It will become a very important part of your mission, if you choose to accept it, to bring these truths in concert with the archangelic realm that we work in concert with; to humanity as part of the process you call the ascension process of your planet.

Many of you are planning important celebrations and ceremonies at certain vortices to receive these wisdoms.

You will, as a part of each of your divine soul plans, be participating in these in addition to the resonances you have with the frequencies that are uniquely a part of each of your divine soul plans via the Archangel Michael, Archangel Uriel, Adama, the mother Mary energy, or any other star frequencies that will be coming into your realm.

You have gone through a great healing, dear ones. You have been tested. You are continuing to be tested in your relationship with self and in your relationship with one another. But you have moved beyond the halfway point of that, haven't you, dear ones? Acknowledge the healing that was necessary for the work you have done and are about to embark upon.

It is an exciting and challenging time. It will be a time of chaos within your frequency as those entities and frequencies that have held control of you end. They are willing and able to fight to the end. Know this truth. It is only your light and the work that you are embarking upon that will support the divine destiny of Mother Earth, who has chosen to ascend to a higher frequency, thus interning all of you within and upon her body to do the same if you so choose.

Endeavors that you have been involved with thus far are only a beginning and a foundation of where your work can and will go if you so choose. We support you. We acknowledge the difficulties you go through within your frequency, and we thank you for making that choice, which you did make many, many eons ago to remain in this frequency and see through the lifting of the veil, dear ones.

It has not been an easy journey, but it has been a necessary one, for you have needed to experience every aspect of the veil in order to prevent returning to it again. As you know, Lemuria and Atlantis, the early stages of Egypt, and civilizations whose names have been lost to you, did not succeed. They failed in their divine soul plans. Many chose to go into a higher frequency to hold the truth that is coming through to you at this time so you do not fail in the creation of your final golden age, when Man Power becomes God Power.

We take our leave at this time and know if you allow, we shall come to you periodically and we shall come to any one of you at any time by simply asking.

Chapter XXXI

True mother love
Is simply the closest thing
To the unconditional love,
Of everything, God love.

MOTHER LOVE DEFINED

With Mother Mary

True unconditional mother love is a direct connection and reflection of the cosmic love the higher God Power realms and *source* have for humanity. A love without control neither wounds nor needs. It is this permanent reconnection with unconditional love that will allow our destined ascension into higher-self God Power existence. As our wounds and defenses now arise for healing, let us allow the balancing of the masculine and feminine energies, which is vital within our ascension process. Celebrate today this cosmic love reflection within mother love and know it is a pathway to our truth and oneness.

Chapter XXXII

There is a cosmic law
Called cause and effect
That automatically balances
In order to prevent a wreck.

THERE ARE NO ACCIDENTS

Mother Gaia

Greetings, beloved children. This is your mother, Gaia, coming to you at this crucial time in the evolution of my body and your bodies as well, dear children.

Oh, what a precious moment it is that you and we have waited so long for in our evolutionary cycle of ascension. How patient your mother has been. How you have abused my body and not realized that I am a conscious, living being like you.

Many of you are coming to the realization that your mother, that your home, is a living, conscious frequency of love and light. We know you are wishing to connect with us because of recent events within your frequency.

We remind you, that there are no accidents within your frequency. There are only tools of learning for how to transcend and ascend the frequency that has kept you in lack and limitation so long, dear children. Now that day of release and revelation has come forward, has it not?

So we ask you, are you ready to release yourselves from all that you have known so that you can just surrender to the unknown and the unknowingness of the truth? All you have been experiencing has been a learning tool, an illusionary learning tool, to return you to the connection of *all that there is*—with your mother, with your home, with your solar system, with your galaxy, and with your universe, dear children.

Any and all events that you have experienced through your multi-incarnational cycles upon my body have simply been to return you to the truth of who you are and why you are here through so many entities and frequencies that you are exposed to in your evolutionary path.

So it is our intention and our prayer for you to fully receive the truth from the many sources, including your mother Earth, that have the same destination, dear ones. It is time to awaken to your divine essence, to your connection with all that is, your God Power, by releasing the duality and separation that has caused the confrontation for so many millennia on your planet.

Your world is not what it appears to be in so many ways. Your view of it has been so lacking and limited that you came to believe that you are lack and you are limited, and neither of these things is true. So as we nestle you in the bosom of your mother planet, we know and realize that how you treat your home is a reflection of how you treat yourself.

And so many archangelic forces, Michael, Gabriel, and many others, have been giving you the tools to allow you to ascend into a loving, self-accepting, compassionate relationship with self so that they may mirror to your home, where your home has chosen to move to a higher frequency of existence. That means everything within and upon our body must also ascend and aspire to that higher frequency.

It is your divine destiny to be a formless, eternal being of light, and there are stages that you are going through that lead you to that reality. Your next step is leading from the third to the fourth to the fifth dimension.

Once connected to the fifth dimension, your true work, your true purpose, your true meaning of being in service to *all there is* will be more fully revealed to you as you eliminate the need for the learning tools, the cause and effect, the karma, and the others you have used within the third dimension. You are becoming ready to transform your Man Power into God Power.

Chapter XXXIII

*The time has come for Mother Earth
To protect and serve herself,
Due to the lack of consciousness,
Among us.*

INTERGALACTIC FEDERATION WITH GAIA 12/21/12

Greetings, beloved humanity. We come to you from the Intergalactic Federation in concert with your mother, Gaia, Mother Earth.

Greetings, beloved initiates of your 12/12/12 and 12/21 portal openings.

We are the Intergalactic Federation working in concert with your mother Earth.

We are above you, dear ones, in a mother ship connected to the inner-Earth frequencies of your Earth, connected to the divine feminine energies from which you have just received a divine message.

Dear beings of the third dimension, heed the words that have been given to you from this beloved feminine energy. We come to give you a bit of oversight, if you will.

Dear ones, you are not from this planet. You never have been. Many of you seeded from your sister planet Venus many millennia ago. As you are aware, Venus is called the planet of love. There is an unconditional loving force on that planet, which many of you incarnated into for millions of years. That unconditional love from Venus was sent to the planet you inhabit now as a gateway, as a network, if you will, for your colonization here.

It was that love force that the two Mary's were speaking of that journeyed you to this planet. It was encoded in the central sun in the core of this planet.

You are only beginning to understand what resides there—what a mighty force, how many civilizations and other frequencies exist within the core of your planet. Remember, dear ones, you live inside a house, not on its roof.

So this love was seeded, incarnated, if you will, into the planet that you now reside on and have for many thousands of lifetimes, for many of you. It is the activation of that Venus love force that the two Mary's are speaking of tonight; that is a part of what you call your ascension process.

It is your God Power; it is your ancient right to know that you are love, to know that we are one. We're actually on a reconnaissance from Venus, meeting with the Lemurian and Atlantean fifth-dimensional frequencies in the core of your planet, assisting you during this period of portal openings. A rare opportunity, indeed, as you just have been reminded of.

You chose to be here. You were born to be here this moment. It is your divine destiny. It is your birthright, dear ones, to receive this. Can you? What the two Mary's and all the higher beings who have taught you and reached out to you tonight are reminding you of is that it has been only you who have stood in the way and that the end time has come.

You have learned all you need to learn about sabotaging yourself. Yes, as you have been forewarned, there will be trials and tribulations, disturbances, and chaos, as your mother, planet Earth, Gaia, must, like you, cleanse herself of the abuses you have inflicted upon her. That is the chaos. That is the potential disruption in the relationship with the self, others, your planet, your solar system, your galaxy, and your universe, dear ones. It is all interconnected.

What is being laid before you now are ancient truths that have been sent to you many times before where you have subjugated or killed the messenger. Now you are truly ready to receive the truth of who you are and why you are here. You're truly ready to realize that everything and anything that is being said tonight through others is being said through you, that you are becoming telepathic, multi-dimensionally connected to this frequency and all the frequencies on out.

Over the next nine days, you will move from three, four, five, six, seven, eight, nine, ten, eleven, and twelve dimensions out and begin to embrace the integration of what all of these frequencies have to teach.

It is a divine moment. So we ask you right now. Put your hand upon your heart. Connect with the beat of your heart. That pulse is maintained and sustained molecularly by the vibration and the beating of the central sun of Mother Earth at the core of your planet. Feel that pulse. What gives it life, what gives it force is what gives it focus for your move from your mind into your knowing heart. When you feel lost, when you are in doubt, when the mental body wishes to sabotage you again, that pulse will take you back home, dear ones, to your origin.

It is a magnificent time, and you have chosen to be here. We are meeting with your world leaders, your spiritual leaders, and your corporate leaders, giving them choices. We cannot interfere with their freedom of choice and freedom of will, but we are giving them choices of how to move into a higher realm of existence where you will be able to manifest all of your needs without the control of others.

We cannot give that to you now because it would be abused, but you are in the process of being the ascended master that through your thoughts and your meditations and the intentions—unlike what you have set forth tonight—will come into reality. That will become commonplace. That is who you are. You will all become channels of the information you are receiving tonight. Know this truth. There is nothing special about anyone being able to do what is presented to you tonight. Some of us are simply way showers to show you how simple, organic, and easy it really is.

So we congratulate you on joining in community. We encourage you to stay connected over the next nine days and to reassemble yourselves on your twenty-first, which will be another activation portal unlike any that you may have ever maintained and sustained in your physical human forms. Be together. Support and love one another.

Channel more frequently. Bring in the two Mary's. Bring in the ascended masters. Bring in the star fields. Bring in the Intergalactic Federation. Bring in the Inner-Earth civilizations. We are all ready to speak, to teach, to remind you who you are and why you are here.

Have a blessed evening, and as you have been reminded, call upon us. We are simply a heartbeat away.

Chapter XXXIV

When mankind, becoming kind,
Has fully awakened and gained further wisdom,
We may join in perfect cooperation
With the magnificent force of Mother Earth,
Creating heaven on Earth,
Being one again.

ANOTHER CHRISTMAS STORY AND MYSTERIES REVEALED

Greetings, beloved children on the surface of my body. We come to you this night with many messages to God-empower you in your process, in your journey, in the choice you have made to be here once again upon this planet we call Earth, upon our body to continue your incarnational cycles.

We are a living being consciousness. We are your mother, and throughout recorded history, your recorded history, we have been abused. We have not been acknowledged. We have been taken for granted in the last millennia of this history of yours. This time of our abuse, this time of our segregation from you, has ended, dear ones, our children.

It is time for us to join in oneness. It is time for you to ascend with us, to move into a higher frequency of consciousness. This is your divine right and an essential part of your divine soul plan, which has been pulled out from the Akashic Records, the Hall of Wisdom, the Hall of All There Is.

This opportunity does not come often, as the channel we are coming through has explained to you tonight. It is a rare opportunity for you to make the choices that you are about to make, if you so choose.

Understand, on this particular planet, you are given a choice of your freedom of will, a freedom of choice, which is not always the case in every galaxy throughout the universes, dear ones. So, we cannot interfere with that. We are not allowed to do that through universal law.

So we honor the choices that you make to move into a higher frequency of consciousness. But we wish you to know, for those of you who choose not to ascend with us, it will not be an easy time upon this planet. You can call that a warning, if you want. It will be a difficult time to stay in this frequency.

It is a time to move beyond this frequency, to move beyond cause and effect, to move beyond the incarnational cycles of your emotional, mental, and physical bodies, which have been your learning tools for millennia on this planet.

It is a time to awaken to who you really are, to know why you are really here. There are many teachers on the planet at this time and throughout history, who have come forward to attempt to teach you this. Many of them have been killed, destroyed, or not believed.

Again, it is your choice to believe the wisdoms that are now coming in from the Inner-Earth civilizations, which is a new concept to many of you. But it is where we reside. It is not so new to you that there are archangelic realms and star realms, which seeded this planet, hold this ascension process in place, and are here to assist you at this divine moment in your history.

This has been a unique experiment within the cosmos, dear ones, and you have all chosen to be an eternal part of it. This planet was seeded by twelve star systems. Most planets are seeded by one. Each star system is represented on a council of twelve, if you will, which brings a diversity of teachings and experiences throughout the cosmos into your planetary plane. As a result of this, you now have a diversity and multiplicity of cultures, languages, religions, and identities of the male and female energies.

It is a unique, divine experiment that many of you have had hundreds, perhaps thousands, of lifetimes upon this planet to experience. We of the Earth consciousness of Mother Gaia applaud the arduous path that you have chosen, and it has not been an easy one, dear ones. But the end time has come for those who so choose it.

Since this is the beginning of your Christmas Spirit, we would now like to tell you another story of Christmas.

The Christ Consciousness has been on this planet and has experienced itself in many incarnational cycles throughout your history—Atlantis, Lemuria, Egypt, Greece, Rome, and civilizations whose names have been lost through the eons of Earth time. The desire of humanity is to once again know the Christ consciousness, to know the teachings of unconditional love within, that we are all individuated expressions of it, unique expressions of it.

We wish you to imagine an extraordinary mother spaceship. Her name is Mu. She is coming from a galaxy that seeded this planet many hundreds of millions of years ago. Oh yes, your planet is much older, and it has had much more advanced civilizations than your history books tell you, dear ones.

You have had many golden ages beyond the civilization you are living in now with advanced technologies you would marvel at, which are about to be revealed to you again. There is free energy available to you, but forces in your world prevent it from being given to you. There are worlds without taxes; there are worlds with immortality that await you. This is your true destiny, dear ones. This is your inherited divine essence that you are awakening to, if you so choose, through this period of ascension.

But now, back to the mother ship. Imagine she is larger than anything you can conceive. This ship is as big as a continent on my body. It is coming from a portion of the universe, a galaxy with many beings captaining this ship, powering this ship.

The Christ Consciousness; the archangelic realms of Gabriel, Michael, Raphael, and Uriel; Lord Sananda; his twin flame, Lady Nada; and many ascended masters whose names you may or may not know; are all on this mother ship.

All these beings are powering this extraordinary spaceship. It is coming closer and closer and closer once again, to the Earth realm, which it often does. The ship is often sighted over the heavens of Mount Shasta in your Northern California. And she's coming once again, as she did two thousand years ago. As she gets closer and closer and closer to your planet, she begins to reflect the light of your star, your Sun.

Dear ones, this is the Star of Bethlehem. This is the six-pointed star, the Merkaba of your existence, the beloved Star of David, whose wisdom and power and truth of being have often been lost.

Many who are anticipating the coming of this wisdom once again upon the Earth plane see this star. They are led to the incarnational cycle of the Christ Consciousness in one you call Jesus of Nazareth. The rest of this Christmas story is almost the same as your present one, except the relationships with the feminine energy have been altered throughout your history.

Jesus of Nazareth was a good Jewish boy, so, of course, he married. And he married his twin flame, beloved Mary Magdalene. His mother, Mary, and his wife, Mary Magdalene, were two very powerful feminine energies. But the patriarchal energy that created your churches and religions quickly subjugated them in order to control the feminine energy.

An important part of the ascension process will be the balancing of these two energies, the masculine and the feminine.

The channel that we are coming through now was led to create two sacred journeys to Mount Shasta, California, in preparation and participation, serving as a proxy for humanity, in order to balance the masculine and feminine energies.

During these sacred journeys, there was also a further balancing of giving and receiving, personal processing and teachings, and tools that would allow your deeper healing to clear all aspects of yourself that prevent you from moving into a higher realm of reality.

It is an exciting and challenging time, dear ones. For all that you have known will change as it changed when 350 million Lemurians lost their lives in one night; the Atlanteans on their ten islands in the Atlantic lost their lives in an instant as well.

Why? Pretty much the same that is going on now, dear ones, the abuse of power. The abuse of the few controlling the many. Whenever our body is in harm's way, which is once again happening, we step in, dear ones, and prevent the annihilation of this planet. Why? Because we wish to reveal to you tonight, the purpose, the meaning, and the value, of this planet you call Earth.

It is a lover-versity. You have come here simply to learn how to love. So far, you haven't done a great job, have you? And the Christ Consciousness energy, which is not exclusive to Christianity, is an essential component of your process. It allows acceptance, compassion, and forgiveness for all that you have chosen to experience.

It is time to know why you are here. It is time to consciously begin to remember the choice you have made to be here and to support those who do not fully understand, who are not conscious of what's happening, by building communities of equality, harmony, and balance as your life shifts and changes. We wish to assure you, the world that you have known will not continue.

It is the destiny of this planet, in concert with humanity, to produce master teacherships to be expressed throughout the universe. Each one of you has signed an energetic contract to *be* these master teachers. This is who you truly are.

You have been murderers; you have been healers; you have been priests; you have been abusers of power; you have been teachers of wisdom. You have experienced every aspect of the God force that we are in service to that you can possibly experience.

The learning time of this frequency is ended, and your real work will now begin as you move into a higher frequency existence beyond 3-D, 4-D when you sleep, or what you call death and on to 5-D into immortality.

Can you imagine if you now brought your wounded behavior into immortality, what type of universe we would have? It would be a reflection of what exists now. That is not acceptable, and it will not take place.

There's work that needs to be done in order to move into the higher frequencies of immortality. Our 5-D governments, our spiritual centers are led by individuals who have achieved the higher realms of wisdom and understand what we speak of tonight.

It is a glorious time as you go into your Christmas, your Hanukkah, whatever religious celebrations you wish to use to connect you to the truth of who you are and why you are here. We, your mother, we, your home, ask you to remember what we speak of tonight.

Most civilizations live inside a house, as you do, on the surface of our body, dear ones. Most of the planets within your solar system have various advanced civilizations within the core of them. The same is true here. There are many Inner-Earth civilizations inside our body. This is why you may not see on the surface of your solar system planets what you call civilizations. Or they may be in a frequency that you are not capable of seeing at this time.

There are many forces in the universes, the Galactic Federation and many others that are surrounding this planet to assist you in this ascension process. We, they, cannot interfere with your freedom of choice and your freedom of will, but we are here to support you by bringing truth and teachings and wisdom to you through many channels and many sources throughout your world.

The most important thing to remember is you chose to be here with so many of your brothers and sisters at this time, dear ones. It's not an accident that you're all here now.

As many souls as possible who have ever lived upon this planet have chosen to incarnate at this time in your Earth history to experience what we are discussing tonight—your ascension into a higher-realm reality.

New truths will soon become common knowledge. It will not be revolutionary at all. When we know, and the forces that are supporting you know, that we can be received as friend and not foe, much more will be revealed. Your energy systems, your financial systems, your ability to manifest whatever it is that you need, will be at your disposal, as they are in all advanced civilizations. How does that make you feel?

The reason you have advanced civilizations at the core of your home, your planet Earth, is because they would be corrupted on the surface. They were once *on* the surface. They've chosen not to be corrupted by your energy fields and to maintain and sustain themselves in the core of this planet, in order to protect themselves.

But they cannot advance until you advance. There is an interconnectivity of all life forms, all conscious beings on this planet. And, dear ones, everything on your planet has consciousness—your minerals, your plants, your animals, your fellow human beings.

The time has come to end thinking one is better or superior to the other, to begin to remember that molecularly and electron-wise, you are all created from the same source, whether it's a dog, a plant, a crystal, or another human being who looks dramatically different from you.

Wait till you really get out into the universe, dear ones. You're going to see configurations, physiognomies of life forms that will astound you, filled with unconditional love, filled with service for all that there is.

We hope what we share with you tonight thrills you as you enter a sacred spiritual season, as you open your hearts, not your minds, to what we are now saying.

For your hearts and the DNA and the RNA configurations of your heartbeat are synchronizing with the heartbeat of *our* heart. Your heart *knows*; your mind simply believes.

As many of you know, the end game has come for the mind being in control. She will now go into service to your heart, for only through the heart can your ascension take place.

Chapter XXXV

Divine essence is the most sacred force
In the universe.
It eliminates all discord
In order to afford perfection
In all directions.

DIVINE DISCUSSIONS

Divine Discussions is a video program in which conscious channel Phillip Elton Collins and spiritual journalist Joel Dennis Anastasi connect with various multidimensional realms to delight and enlighten us. The following are transcripts from some of those shows:

DIVINE DISCUSSIONS #1:

Mode of Expansion; Adama, the Council of Twelve, and the Archangelic Realm of Uriel

Greetings, beloved humanity, this is Adama, the high priest of Lemuria in Telos in combination with the Council of Twelve, in combination with the archangelic realm of Uriel. We are pleased to come to you at this most auspicious time in your Earth's history. At this time when your calendar is moving from your winter to your spring, a time when you are moving from your Man Power to your God Power. And energetically, dear ones, what exactly does that mean? It means the energy from the core of your Earth is now coming from inside out through you, through the interior of the planet out into the cosmos. During your winter cycle, that reverses, as you know. It goes from the outside into the core of your Earth. So you are in a mode of expansion. And expansion, dear ones, is exactly what we are going to be talking and teaching about today. For you are expanding, dear ones, into your God Power. You are expanding in a way you never have before in your recorded history.

Many, many millennia ago, you had more chakras than you have now. You have one through seven in your formatting at this time, which had been shut down by various forces, veiled if you will, and that can be a separate teaching.

But now that veiling is being reawakened, and the seven chakras that you have are now going to go into completion and expansion, dear ones, with the twelve star systems that seeded your planet.

For, dear ones, your planet is an amalgamation of twelve diverse star systems that bring all of their diversity and all of their intention into one planet, which you call Mother Earth.

And it has been an arduous, divine evolution where you have gone through six previous golden ages, which have lost themselves because of their disconnection to *source*, their disconnection which maintained and sustained them at that time. You are now approaching your final God-Power golden age, your final golden age, which will allow you to be permanently connected to *source*, to the forces that maintain and sustain you, allowing you to go into full service to this source, to your God Power.

So what are the tools, what are the teachings, what are these mechanics, if you will, the science that is exactly taking place? So many of you know about the seven existing chakras. Now you're going to be connected with eight through twelve to complete the twelve star systems, which seeded your planet. So we shall start with the eighth one just above your crown seventh chakra, which goes out in various degrees of what you call distance, depending on your individuated soul plan. For some of you, it may be a few inches beyond your physical body or few feet out for others. But that matters not. Then we go out into the ninth chakra, which goes out toward your satellite, known as the lunar, known as your moon. Then we go out to the tenth, which incorporates your solar system, from your closest planet to your sun (Mercury), going all the way out to your farthest planet, realizing that additional planets are in the process of being discovered. Then we go out farther to the entire galaxy holding your solar system and millions and billions of other solar systems within this galaxy, yours being called the Milky Way.

Then, as we go farther out into what is called the universe, containing again millions and billions of galaxies, you have this system of awakening.

So you have twelve, eleven, ten, nine, eight coming into your beingness and this process called ascension, which will fully awaken your beingness and give you the reconnection to source and the tools that you need if you so choose to apply them to go into your higher-frequency existence into an immortal state of light being. This is your destiny, your God Power, which is your divine right at this time.

Now, needless to say, the discussion of the star systems and the discussion and the science of each chakra system are lessons and teachings that can fill volumes.

But for the moment, what we wish to do, we in the Inner-Earth in connection with the archangelic realm of Uriel, combining below and above, if you will, "As below, so above," if you will, we're combining these forces just again to give you, for those of you not aware of this, and many of you are, exactly what is taking place and why it is taking place at this particular time, feeling it strongly now in your mental, emotional, physical body as you move into your spring as the energy from the core of the Earth moves out from the interior of your planet to the surface of your planet through your bodies, for this process largely has to be experienced through your body, housing your mental, emotional, and etheric bodies out into the cosmos, out into the universe, if you will, connecting...to this twelfth chakra.

Now each of you, depending upon your soul plan and your evolutionary path and your incarnational cycle, will be at different points at the awakening of different chakras above seven, eight, nine, ten, eleven, twelve, and so forth. Don't worry which chakra you are at. It's not a question of a competition or a race. You will all get to the same destination whenever you are supposed to. But it is your divine right. It is your mission to awaken these, which had been "dumbed down," if you will, which had been veiled, which had been shut down, by various forces that had attempted to control you, and you see vestiges of that control in your governments, in your religions, in your corporate systems, that are at play now, but this is diminishing, this is being released.

So it is the intention of your planet, which is in the process of ascension, moving into the full body of light, that she is to become the star that she is, thus everything within and upon her body will become a light body as well and move into its God Power.

So, in effect, you are all aspects of the star systems that seeded this planet, in effect, star beings. And how does that make you feel, dear ones? To realize this is the gloriousness of you. This is your divinity. This is your divine right to know this truth and how this will transpire at this time.

Many, many teachings from the interior of the Earth and the expanded realms beyond the interior of the Earth, archangelic, intergalactic, and star systems, are all combining together in this integration process, to allow you to awaken to the truth of exactly what is happening as your Man Power becomes your God Power. And, dear ones, that is why there are so many of you on the planet at this time. There are billions of you here at this particular moment.

Many and most of the souls who have ever incarnated on the planet are here presently in one format or another in order to experience this. You may also be aware that there are many leaving your third-dimensional frequency at this time, for they are not able or capable or ready to make this transition, this transformation, if you will, into this ascension process (Man to God Power). So they are going to leave this frequency; they are leaving this frequency, going into the fourth or fifth dimensions, gaining the empowerment they need, making the decision whether to come back here in their final incarnational cycle to complete their ascension process. Many of you are making it in your present bodies, in your present formats at this time. Again, it doesn't matter which, the destination is the same for all of you.

So it is a glorious moment. We are combining and getting dispensations with these different frequencies and layers of consciousness to come together at this time like never before. That is why we are able at this time to combine below energies, if you will, and above energies. So we just want you to take a moment and ground yourself, imagine yourself completely cored and planted on the surface of this particular planet on which you have chosen to experience this evolutionary path, this divine journey from Man to God Power...

And imagine the energy going down into the core of the Earth, transcending all the way through the Earth, out the other side, out into your solar system, out into your galaxy, out into the universe, which houses all of these galaxies, circling back around, collecting chakras, twelve, eleven, then nine and eight, and bringing them, dear ones, down into your crown chakra seven, down into your chakra six, down into your chakra five, down into your chakra four, down into your chakra three, down into your chakra two, and down into your chakra one. And allow the integration, the amalgamation, the transformation of you to receive these higher chakras, dear ones.

Take a deep breath, and know that it is time for this process to take place. Now, we do alert you that various symptoms, if you will, depending upon your defenses that you have created through your various wounds, through your various incarnation cycles, may occur. You may be experiencing various symptoms mentally, emotionally, depending upon what your specific defenses are. And again, this is another teaching, which will be brought to you soon if you're not already aware of what these defenses are that allow you to maintain and sustain yourself in this particular frequency called 3-D—third-dimensional, which you are in the process of moving through, moving beyond, that the timeline has come, that the end time has come.

So having introduced this new paradigm, having introduced this new format, and again for many of you who already know this, for those of you who do not, welcome to the new knowledge. It is time for the truth, the full truth of who you are and why you are here as a species and the mission of this planet comes fully forward in your moments of now. For there has not been much truth in your histories. In your current dialogues and through the communication, the transportation systems, which are advancing and will continue to advance, more and more truth will come forward. More telepathic ability will come forward, which will eliminate deceit and denial of deceit, for you will each know what the other is thinking. So having said that and introduced these wonderful new adventures, if you will, in your journey of humanity, we would like to open this process to any questions that you have at this time, dear ones. How may we help you? How may we serve you? How may we clarify?

Joel: Adama, we're thrilled that you came through. Thank you so much.

Adama: You're welcome, dear one. We remind you we are here also with the archangel realm of Uriel and the Council of Twelve.

Joel: Yes. Well, we welcome and thank all of the entities for joining us.

Adama: It is our service to be here.

Joel: I think for the folks who will be watching this, we are exhausted with duality. We've had it! We've had enough. We are so ready for what you're saying, for the truth to finally come through. Thank you for being sources of that for us, so that we who are experiencing all of this feel that there is some purpose to what sometimes seems to be a veil of tears.

Adama: Let us discuss how to handle this fatigue, dear ones. To handle the fatigue, we would suggest that you really engender a compassion for self by speaking your truth and your needs and your boundaries. Every moment of now is a reflection of the loving relationship, which many of you are teaching as light workers and way showers at this time. And to rest and to rest and to rest and allow your bodies mentally, emotionally, and physically to integrate these new energies so that the fatigue, so that the exhaustion as you move from a carbon-based reality into a crystalline light body reality is assimilated, dear ones. So take care of yourselves. Balance your giving and receiving. Balance your feminine and masculine energies. All of the teachings that are coming forth now, apply them and truly be your messages, dear ones. And you will find that your exhaustion and your fatigue are transformed into joy, energy, and bliss, dear ones. Remember, you are moving from your Man to God Power.

Joel: Well, thank you, because I feel the exhaustion quite a bit, and those in my soul family often report the same thing. So the issue of taking care of ourselves is really critical through all this process?

Adama: Like never before. For many of you have been taught to give and to give and to give, particularly those who have received the mission, if you will, to be light workers and way showers and healers and teachers, and you have not learned fully how to balance the giving and the receiving, particularly the receiving as a giver, and you have exhausted yourselves near death, dear ones, in reality. But it is time now through the loving relationship of self, which has been taught through many venues through the channel that we're coming through, and many others, through the divine soul who is asking these questions and many other entities, all this truth is coming forth of exactly how to care for yourself during this momentous event, dear one.

Joel: And, of course, it's also so important for us to get the support of our soul family.

Adama: Absolutely, and the support of us, dear one. We remind you that all of the past golden ages demised, if you will, as a result of their lost connection, that their mental bodies thought they could do it a better way. Remember that all the energy that maintains and sustains you comes from the frequencies that we reside in and further out into the frequencies of *source* and *all that there is*, which we are in service to at this time. And that will be your destiny as well as you transcending from the frequencies you are in now. Does that help you, dear one?

Joel: Yes. You know, it may seem simplistic, but you just suggested that we call on the support of all the other multidimensional realities. What are effective ways of doing that? It is such a vital source of support for us.

Adama: By simply asking, dear one. By simply, simply asking. So many forget to simply pause, take a deep breath, and simply ask us, dear ones, to be present, and we shall be, dear ones. You can command us. You can demand us, by simply asking. That is how the ascended masters maintained and sustained their limitless power. For they have learned how to simply ask and connect the atoms and the electrons, the electrical magnetic frequencies of the universe and manifest anything in service to humanity and source, dear ones. Does that help you?

Joel: Yes. Thank you. You know you made the statement that it's time for the truth to fully come through now. We're reading on our Internet messages from all kinds of spiritual sources, and many of them continue to allude to that fact that there is going to be some disclosure coming as though some outside dimensions are going to come into the third dimension and bring this truth to us. Is that a reality?

Adama: Dear ones, the process is from the inside out, not the outside in. Those who would experience the phenomena or events that you are describing will be a result of the preparation that they have achieved within themselves to be able to directly connect with us and these other frequencies; by the state of readiness and commitment and beingness of their message, which will allow us to come forth fully, to allow your Man Power to become God Power. Does that help you, dear one?

Joel: So the truth that will be coming through will be our opening ourselves up. It's the inner work that makes us receptive and the ability to bring the messages from the multidimensional realities into the third dimension. Is that what you are saying?

Adama: It is a reflection of self is how we would word it, dear ones. Does that help you?

Joel: Right. So what can we be doing? It might seem rhetorical, but let me ask you anyway. What can we be doing to encourage the truth coming through to mankind?

Adama: First and foremost, do absolutely nothing, dear ones. Be in a state of beingness, which you know. And it's not just a format of linguistic expression when we say "being versus doing." Allow yourself, through the state of beingness, to connect to the vibratory frequency of the consciousness of the wisdoms that will allow you to transcend and transform into a higher format of existence. So many of your teachers, so many of your messengers, are not truly being their message in all aspects of their life. They may have a personal persona and a public persona, which may not support one another. It is time through this beingness of teaching. It will be through that resonance that others will come to you. Not necessarily what you're saying through doing but what you are actually energetically being, dear one. Does that help you?

Joel: Yes, you alluded to the high-vibration energies, the powerful energies that are coming into the Earth plane, and I think you mentioned the spring equinox, which is next week. What can you tell us about the energies and the effect they have on mankind?

Adama: Well, the cycle is in breath and out breath. That's how your planet breathes with these different seasonal cycles and different hemispheric locations upon your planet. It is simply the way your planet breathes; it's the way she inhales and exhales and expands and contracts and expands and contracts, which is the rhythm of creation in the universe, dear ones. Does that help you?

Joel: Right. I was reading about the (God) power energies that are coming in next week with the equinox. Because they are higher-vibration energies, they help to raise the consciousness of mankind. What would you say about that? Is that correct?

Adama: They are unique opportunities happening now in this portal in this opportunity of what you call ascension, which is not always available; as a result of this, there are more God Powers coming through but the cycle of the expansion and contraction in breath and out breath has taken place since the beginning and creation of your planet, dear ones. But it is a unique opportunity at this time through the dispensation and the combination of energies being able to come together, again, the twelve star systems that seeded the planet, the archangelic realms in service to this planet, the Intergalactic Federation, who are sort of the stewards of all this God Power information.

And the inner-Earth civilizations, which in large part are totally unknown to humanity and now are connecting below and above, are completing the connection. That is the reason why we earlier took you through the exercises of connecting, going through the planet below pushing through the planet, out into your solar system, out into your galaxy, out into your universe and then circling back into you, dear ones. Does that help you?

Joel: Yes. You referred to this as a unique opportunity. Is there anything in addition to what you explained, the exercise you put us through, etc., that we might be doing in terms of consciousness to maximize the benefits of this high-vibration energy?

Adama: To be the message. To be the teaching, again, at the risk of sounding redundant, of the teachings that are coming in. Each golden age prior to the seventh and final golden age for your planet was given these opportunities of ascension as a preamble, as a preparation for going into their golden age, to connect with the higher realms that facilitated, that made that golden age possible. That is what your scientists and your historians are attempting to figure out; as they look at these structures, as they look at these temples, as they look at these pyramids, as they look at these artifacts, they cannot figure out exactly how they were created, knowing they're not possible in your realm now. What they're missing is the connection to the higher God Power realms that made all of that construction and wisdom possible, dear ones.

Joel: Well, they're missing it, but then they're totally closed to the possibility of the role that energy played in it all.

Adama: That will shift and change and is in process now, as more and more of these civilizations are really revealed to know that they actually existed, that they are not completely buried in myth or in fairy tales, if you will, or in legend, that more and more the information and the wisdom and the consciousness from these prior golden ages, which still exist in certain frequencies and bands of consciousness will also come forward, dear one.

Joel: You alluded to the remnants of control that still exist in government and religions and so on. The Catholic Church just elected a new pope, and it's filling all the airwaves and the media and so on. I am going to ask you to do something. I realize you don't make judgments, but the Catholic Church of course has been a huge instrument of control over the ages. I certainly thought it was hopeful that a Latin American pope was selected, and in some ways, he seems to represent new things. And then I heard him make statements about homosexuality, which were the same old narrowness and bigotry. It raises questions in my mind whether or not the Catholic Church understands what spirituality is all about fundamentally.

So what observations would you make about the role of the Catholic Church and to what degree it does seem to be opening up to a greater embracing of all spirit.

Adama: Dear ones, the core issues with your organized religions on your planet all share the same misconception or the same lack of truth, we should say: that you are God experiencing itself. And their attempts to control you and manipulate you and to control humanity are, in effect, to control God. Until a religion is completely inclusive to all aspects of the diversity of humanity upon this particular planet, they are not representing *source/* God Power; they are not representing *all that there is*. They are representing hypocrisy, deceit, lies, and nothing that has to do with God, dear ones; it's all about Man Power. We do not wish to offend anyone who has received solace through certain organized religions. For there are many good deeds being done through these religions. We are talking about the elite at the top, who control these religions. Until there is an equality of the masculine and feminine energy in all religions, they cannot represent the intentions of *source*, of equality, harmony, balance, and love for all, dear ones. It is at best a distortion that began with a spiritual truth and foundation to love one another, which your Christ Consciousness brought into your realm again two thousand years ago and many times before that, dear ones.

That was not the first and only expression of the Christ Consciousness on your planet. It expressed itself in every golden age prior to this one we're going into. So it is a control mechanism. The religions are a form of government, and they reflect the people they govern. So if the people wish to make a change and accept their God Power within themselves, their divinity within themselves, their holiness within themselves, they will find that they can transform the existing religions on this planet or simply not need them any further, dear ones. Does that help you?

Joel: Yes, it does. So if we want to make an evaluation of any of these organizations, we simply have to see whether or not they are creating community, harmony, balance, and love?

Adama: And follow your resonance—your internal gyro system within you, which is your connection to *source*. Check in with your solar plexus.

Check in with your heart, and ask her, "If this is true for me, does this resonate? Or should I make another choice? Set a new boundary? Create another path?"

Joel: So it always comes back to us? Doesn't it?

Adama: Indeed. As soon as humanity awakens to this truth, the only relationship you're having is the one you're having with self. There will be great, great revelations, dear one.

Joel: Well, thank you so much. Is there anything you'd like to say in closing?

Adama: What a remarkable time you have all chosen to be here! Stay open, dear ones. Allow your resonance to decide your path in what you assimilate and absorb within yourselves, not what's being said here. If it does not resonate, don't apply it. If it does, do. For you each have your own divine paths and your destination is service to source as your Man Power becomes God Power...

DIVINE DISCUSSIONS #2:

Final Golden Age: Archangel Michael, Adama, Lord Sananda, and Saint Germain

Greetings, beloveds, from the archangelic realm of Michael in concert with Adama from the inner-Earth realms, Lord Sananda of the Christ Consciousness realms, and beloved Saint Germain of the ascended master realms.

We all gather today to talk about your next and final golden age on planet Earth. Dear ones, you've all chosen to be here whether you are aware of it or not to participate in one of the most exciting adventures your planet has gone through. You have gone through six previous golden ages, which have had their life and death, if you will, as a result of their connection and disconnection to *source*. Now it is your destiny, now it is your blueprint, now it is your divine right, dear ones, to go into your final golden age, which will allow a permanent connection to your God Power.

We would also like to talk about what America, the United States, and the Americas at large really mean within this journey into your final golden age. Dear ones, what you call America was once what you called your Garden of Eden. What was integrated into the geographic location and energetic portals and vortices of what you call the United States was and continues to be the Garden of Eden, which is being reactivated at this particular time in a process you know as ascension—ascension of yourselves from inside out in concert with the ascension of your planet for both to return to the beings, the eternal beings, the immortal beings of light that you are, dear ones...for Man Power to become God Power.

Oh, what an extraordinary journey this has been. So what is the meaning, value, and purpose of this united, this union of states called America? What does the word *union* mean? What does the word *united* mean, dear ones? It means the connection of your divine selves with source, your Man Power to your God Power / creator. It is not the United States; it is the "united divinity" of you in combination with the source, your God Power, which maintains and sustains and creates you.

What is happening now is a reactivation, a rebooting, a new downloading through various portals and vortices within your continental United States to assist humanity in clearing and cleansing your duality, your separation, your confrontation, your wars, and, through the resonance of this, to allow the entire planet to go into this final golden age, for your Man Power to become your God Power. That is your destiny.

This is reflected in the forefathers' documents, which founded the United States of America. Your forefathers and we—Michael, Saint Germain, Lord Sananda, and others—gathered in concert to inspire your forefathers with these documents, your Bill of Rights, your Constitution, these inspiring papers, and to give such individuals as George Washington the inspiration to know the destiny of this particular country you call America.

So how exactly will the advancement of your country take place? It will take place through a clearing and cleansing of the selfish Man-Power consciousness of humanity, which has kept you in separation and limitation to allow you to go into a constructive God Power endeavor of self that will be reflected out to the entire world.

Once you maintain and sustain through this healing process of self—which we of the archangelic realm of Michael have taught you for many, many eons now of moving from the mental body to the heart space—once this process of the individuated self moves from the harmful self to a constructive self, we of the fifth-dimensional God Power realms will continue to be forthrightly available to you to assist in this endeavor of ascension.

This is what is taking place at this time. This is why there are so many tools and teachings coming through to humanity through various fifth-dimensional sources. So it is a great time to move from your limitations, your separations, your lack, into an immortal state of being that will allow you to stay permanently connected with us in a final God Power golden age, which will prevent the death and destruction of this age as has happened in the six previous golden ages.

It is a divine moment in your history where you will become telepathic, and the mistruths and the deceits and the denial of the deceit taking place in your communication systems and with one another will no longer take place, and truth will reign supreme, dear ones. And truth will set you free.

You will also be gifted, once this connection is complete or in process, with free God-Power energy sources, which will change the structure of your financials and your relationship with self.

A small percentage of you will no longer be controlling the vast majority of you, so you will no longer be giving your God Power away to Man Power. For right now, as you know, within your governments, your corporations, your religious organizations, there is much mistruth and deception taking place, which will be cleared with your direct connection to source, through your God Power, dear ones.

So you all chose to be here for this distillation, for this creation of your final golden age, to move into a process of ascension to go into an immortal state of being to really begin your true service to source, dear ones. And we ask you as we join our energies to accept with compassion and to forgive the process you've had to go through for the various reasons you've had to go through them and know that the end time has come, dear ones.

This is the time of the healing of the self in order to move into a oneness with all in order to have a connection with source / God Power and allow the archangelic realms, the star realms that seeded your planet, the inner-Earth realms that were once upon the surface of your planet, to all work in concert to assist you by you merely asking us in a constructive format, a format that does not include harm of others, dear ones.

Oh, what a marvelous, divine moment this is for humanity. So we ask you—no matter how things appear outside as Earth's final clearing and cleansings of your third-dimensional frequencies, your past and present lives as well—we ask you to be aware and not to doubt this process.

For one iota of doubt can interrupt the process within yourself, dear ones. Accept and know within your hearts that the time has come now.

So let us briefly open to some questions and answers, for this is how you best integrate wisdom and truth. For we have brought you these messages many times before. But now are you ready to receive them? Now are you ready to know the truth, dear ones? How may we assist you in this question-and-answer format?

Joel: Well, we certainly would like to thank you all for joining us. It's a thrill to have such wonderful, God-Powerful, loving entities joining us.

Entities: You're welcome, dear one. We have a wonderful dispensation enabling us to be joined together with you. As you have experienced in the past with your Angel News Network, you had some fourteen frequencies come together with a united Twelve Life Lessons teaching. It is indeed a very exhilarating moment that we can join our forces in oneness as well with you to assist you in this process.

Joel: Michael, Adama, Lord Sananda, and Saint Germain. We are indeed blessed.

Entities: We are blessed to be in your presence, dear one.

Joel: Well, my questions, of course, are coming from the third dimension. So let me apologize ahead of time for having the limited perspective that represents. You've told us, don't doubt the process because that just retards it and that the time has come for these changes that you have outlined. You've talked about the role that the United States is playing in the unfolding of the new golden age and what the word *united* truly means. You have told us that we have chosen to be here.

We are watching the Man-Powerful continue to abuse their power, to continue to pollute our beloved Gaia, continue to pollute the air, the water, the land, simply to increase the storage of money they've got piled up in their reserves and to increase their power and influence over us all. Those of us who are light workers and way showers certainly want to be able to do what we can to speed up the coming and the growth of the new golden age. What would you counsel us to do to add our energy to the changes that are happening here?

Entities: It has to do with the amount of humanity, which is able to go into an awakened state of consciousness. When it reaches a certain percentage, a certain quantum shift point, if you will, then we shall be able more and more to work with you directly by you simply asking us to work with you directly to eliminate these old paradigms of control, dear one. They will be eliminated.

The process is in progress...those forces will no longer be able to control your planet. You do have freedom of choice and of will that we cannot obliterate. But we can work in concert with those who have raised their consciousness to a point to work in concert with you. Do you understand, dear one?

Joel: Yes, I do. You've given us this guidance before. But I guess we constantly need to be reminded. What are some effective ways that those of us who are trying to raise our consciousness around these issues can join our energies together to accelerate this process, to help you, to join with you more God-Powerfully.

Entities: More fully help one another, dear ones. Really join with like-minded, like-spirited individuals through your resonance, through your internal gyro system, if you will, and really form communities and groups, which will empower you through the processes and the teachings that have come to you beforehand. Use them in a loving relationship with self, and allow that to mirror to one another.

You will not go forward with this process without eliminating the conflict with self, others, and endeavors, such as war, dear ones. That simply will not take place in the future. Does that help you?

Joel: Yes. Certainly, we understand the wisdom of that. You know what we at the Angel News Network are being and doing in terms of the various activities we've been involved with, with the channeling activities, the workshops we've created of Life Mastery, the We Consciousness Light Workers and Way Showers Support Forum, and the other programs that Michael and other spiritual entities have given us. We feel as though we've been laying the foundation, and now we need to step out in a stronger, broader way to reach the world. What guidance would you offer in terms of how we can more effectively do that?

Entities: You are moving from the light worker into the way shower and combining the light worker with the way shower, are you not, dear ones? You are moving from your Man Power to your God Power.

And through your individuated talents and gifts, you will find endeavors that will allow that way showing process to take place through your specific talents and gifts. Whether it is writing a book, producing a seminar, having a show of some kind, a workshop through your cyberspace, which has been gifted to you from the realms we come from at this time—the Ethernet, which frees you from the frequency of 3-D, which you are in, which allows you all to be in concert simultaneously bypassing many of the control mechanisms.

But what has humanity done with a lot of cyberspace? They have abused it and misused it as they have many other tools they've been given in the past. So we ask you to check yourselves as to how you are using the gifts and talents that you already have and apply them into the constructive endeavor of ascension, dear ones.

Joel: In the beginning, we were using the more traditional vehicles. We were publishing books. We've been doing seminars in brick-and-mortar buildings with limited audiences. We are, as you say, now at the threshold of taking these teachings into cyberspaces to send them out into the world in more powerful ways to reach larger audiences. That certainly makes sense in terms of where we are going.

Entities: Yes. Each of you will have a reflection of your soul plans and the defenses that you are healing at this time. You will find your path. You will find your journey. Love and support one another in that by simply asking one another what you need and supporting each other within an egoless environment. Much will happen, and much will be revealed. Remember, things are moving exponentially at high speed now. Pay attention to your emotions and the thoughts that your emotions create, the physical symptoms that you create. Remember, you are moving into a higher state of being your God Power as you move from a carbon format to crystalline format. This will make many things possible that have not been possible in the past. If you simply pay attention to your present now as opposed to how things have been in the past, you will see things are moving exponentially at a nice clip and pace, as you would say.

Joel: You have pointed out more fully than I've heard before the role of the United States of America in the new golden age. I think you said that the United States was the Garden of Eden and that it is being reactivated. Is that what you said?

Entities: Yes, dear ones. Your myth of the Garden of Eden is really the beginning of the energetic God Power, which is now your United States. Humanity came into planet Earth through the geographical area that you are in now, through what you call America. That was the beginning of humanity and the civilization that came through hundreds of millions of years ago. That force field, if you will, that vortex, that portal, is being reactivated. The memories of that initial golden age, the memories of that original Garden of Eden, have never been lost and are in the process of being reactivated now, dear ones. Does that help you? We realize that this is a new story for you. We understand.

Joel: You say America is going to lead the world into a new golden age. But I'm looking at this logjam that we call democracy in the United States. I see it as the forces of separation fighting the forces of unity, which are trying to bring us all together so that all the people can be served equally. We don't seem to be able to get anything done in America at this point. What observations would you make about how well our democracy is working at this point?

Entities: It is the last hurrah of duality. It is the last hurrah of separation. It is the last hurrah of confrontation. Your worlds are now becoming more and more hesitant about going to war, which is your most destructive form of confrontation. You're beginning to realize that it simply doesn't work. So you're having old Man Powers, old paradigms in their last hurrah bellowing, knowing that the end time is here, dear ones.

Joel: I don't want to shy away from naming the facts as I see them. The fact is corporations maintain so much control in our country and direct a disproportionate share of the resources of our democracy toward feeding their needs and agenda rather than the needs of most citizens. We now have a far more diversified population in terms of race and religion than we've had in the past, while the old guard composed mainly of older white males is trying to hold onto power. That's where most of the resistance to equality seems to be coming from, from my perspective.

Entities: Energy will not be given to Man Powers that do not support God Power oneness and the ascension process, dear ones. Each life force, each life is given, through the realms we reside in, life substances, which maintain and sustain life and your ability to move and be in this frequency.

God Powers, life substances, in the future will only be given to endeavors and individuals, which or who serve the ascension process. It is your destiny that this takes place, dear ones. Know this truth.

Joel: All of the programs that Michael and others have been bringing to us have always talked about creating a world of community, harmony, and equality. Isn't that really what we're all heading for?

Entities: The foundation of that is the relationship with self, mirroring into those communities of equality, harmony, and balance. Yes.

Joel: I think we've pulled together a lot of the themes in your opening introduction to us. We're so grateful that you've joined us. Is there anything that you would like to add before we bid you farewell?

Entities: Just to reiterate that this is your final seventh golden age moving into a mortal state of God-Power beingness. You're in process with that, and you have chosen to be here for that. All of you who are here now, whether you are conscious or unconscious of that, what is called the United States and the Americas at large will be instrumental in creating this paradigm of resonance, which will lead the planet back to an original state of Garden of Edenism, if you will, that began many millennia ago and is being reactivated at this time. That is new information for some and not for others. But this is what is taking place.

We ask in your constructive endeavors to call upon us, the archangelic realms, the star realms, the inner-Earth realms, for us to assist you and support you in your endeavors of unity, equality, harmony, and balance in these communities that you are creating. We are here to serve you. We are here to support you if your endeavors are constructive, dear ones.

So as we take our leave, know this truth. Know that we are here. Know that the veil between us is as thin as it has ever been. And soon, we shall all join in God-Power oneness.

DIVINE DISCUSSIONS #3:

Ascension Process, Giving and Receiving; Great White Brotherhood, Saint Germain

Greeting, beloveds. We come to you at this time from the Great White Brotherhood in combination with the Ascended Mastership of Saint Germain.

We join together with a teaching to support you in your ascension process as you are moving to a higher frequency of God-Power reality with a discussion of giving and receiving, dear ones. We realize many of you have been dealing with the universal equation of giving and receiving, and you already have some understanding of what this is. But we wish to take you to a deeper level of understanding of giving and receiving. Most of humanity who chooses to *give* has that down pretty well, as you would say.

We would like first to focus on *receiving* and your God Power I Am Presence. What is this thing, what is this phenomenon, what is this aspect of yourself called the I Am presence? Is this your connection to your higher self or to the God Power that created you and continues to maintain and sustain you?

The atmosphere of your planet of Mother Earth is composed of every thought and every emotion that humanity has experienced for millennium. This atmosphere creates your weather and creates and supports many of your natural events, your acts of not-so-God, if you will. We're asking you now to become aware of your thoughts and your emotions and how they affect you physically, how they affect your planet and your weather, and, most important, how they affect one another.

It will be through the *receivership* of your I Am Presence, your God Power divinity, if you will, that you will connect to the forces that maintain and sustain you, that give you your life substance and allow you to move into this ascension process and your final golden age, your seventh golden age. This will allow a permanent *connection* to your I Am Presence and God- consciousness and the presence of the creator, who maintains and sustains you.

It is the absence of this connection that brought about the demise of your previous golden ages, called many names, which you know: Lemuria, Atlantis, early Egypt, early Greece, Mayans, Aztecs, and many other divine civilizations; humanity simply does not understand what happened to them. What is the mystery associated with the disappearance, the ending, of these apparently extraordinarily evolved civilizations, which in many ways achieved beyond what you have at this point and then ended for various reasons?

The basic reason, the core reason, for the ending of these civilizations was their *disconnect* from the I Am Presence, the disconnect from the *creator*, who maintained and sustained them. The mental body of humanity felt that it could do it on its own, its own way, a better way. Through your freedom of choice and freedom of will, you were given that opportunity. The time of learning this way through repeated Earth lives is coming to an end.

The reason and the function—the meaning, value, and purpose—for repeated Earth lives, for repeated embodiments, is for you to learn in each lifetime what you need to learn and then to review it when you've left your physical form so that you might decide what was incomplete that you might address in the next lifetime—and for that to go on and on and on. Dear ones, that cycle of reincarnation, of re-embodiment, would have gone on for eternity if it were not for the aspect of the God-Powered I Am Presence, which is *connected* to *source*, allowing the end time of re-embodiment, reincarnations.

What a glorious moment it is. For once you become immortal and no longer have to go through repeated Earth lives to learn what you didn't learn in the past, you maintain and sustain your connection to source through your connection to your I Am Presence. Your true service to *source* will fully be engaged, and your Man Power has become God Power.

Right now, much of humanity, which is awakening, is involved in something called world service, which is a precursor, a preamble, to *universal* service.

As has been discussed with you in previous teachings within the *divine discussions*, you are assimilating and integrating five additional higher frequencies, divine chakras, if you will, to move down into the chakras that you are familiar with, one through seven. This will allow a more conscious *connection* to your I Am Presence and to *source*.

Now, there are many more chakras than twelve. So why is twelve important at the time? It is important because the twelve chakras that are being integrated at this time reflect the twelve star systems that seeded and diversified your planet, which diversified your blueprint of your learning to love. That is the reason for your planet. That is the reason for your habitation of this particular planet, coming from other galaxies, coming from other planets within your solar system.

So as you *reconnect* with your solar systems, your galaxies, and your universes/multiverses at large through this extended, elevated chakra system, you will more fully *connect* with your I Am Presence and to *source*, your God Power. You will reverse the dumbing down that has taken place in the past for various reasons, and forces and entities that have attempted to control you will stop. Many of those forces of the few controlling the many are still in play on your planet now. But the end time of that is in process. So having given this introduction to the I Am Presence and the balance of giving and receiving and the importance of universal law, we would like to open this up for questions and answers so this may be more fully integrated for you, dear ones. How may we help you?

Joel: Welcome and thank you for joining us.

Entities: You're welcome.

Joel: The Great White Brotherhood and Saint Germain.

Entities: Indeed.

Joel: It was Gabriel who first told me about the Great White Brotherhood. I never quite understood what the Great White Brotherhood is. Can you tell us what the Great White Brotherhood is?

Entities: Yes. It is a God Power that supports the Christ Consciousness, as many other entities do. It is a God Power that has been housed, if you will, in many sacred temples and particular vortices and on the geographic areas known as the United States. And it is a force that works directly with the ascended masterships, which are in service to humanity to allow you to move into your divine blueprint of ascension, immortality and service to *source*. Does that assist you?

Joel: Saint Germain, of course, has quite a historic association with the Earth. For those who don't know, can you just give us a brief summary of Saint Germain's role and association with planet Earth?

Entities: When you review our incarnations on this planet, you will see that the embodiments of Saint Germain have occurred throughout your history to enlighten you, often not to particularly receptive ears of those in control and power. But we who love you unconditionally, we who inspired your United States, we who inspired freedom, we who inspired the statue of liberty, we who inspired unity and union to *source* and inspired the concept of a *more perfect union* of the United States are Saint Germain.

Joel: We are getting more and more information coming to us through various spiritual sources about the pivotal role that you played, Saint Germain, with our founding fathers and the creation of our founding documents.

Entities: We were instrumental in inspiring the individuals who laid down the documents, your Constitution and your Bill of Rights, to reflect universal law, to reflect a blueprint for this final golden age and to inspire the forefathers of this country to understand this task at hand. Needless to say, the ideals of these documents, of these words that have been brought from higher frequencies to humanity have not been fully realized. They have been partially realized.

But it is your destiny for them to be fully realized and incorporated in this country you call the United States and to allow that truth and allow that resonance to ricochet through your world.

Joel: Well, if it's going to ricochet around the world, we've got a lot of work to do here. Our Congress always seems to be in a logjam. Right now, our Supreme Court is going to be addressing another issue of equality in terms of gay marriage. We seem to be redefining all the time what freedom, equality, and liberty truly mean.

Entities: Dear ones, the monsters of humanity are doubt, fear, and ignorance. They have interrupted you throughout the millennia and all along your true path. So we ask you to have no doubt, to have no fear, to know that your thoughts and your emotions accumulate in your atmosphere collectively and influence the entire world. It is time to know and to trust and to surrender to what is being given to you from the higher realms at this time. Do you understand?

Joel: I do. Now Saint Germain, I am going to go out on a limb here because I didn't know you were coming through today. I've been so inspired by the fact that you were the inspiration of our founding principles. Of course, the equality of all mankind is central to them. Our Supreme Court right now is going to be addressing the issue of marriage equality for gay people. What would you say to the Supreme Court justices who are making the decision right now?

Entities: What we would say to the Supreme Court, if they would allow us an audience, is that the diversity of all of God's beings, of all of *source's* beings, must maintain and sustain equality, harmony, and balance, or humanity cannot go forward. There can be no aspect of humanity through your evolutionary path that can be subjugated further by Man Power.

And the base and foundation of all this separation is the imbalance of the masculine and the feminine energies that radiate out in all of your prejudices, in all of your eons of separation and duality, whether it be sexual preferences, religion, gender, too big, too small, too dark, too light, too this, too that. The "too's" shall end, dear ones.

Joel: Very powerful. Saint Germain has spoken. You said that the purpose of our planet is to learn to love. Is the universe observing us in terms of our long, long struggle to learn that process?

Entities: We need to explain the purpose of love. The purpose of love is the building block, the electro-magnetic God-Power building block of everything. And, yes, indeed, the entire universe is watching and looking very closely at your planet, for many of them are an aspect and a component of its creation. And the very best, if you will, the highest component of them was brought into the creation of what you call Earth. That is why you have reflected many previous golden ages, which embodied all of that through beauty, through truth, and through oneness. Only through this understanding and the activation and the manifestation of love can you build this new paradigm of ascension of oneness in service to source, dear one.

Joel: I believe I heard you say that the cycle of repeated incarnations was going to be ending and when that happens, we would be able to be in fuller service to *source*. Could you expound on that, explain that?

Entities: Most of humanity has had hundreds, sometimes thousands of embodiments and reincarnations to learn what you came here to learn. That karmic disposition, that cycle of re-embodiment, is coming to an end. Every planet in the solar system, in the galaxy, in the universe, if you will, goes through very similar cycles to what you've gone through to become, to return to, if you will, being beings of light, bodies of light. Once you become these bodies of light, having repeated dense, physical lifetimes is no longer necessary.

Joel: What does fuller service to source mean? Could you explain what that represents?

Entities: There are millions and billions and trillions of worlds out there that are going through various processes not unlike your own, some behind you, many ahead of you. You would be in service to supporting those worlds and continuing to support the evolutionary path of your own planet. Some of you would choose to go elsewhere. Some of you would choose to be here.

Remember, dear ones, the universe is ever expanding, ever growing, which invites all higher frequency and service to it. The universe is an ever-growing and expanding being of consciousness. The work to support that growth and expansion is eternal and limitless.

Joel: So if we are to truly understand what you're saying, we would have to understand ourselves, first, as being spirit and, second, as being expressions of God, so that we would, in effect, be functioning as God throughout creation?

Entities: As has been said to you many times before, it is a process inside out. It starts with an individuated divine soul plan, which connects to a planetary plan, which connects to a solar system plan, a galaxy plan, and a universal plan, dear one. It is much more complicated than humanity is aware of. Not so much complicated as marvelous and miraculous, and all this is being revealed to you.

Joel: I think we've attempted to understand as much complication as we're capable of right now. So let's thank you very much, Great White Brotherhood, and you, Saint Germain, for joining us, and thank you so much for your teachings.

Entities: We're delighted to be here with you and in reiteration for the further integration of our teaching today, remember the importance of *receiving* your I Am Presence, which is your God-Power *connection* to your higher self and the *connection* to the *source* that maintains and sustains you and gives you life substance each and every moment of the now.

DIVINE DISCUSSIONS #4:

Powering Up New Chakras; Keepers of Creation

Greetings, beloved Earthlings. We are the Keepers of Creation.

We come to you at this time as your chakras are growing and expanding from seven, eight, nine, ten, eleven, and twelve, connecting you more vastly to your solar system, to your galaxy, to your universe, and to your God Power. For the time has come for you to know more about your reality, to know more about creation, what creates creation and what your involvement in it is.

What is creation, dear ones? It is cosmic love. It is the consciousness of your creator through cosmic love. And what is love? Love is a vibration of frequency in combination with light, which creates all matter, seen and unseen. Most of your universe is unseen. But there is much of it that is seen that you are aware of now. So it is a time to connect with the God Power of creation, which creates creation through something called love, through a combination of love and light. This creates density, which creates you and all the life forms, the minerals, the plants, the animals, and those around you.

It is a time to know the relationship of these vibrations of love, which are experienced through your emotions and your thoughts, which accumulate in the atmosphere of your planet and create your reality. You are each given in each reincarnation cycle a portion, if you will, of God Power creation, of love's life—and what you do with it through your freedom of choice and freedom of will is your decision, dear ones.

It is your decision to do what you will with this life substance through your thoughts and through your emotions. More and more your reality is learning through teachings from other realms, such as the archangelic realms of Gabriel and Michael, exactly what is the relationship of your emotions and thoughts to your physical being and the reality that you create through the God Power of your own creation.

For this cosmic love creation, this consciousness of the creator, if you will, is the building block of all that there is. This consciousness forms the building blocks of the galaxies, solar systems, and individual planets going through their evolutionary ascension processes, which your planet is involved in now. As you raise your consciousness in connection with the consciousness of creation of your creator, more and more of the science of the interconnectivity of creation will come to you, dear ones.

It is a time for you to know what you have not known or chosen not to remember or which has been veiled from you in the past. This is an exciting moment in which you have all chosen to be here and to understand who you are within this process, why you are within it. For as your higher chakras open up—chakras seven, eight, nine, ten, eleven, and twelve—it will allow your connection to all the God Powers, the wisdoms, the sciences of creation.

For this thing called love begins with the love of self, which you most recently have been taught through this endeavor called the Angel News Network. It is important to understand the foundation and value of this relationship of love of self and how it mirrors or reflects out to others, reflects out in the love and compassion for your planet and then goes forth out into your solar system and into your galaxy, then beyond your galaxy into the universe at large. Then you really begin to master creation yourselves. For you are creators, dear ones. You do not create the energy that is given to you, but what you create with the energy through your freedom of choice and freedom of will is your choice, isn't it, dear ones? And there has been a great abuse of this freedom of will and choice in the past.

But now, as you are connecting more and more to self and one another and realms beyond self and farther out into your solar system and your galaxy and your universe, you're beginning to understand what this building block, what this glue, what this God Power called love really is and how it relates and assimilates into your emotions, the faults that your emotions create, and your physical bodies, the symptoms, the illnesses, the ageing and, ultimately, what you call death. All this is opening up in preparation for your immortality to be connected to *all there is*.

It is a magnificent time, and there are many volumes of wisdom in our crystal libraries throughout the solar system and galaxies of the universe. For there was and is a parallel universe from whence this love God Power came. Your planet and universal wisdom is called the "lover-versity," dear ones. For the whole purpose of your planet and yourselves living upon and within it is to learn to love—self, others, planet, solar system, galaxy, and universe/multiverse.

Once you reach this level of universal wisdom of connection, as you would say, the whole shebang opens up.

So we'd like to open up now to whatever questions may come to you and allow a further integration of the process of these new truths, of these new wisdoms. For your world is also on the brink of something called equality, which is a reflection of God Power cosmic love. The significance and importance of equality is that no life form can see itself as being better than another. Once you go into equality and oneness consciousness, you see the interconnectivity of all; you see the oneness of all through love. You see your Man Power becoming God Power. How may we help you with your questions at this time, dear ones?

Joel: Well, it's exciting to have you join us.

Keepers of Creation: And we as well. We have not always been able to approach you, and at this time, we are.

Joel: That suggests a question to me, but the one I want to start with is, the Keepers of Creation is a new term for me. Could you define what that represents, what that means?

Keepers of Creation: We are attempting to explain our God-Power consciousness, our frequency, in your language, dear ones. So we have chosen the new phrase, Keepers of Creation. We are very close to the God Power creator, creation itself. So we see ourselves as a band of a realm of consciousness closely connected to the creation process through love. We know that human beings love to personify, give a name and give a label to the different realms, the different higher realms. But soon, when you release yourself through telepathic ability, language will not be necessary and you will connect to us through resonance and feelings, dear one.

Does that help you?

Joel: Yes. When Archangel Gabriel talked about the various archangelic realms, he referred to them as hierarchies of consciousness. He said that each hierarchy had a mission or role. Do you have a mission or role that is uniquely your own?

Keepers of Creation: As we have done with this opening statement, our mission is to explain creation and your relationship and participation within it as creators of your own lives and how the macro and the micro integrates and interrelates, dear ones. Does that help you?

Joel: Yes. I believe you said something about your being able to come forward now. Why is that? What is unfolding now that permits that?

Keepers of Creation: It is the dispensation of the ascension process of your planet whose soul plan is in process to return to a being of light; thus, in turn, everything within and upon your planet's body will do the same. As a result of that and the opening of your higher frequencies, you are connecting further and further out beyond your solar system, beyond your galaxy into the vastness of universal wisdom, dear one. You are becoming God Power.

Joel: And what effect is that having?

Keepers of Creation: This explains truly who you are and where you came from. It explains that the adventure and the experiences you've had on this planet called Gaia and Mother Earth are an *aspect* of the whole, not the whole. And once you've become amalgamated, if you will, and integrated with the wholeness of universal truth, then the great journey truly begins.

Joel: You referred to love. Most of us humans think of love as being a feeling. Of course, Gabriel and others refer to it as the glue of creation, etc. You used the word *glue* as well. Love is so fundamental to this whole ascension process as it is unfolding, isn't it?

Keepers of Creation: Yes, the human understanding of love is a very dense shadow, a shadow of what we're speaking of as cosmic love.

It is not necessarily integrated with human feelings or a misinterpretation or even a misuse of what love is. Love has often been confused with control and fear in your frequency, dear one. It is the building block. It is, indeed, creation itself. Love is God Power.

Joel: Learning to love is our job here, isn't it? You referred to the fact that we come here in one incarnational cycle after the next and what we do with it is our opportunity, our responsibility to use our freedom of will to learn to love.

Keepers of Creation: You are given a portion, a quantity of this God Power life substance, of this life force, and through the freedom of will and freedom of choice you have on this planet, it is up to you what you do with it, what you are with it, dear one.

Joel: Well, it's such a huge opportunity, and so many of us have squandered many of our incarnations. At least I see them as squandered.

Keepers of Creation: Well, that is why you had so many repeated incarnational cycles to attempt to accomplish what you intended to accomplish the last time that you didn't. But this karmic cycle is coming to an end. It is time to be connected to the God Power from which you came and integrate it within you so that you may break free from the need of repeated Earth lives.

Joel: That's the exciting moment that you referred to earlier in your introductory comments? We're moving into the opportunity to break away from these incarnational cycles?

Keepers of Creation: It will be an exhilarating moment for us and many of the higher-realm forces in combination with your human species to support you to awaken to the truth of your eternal immortality / God Power and for you to begin to express this love. Your ascended masters once walked the Earth as humans and through a process of self-empowerment and self-development and persistence have used this life force of love to free themselves from the frequency in which you exist in order to be in service to *all that there is.*

As a result of that, they have been given the gift, the God Power of creation, through the ability to manipulate atoms and electrons to manifest all in service to all that there is, as long as it is constructive and does no harm.

Joel: You defined equality in such an interesting way. I think you referred to it as a reflection of cosmic love. This country, the United States, was founded, in part, to establish the idea of equality among humankind. It has been such a long battle. The expansion of equality has moved from a very small group to an ever-wider percentage of our population. That to me has been one of the great struggles of mankind—between those who have resisted the expansion of equality to include everyone and those who have tried to include everyone. That has been the whole struggle of America, the world, and humanity.

Keepers of Creation: We would make the observation that it's happening faster and faster as equal rights for your races and for sexual preferences come up. You will see it exponentially reaching a quantum shift faster and faster as the consciousness of humanity increases, dear ones. But yes, equality has not taken place in your country, in your world yet, and there can be no advancement into full higher realms without equality for all. For no one and no laws upon the land supporting inequality can be allowed any further.

The law of the land and the consciousness of humanity must reflect oneness. Of course, the foundation of this oneness is the balance between the masculine and the feminine energy, which throughout millennia on your planet has expressed itself in national differences, religious differences, all sorts of differences, the myriad of ways that you have separated from one another and have often gone into confrontation and war, which is futile.

Joel: That balance of the masculine and the feminine seems to be growing as the feminine seems to be gaining greater and greater influence all around the world in all kinds of activities.

Keepers of Creation: It is the foundation of equality, dear one. All prejudices and forms of duality branch off, if you will, from that inequality of those two energies, male and female, masculine and feminine.

Joel: Are you as Keepers of Creation going to be showing up more in terms of your interaction with humankind all over the world? Are we going to be hearing more from you?

Keepers of Creation: It's up to you, dear ones. Do you resonate with what we're saying? Do you resonate with being connected with us? Many of the platforms of the relationship with self through your endeavors of the Angel News Network and schools and teachings throughout the world have laid many, many foundations. Are you ready to open up to the cosmic experience of love, the cosmic experience of self? If this resonates and you ask for it, it will take place, dear ones. We're merely peeking in the window and saying hello today.

Joel: Well, we're delighted you're peeking in our window. The ascended masters and the angelic realms have been showing up for us when we show up. We don't necessarily ask specifically for them. Are you suggesting that we need to ask for you specifically? Or just have an attitude and consciousness of openness to you?

Keepers of Creation: Both, dear one.

Joel: Well, we certainly hope that we can look forward to your wisdom whenever there is something valuable to say, which I would guess is always.

Keepers of Creation: Remember our dispensation comes from the higher chakras, which reflect the twelve star systems that seeded your planet, moving from your seventh to your eighth chakra beyond your physical being out into your lunar, out into your solar system, out into your galaxy, which you call the Milky Way, and out into your universe, which contains trillions of galaxies. So creation through this love force, through this glue, through this building block, is ever building and growing and expanding in a limitless capacity beyond the comprehension of humanity. So we hold you in love; we hold you in light, the building blocks of your density. We hold you in the God Power love that you are not capable of embracing in yourselves and others until you are fully there yourselves.

DIVINE DISCUSSIONS #5:

Connection to Higher Realms; Saint Germain

Greetings, beloved. This is the ascended mastership realm of Saint Germain coming to you at this time in your evolutionary path as a planet and as a species of humanity. Today, we would like to speak to you about your connection to God Power realms, such as ourselves and the realms of source, the I Am Presence. We would like to speak to you about your connection to the realms and the God Power source, which maintains and sustains you.

It is this aspect of self that humanity is in the process of rediscovering, awakening to—your divine connection to *all that there is*. For you are the arms, the legs, the feet, the lips, the thoughts, and the emotions of *source* / God Power. That is your reason to be here. The connection to source, the connection to the I Am, allows you to escalate, to advance into a state of golden age-hood, if you will. There have been six previous golden ages on this planet, which were maintained and sustained through the connection to all that there is. Realms and bands of consciousness, such as ourselves and beyond, enlightened, taught, and protected these past golden ages. The disconnection to *source*, the disconnection to the God-Power higher realms was the reason for the ending of these previous golden ages.

You are in the process of remembering your connection to these (golden ages). What makes it different now from past ages is that it is your soul plan, your planetary and species soul plan, to develop a *permanent* connection to *source*—a *permanent God Power* connection to the I Am.

Your planet and your species upon this planet, as well as the elementals, the minerals, and the plants and animals, are involved in an ascension process at this time. You are all in the process of returning to being beings of light, which are directly connected to life substance from *source* / God Power. All this is happening because your planet has initiated its ascension process.

Many of you have heard the phrases, "moving from your dense reality to a crystalline light reality," reconstructing your DNA, reawakening certain aspects of what is called junk DNA, now known as spiritual DNA.

You have heard about connecting your seven existing chakra systems to five additional higher chakra systems, moving you further and further up into the connection to *source*.

So with all these events taking place, your awakening of your spiritual DNA, your reconnecting to your higher chakras systems, all of these are to allow you to be permanently connected to your I Am Presence, your God Power—to be currently and continuously connected to the *source*, the life substance that maintains and sustains you, and to realize that all of your thoughts, your emotions, and your beingness have been an expression of this *source* and, in effect, your divinity.

So it is a wonderful, exciting time. Much is going on. Portals and vortices throughout your world are opening with wisdom and reminders that support this process. Ancient teachings are coming forward again to assist and facilitate your moving into this permanent connection to the I Am, this permanent connection to *source*, of which you are an aspect, a representative, an essential part.

So having laid this platform, this foundation, we'd like to open up to more truth. We'd like to open up to questions and answers that can be revealed through the truth of what we're speaking of at this time and knowing through your participation, through your questions and our answers, the integration process of being able to accept and more deeply understand, incorporate, and integrate what's being said can take place. How may we help you, dear one?

Joel: Welcome and thank you for joining us.

Saint Germain: You're welcome, dear one.

Joel: I'm going to be asking questions from a very innocent place. It will be ten years tomorrow that I conducted my first interview with Gabriel, which was my first exposure with a spiritual entity from another dimension. I feel comfortable doing that because when I asked Gabriel for advice, he suggested I proceed as a little child.

Saint Germain: And why would you think he would say that, dear one? What would be the meaning in "being as a little child" dear one? What would that mean to you?

Joel: I knew I didn't understand very much. He gave me the courage to ask anything fearlessly.

Saint Germain: Exactly, because the ego defenses of a child are not fully formed and defended. So the child is open. As has been discussed in previous divine discussions, the elements of fear, doubt, and ignorance are the monster elements of humanity that have kept you in lack and limitation, that have kept you in duality and confrontation. So the child has less of the fear, less of the doubt, and an openness to learn, dear one.

Joel: I've discovered that when I ask a simple, basic question, spiritual entities like you use it as a platform to present all kinds of wisdom. So I tend to ask some pretty simple things, and I am about to do that again now. What you just spoke about, I am fairly familiar with because I read spiritual material almost every day, and I read the messages that come through you and other ascended masters and other spiritual entities through various channels. But I can hardly think of more than a handful of people with whom I could discuss what you've just said who would have any idea of what I was talking about. I'm telling you this because, yes, I think we are at the threshold of a new age, and, yes, all these things are happening, and, yes, I have a sense of that. But almost none of my family, friends, or acquaintances do. That saddens and frustrates me because I feel like there's so much work to do. I just need to express the feelings I have about that.

Saint Germain: Much of humanity is in the place that you have described. So what you are expressing is your need to be in residence with communities of like-spirited, like-minded individuals who are in a similar position, if you will, a similar point on their light path as you are, and that is what will take place. You will follow and be directed toward those of like resonance, will you not, dear one?

Joel: Yes, that is my wish.

Saint Germain: So that is the purpose of it. We will support you. We will guide you through that process. So as you resonate with the higher-realm messages and tools and teachings, which you have been involved with for quite some time now, the individuals you choose to spend time with, to create endeavors with are those who resonate on a similar point on their path. There is no right or wrong in this. The destination will ultimately be the same.

Joel: Could we talk a little bit about guidance? Because I have only recently begun in a regular way to turn to my guides and ask for their support and guidance. What counsel would you give those who are watching who could benefit from the guidance of the higher dimensions? What would you counsel us to do to get more guidance?

Saint Germain: First and foremost, through your freedom of choice and your freedom of will to use your own discernment, allow your discernment, your resonance, your inner gyro system, if you will, to know what is truth for you and do not be guided to anything that does not resonate for you. So assuming that you are resonating with what we are telling you now, listen to the resonance of the words and teachings, and apply them, dear one.

Joel: What kind of guidance is available to us, those who are seeking to learn from the higher dimensions? What guidance is available?

Saint Germain: The guidance is for you to fully know who you are. The guidance is to fully know why you are here. The guidance is to recognize your uniqueness.

The guidance is for you to know your divinity, thus, in turn, your connection in relationship with creation and have that as a platform or a foundation to create service to your world, to yourself, to one another, to your solar system, to your galaxy and to the universe at large, dear one. It is limitless, ever expanding, ever growing.

Joel: Does each soul have guides that are assigned to him or her?

Saint Germain: Your higher self is the most important aspect of yourself. Your thoughts and your emotions are a denser version of that higher aspect and a denser aspect of yourself.

You are moving through an ending of the lesser aspects of humanity that have created discord and destruction and are moving into a more constructive format of expression of self. As many of you have been taught, the loving relationship with self is the foundation of all and the mirroring and out-picturing of that into the world is essential.

Joel: Some people may not understand what you mean by the higher self. How would you define the higher self for them?

Saint Germain: Your higher self, dear one, is your eternal beingness that never dies. It is the portion of you that collects the information from every incarnational cycle that you've had, reviews it, and decides what you have to learn—what you have not learned and what you need to still learn in your process of moving into higher realms and service to *all that there is*. That is your higher self.

Joel: That sounds like such a valuable resource. How would you counsel people to be in contact with their higher selves so they can get this guidance?

Saint Germain: First and foremost, recognize that it exists. And then, through that acceptance and compassion for it and gratitude for it, develop a direct communication with that aspect of yourself, which is eternal, which always serves your highest good and the highest good of all.

Joel: The ascended masters and others have talked about the fact that there is a lot of control of our world that we are not aware of and don't truly understand. They say we are not nearly as free as we think we are but that control is being dispelled as more transparency is coming into our world and we are becoming more and more aware of this.

We've been hearing for the first time in quite a while some pretty bellicose dialogue between North Korea, Japan, and the United States, threatening nuclear war and so on which would, of course, have a cataclysmic effect on mankind.

What would you say about the role individuals like us could play in bringing a higher level of consciousness to counter this kind of bellicose communication?

Saint Germain: Understand how and why it happens. You are dealing with a child (the Korean leader) who is asking—who is screaming, if you will—to be loved, to be liked and accepted, to be supported. And if these needs could actually be understood through the bellicose threats and understood that this is a wounded child who is bringing defenses that he has created in a position of leadership that can affect his entire country or possibly the entire world. In your negotiations and communications with this being, simply sit down and ask him, "What do you need? What is it that you fundamentally need?" And you will find it is the same needs that everyone else has, dear one.

Joel: That's the same kind of exercise that we have in the life mastery program where we talk to our own wounded child.

Saint Germain: Exactly. You have a group of wounded, often masculine-energy little boys running around with big toys bellowing, "Love me! Like me! Accept me! I want to be like you!"

Joel: So almost all the conflict in the world virtually springs from the woundedness that we contain in ourselves.

Saint Germain: That is the process you are going through in this golden age, so that those who are in leadership are spiritually astute enough to have healed and processed permanently the aspect of self that we're describing now, so they cannot bring that into higher realms. It is simply not allowed. Soon, you will create a world where that behavior will simply not be allowed.

Joel: We've been talking about the personal responsibility that each one of us has as a soul as this new age approaches. Are you able to make any observations to us about the consciousness of the leadership that we have in our own country and elsewhere? Do we have some enlightened figures on the international scene including our own president?

Saint Germain: There are various degrees of the ascension process within each individual divine soul plan, so it would take a long time to go through each and every one.

Generally, we would say it is that loving relationship with self that allows you to move from the unhealed narcissistic me awareness into a healed we consciousness and allow that united union of your entire planet. The national boundaries that you have—the linguistic boundaries, the economic, religious, sexual preference, whatever these boundaries may be—are disappearing. You are moving into a union of the planet into oneness.

This is a process that will take time in your realm. This is a process that is essential for you all to see yourselves interconnected. What affects one, affects another. And there will be certain aspects of your planet, such as the union of the Americas at large, that can serve as a way shower into this final golden age. There are certain vortices, portals, and energetic openings taking place in certain geographic locations that will help with the resonance, that will help create this united planet rather than a large group of individuated nations fighting for their identity. This is a process of Man Power becoming God Power.

Joel: We've been receiving at the Angel News Network the teachings from the archangelic realm of Michael about this giant movement from me consciousness to we consciousness. That is really what you're talking about as we approach this golden age.

Saint Germain: It is the essential process of moving into your final golden age, moving from the me (Man Power), which is driven by the ego, which is driven by emotions, which is driven by thoughts, and moving into your higher self, connected to the we (God Power), where those lower aspects of self no longer exist.

Joel: It comes back to those teachings that are now thousands of years old. "Love one another."
Saint Germain: Indeed. And how is that actually taking place?

Joel: Well, we know, don't we? It's been the history of mankind. Well, Saint Germain, thank you so much for joining us. Is there anything else you want to say to our audience?

Saint Germain: Become conscious of this wonderful, divine process of connecting with your higher self, your divine self. The DNA transformations are taking place. The chakra transformations are taking place. The geographic portals and vortices are opening up. It is indeed a blessed opportunity to move into the most enlightened and delighted aspect of you and your world that has ever been. You are now getting ready to move Man Power into God Power.

DIVINE DISCUSSIONS #6:

Golden Age of Gaia; Mother Gaia, Adama

Greetings, beloved humanity. We come to you from Mother Gaia in concert with Adama and the Inner-Earth civilizations.

The Inner-Earth civilizations are so close to the heart of your Mother Gaia, your mother Earth. We are in a time of transition and shifting, which is affecting humanity and your evolutionary path, into the Golden Age of Gaia, the final and permanent golden age connected to us, connected to *source*, connected to *all that there is*, connected to God Power so that your lack and limitation, your suffering, your duality, your separation, your confrontation may end.

How does that sound, beloved children, to know that there is an end time in place? There was a time upon my body when all of our continents were joined together in a great union, a great united landmass, which reflected the consciousness and the unity of the civilizations that were on my body at that time. Then those landmasses began to separate, and they became what you experience today in your geography.

But with this new Golden Age of Gaia, this final golden age, this God-Power epoch, the landmasses are beginning to reverse themselves and are joining together again. Your geologists are aware that your continents are heading toward one another and will join. There will be upheaval, transformation, and transition as that happens. That transition or transformation is also happening within your human bodies—your physical, mental, and emotional bodies as well, dear ones. There is so much going on in your world today that we would like to discuss. Then we will go into a question-and-answer session with you, which will allow an integration of our teachings.

It is a process of the self, moving from your narcissism, Man Power, moving from your separation, moving from your selfishness, if you will, to what has been called oneness and we consciousness—moving from the me to the we as the archangelic realm of Michael is teaching you so beautifully.

Adama and we are joining here together to remind you to be accepting and compassionate as to where each and every one of you is on your path. Some are choosing this golden age and are being guided by fifth-dimensional frequencies and energies, such as ourselves. And some are choosing to stay right where they are.

Many of your current events, your geologic events, and your weather events are reflecting their need to stay where they are. In the end, it will not matter. For in the end, you will all end up in the same destination of oneness, in the arms of God Power.

Your cycles of so-called death, dear ones, are a wonderful reflection of where you are. You have had to repeat cycles, to repeatedly come back and learn what you did not learn in the last embodiment on my body. And when that is able to end, which is the gift being given to you, you'll be connected to *source*, you'll be connected to all that is; you'll be connected to the consciousness of Mother Gaia, the Inner-Earth civilizations, civilizations extended throughout your solar system, extended throughout your galaxy, and extended out into the universe at large.

The narcissism, the arrogance, the ignorance, if you will, of the human mind, believing or thinking that you are the only life force within your solar system, your galaxy, or your universe, is naive, dear ones. It is through the connection, the coming together of all these civilizations—some far more advanced than you are, and some behind you—that will enable your awakening. For once you are connected to all that this is through what is called your I Am Presence, your higher self, your God Power, you will then begin your service to *all that is*.

Dear ones, you cannot accomplish the ascension process by yourselves. You simply cannot. The process will be done in concert with we fifth-dimensional energies fueled by God Power, loving you unconditionally beyond your ability to love yourselves at this time.

These fifth-dimensional frequencies and beyond are the frequencies that guided, supported, maintained, and sustained your golden ages in the past, which ended because of their disconnect from this wisdom.

Now you are being given the blueprint, the soul plan, if you will, to be permanently connected to *all that there is* for this final Golden Age of Gaia, this final golden age of your planet, which is returning to light. Thus, everything within and upon our body will be of the light. What a glorious time it is. Only through your doubt and fear and ignorance of this process can you once again impede it *individually*, but you cannot impede it *collectively*, for it is destined for this to go forward.

Because some have chosen not to go forward, to continue to be in duality and confrontation, it is important that you light workers and way showers join together in communities of harmony, equality, and balance, in order to define your needs and to set your boundaries with those who are choosing not to go forward. You do not need to resist them. You simply need to be collectively connected together.

We intend that this makes sense to you. And we intend that the communities that you will create will be connected to us in the God-Power fifth-dimensional frequencies, whether it be those of us in the Inner-Earth, the archangelic, the intergalactic, or the star systems, which seeded your planet as well as the parallel universes reflecting into your universe. All of these will come together into a mighty I Am mass ascended consciousness. We repeat, a *mass ascended consciousness*. So let us take a moment now to open to your questions and allow you to further integrate our opening statement. How may we help you, dear ones?

Joel: Mother Gaia, Adama, and the inner-Earth. Wow! We are so honored by your presence. Thank you.

Entities: We have been hidden from many for a long time, dear ones. Many of us walked upon your Earth, on the surface of Mother Gaia, and now it is a time for you to directly know that we are present.

Joel: Mother Gaia, would you explain something to us? The idea that Gaia, Earth, is a living being with living consciousness is so foreign to most of humanity, as you know. What can you tell us about that to help us understand what that means?

Entities: As soon as you know it within yourselves, dear ones, that you are a conscious being of light, then you will know it of the planet. Stop and think about it. You pull resources from my body constantly. You negate that the planet is a reflection of yourself, of the interconnectivity of us, that you and we are living and conscious, that we both have organs. The Earth has organs—the minerals, the water, the air, the electromagnetic fields. This naïveté, this hidden truth, of the exact structure of your world is coming to an end. That knowledge will allow you to be more responsible and to reduce the consequences of not understanding and treating the planet as your home and mother.

Look what you have done with the feminine energy, which is your mother! You have subjugated this energy as a reflection of how you have subjugated your mother Earth. You are beginning to understand the deeper meaning of equality and harmony, of the balance of the masculine and the feminine. It is the core issue of all of the imbalances and the selfishness and the cruelty in your world today and among yourselves.

Joel: I am very aware that Gaia is a living being. I'm lucky enough to live near a beautiful beach, and I walk along it almost every day. It is so easy to celebrate your beauty, and it makes it even more painful to contemplate the violence you are talking about. How we assault our Earth, how we pollute your air, your water, your land—it's such a grievous thing, and we who think of ourselves as light workers and way showers are all feeling this pain. What can we do to stop this assault on you?

Entities: When you walk along that beach, dear one, you are actually connecting to the megahertz vibrations of the planet, which assists the very pulsing of your heart. Simply stop and connect the beat of your heart with the megahertz frequency of the Earth through the ocean, for the water is a conduit of the vibration to you. You will begin to feel our connection.

You will begin to see our body as your body and that your body is an extension of the Earth, of Mother Gaia, for you are molecularly, structurally, made of the same components.

The inner connection between humanity and the planet are inseparable, dear ones. When you go out into other solar systems and other galaxies, you will see a different configuration of planets to humanity and structure and molecular composition, as many diversified life forms as you can possibly imagine. You get some inkling of them in your Earth now as you go into the deep waters or the higher skies of this particular planet. Does that help you, dear one?

Joel: Yes, I have some sense of that diversity. I watched a documentary called *The Blue Planet* last night, and I was amazed at the incredible variety of sea life that I haven't seen before with their amazing structures and designs. It was extraordinary.

Entities: Dear ones, there are more life forms on your planet undiscovered than discovered.

Joel: My fear is that we're killing them off before we can even discover them.

Entities: That will not take place. It is not the destiny of this planet for you, humanity at large, to allow that destruction. There are life forms on my body that are choosing to go and return to their original planets and solar systems and galaxies of origin. But all of these life forms have been uniquely essential to the evolutionary path of this planet and humanity, just as each and every one of you is uniquely necessary for the progression of this planet and humanity.

Joel: You created an incredible image for me when you spoke about the separation of the continents reflecting the separation of the consciousness of mankind on this planet. That is quite a powerful concept.

Entities: That is the reason why we brought that forward. You are beginning, through your sciences, to realize some of the history of this planet and how the continents were joined together.

Now, through your scientific measuring tools, you're able to begin to understand and to believe that the planets are returning to reform a large landmass, which reflects the evolutionary blueprint of the ascension process of this planet.

Every planet goes through an evolutionary path not unlike the one that you are going through. The time comes in the history of that planet when they, too, will ascend, and the vehicle for that ascension is love.

It is love of self, ringing out through the love of planet, love of one another and love of the cosmos. Love is the tool that will bring you forward and to your God Power.

Joel: I don't think mankind's science is aware that man was even on this planet when all the continents were joined. That was many hundreds of millions of year ago, I assume.

Entities: Indeed, dear ones, and far beyond that. Earth is an ancient being, an ancient source of love reflecting, a "lover-versity," if you will, reflecting throughout the cosmos. So many entities and star systems came together to create this divine planet called Earth, called Gaia. And we are all waiting in bliss and joy for your awakening to this truth of what a divine experiment this planet has been, a blue-green ball of love reflecting out into the cosmos.

Joel: You said that the continents were reconnecting again. Hopefully, it's not going to take as long for mankind's consciousness to reconnect as it took to separate the continents in the first place.

Entities: The energy of that, the electromagnetic God Power, is in process. It will be an individual decision that each person makes as to when his or her transformation takes place. You are experiencing, in your current events, those who are choosing to continue to destroy one another through war and through acts of violence. That is where they are. They are staying in their wounded child, their wounded cocoon of betrayal and abandonment. They are choosing not to awaken to use the tool of a personal process to free themselves from these Man Power wounds in order to move into an ascension process with the assistance of the fifth-dimensional frequencies. This is very clear. Do you understand?

Joel: I do. Of course, the violence you're referring to is occurring all over the world. We have it in our own country, the United States. Recently, we had the horrible bombing at the Boston Marathon, and, of course, all this battle going on over guns and the so-called right to bear arms, etc. In my view, it's all feeding into the consciousness of separation, violence, and fear.

Entities: It is the consciousness of me, the consciousness of the wounded me, reflecting wounding's of past and present lives and making a conscious or unconscious decision to stay there, to be there—as opposed to those of you who are awakening and wishing to heal those wounds and taking ownership. Also, there are Man Powers on your planet that have attempted to control parts of humanity, to keep them dumbed down, if you will.

Not to belabor the drama of that, there are some people stuck within the astral fourth-dimensional aspects through addiction, through mental control, through RNA and DNA control. But with the awakening of the expanded chakra systems eight through twelve and the awakening of your spiritual DNA, Man Powers will no longer be able to control these individuals or portions of humanity. The cabal, the illuminati, the hidden forces that are now being revealed, it is their last hurrah! For they know that many of you light workers and way showers know the truth. So they attempt to create events to constantly distract you, to impede you, to frighten you from your ascension process.

Joel: We've been hearing about this last hurrah, the dark forces, for quite some time. Of course, many of us are saying, so when is it over? When is the last hurrah done? I realize it's a process, but what can you say to those who are asking that question?

Entities: It's over the minute you to decide for it to be over, dear one. It's over in the now. For it's the Man Power mental body and the addiction of the mental body and the alter ego within the mental body that wants to know when. Move into the heart space. Take a deep breath and know that it can be now. If you simply make the decision *now* to be in peace, to be in love, to be in unity, to be in the *we*, to be in God Power, dear ones. It is now. It always has been.

Joel: So that's what we have to do.

Entities: That's what you have to *be*, dear ones.

Joel: That's what we have to *be*. And that's the message for today, isn't it?

Entities: Indeed. The abuse of my body is over. The time line has ended. We have been patient long enough within your freedom of choice and your freedom of will. We shall not and cannot allow the destruction of our body. The Atlanteans attempted it, and their civilization was ended prior to their ability to destroy Earth, dear ones. Take heed. Many of your activities, in your altering of genes and DNA and the abuse of your home, your planet, are reflections of that assertive Atlantean energy rearing its head one more time.

Joel: Well, that issue that you're raising about genetic modification has become a huge issue around the world, involving our crops, our experiments with animals, maybe even with people, for all we know. Could you speak about that?

Entities: Humanity, you do not own the creations of God.

Joel: So we're going to create the disaster that Atlantis experienced if we continue it?

Entities: It's a possibility. So what do you choose through your freedom of choice and freedom of will, dear ones? A world of continued separation and confrontation and the insanity of wars, which don't work? Or do you choose to open your hearts, to think with your hearts, to become God-Power conscious beings of light and celebrate who you truly are?

Joel: Well, thank you so much for visiting us today and speaking to us so powerfully. Is there anything more you would like to say before we close?

Entities: Remember that we are all intrinsically connected—your Mother Gaia, your planet, your home, humanity, the inner-Earth civilizations, your solar system, your galaxy, your universe, your God Power. Stay tuned for more of the revealing of this miraculous truth.

DIVINE DISCUSSIONS #7:

Temple of Sun, Goddess of Liberty, Christ Consciousness, I Am Presence, Archangel Michael

Greetings, beloved Earth beings from the Temple of Sun. We're going to take you on a journey today to the Temple of Sun in concert with the Goddess of Liberty. So take a deep breath. Join with your Christ Consciousness. Join with your I Am Presence. Join with Archangel Michael, the legions of the Blue Ray Angels, Goddess Liberty, and your God Power to join us in the Temple of Sun.

What is the Temple of Sun, dear ones? It is a temple that existed in the time of Atlantis. It was the western boundary of Atlantis. With the destruction of Atlantis, it was etherically recreated in what you call the island of Manhattan. So, in effect, the island of Manhattan is and was an aspect of the Atlantean islands. And this Temple of Sun, our Temple of Sun, has been recreated in an etheric format over the entire island of Manhattan—what you call Manhattan today.

The central altar of that island is the Statue of Liberty. But this etheric Temple of Sun goes the full length of the island of Manhattan and actually filters over into what you call New Jersey. As you know, the Statue of Liberty, your Statue of Liberty, today is encompassed in both the states of New York and New Jersey. Held in the hand of the Statue of Liberty is a book, a book called the Book of Law. And within the Book of Law are all the master teachers and ascended master teachers to lead your country called America into its final golden age, and, in turn, to lead, through its resonance of equality, harmony, and balance, your entire planet.

What does this island of Manhattan containing this Temple of Sun really represent for your world? Bring us your huddled masses yearning to be free. Bring us your wretched, your outcasts yearning to be free. This Temple of Sun has allowed the eastern aspects of America to be the refuge of all, to be the sanctuary of oneness, to be the final golden age of your planet. That is the connection between the island of Manhattan and this temple.

Contained within the Temple of Sun are various altars, which represent the suns and solar systems throughout galaxies and throughout the universes, for every planet has a Temple of Sun, dear ones, which allows the forecast, it allows the destiny, if you will, of that particular planet.

Your planet is in the process of ascension, of which many of you are aware. As a result of this, there are many God Power activations taking place, but this particular portal, this particular vortex called the Temple of Sun housing the Goddess of Liberty, is fully rebooted at this time to lead this final golden age as America is the heart space of the planet to allow this resonance of oneness and we consciousness to spread out. It is a mighty time. It is a joyous time when many higher frequencies come together within this temple to be refreshed, to be rejuvenated, so that we may guide you.

We support you in this process of ascension, through the energies radiating out in the Temple of Sun. Many of you have not been aware of the presence of this particular temple as one of the most important vortices or portals on planet Earth. So now you know. Now you know that this Book of Law held in the arms, in the hands, of the Statue of Liberty guides all those who are seeking freedom, unity, and oneness to your shores.

Your country is in the process of reevaluating its immigration laws at this time. We of this temple, the Christ Consciousness, the I Am Presence, the archangelic realms of Michael, the Goddess of Liberty, are supporting and reminding you of the birthright, of the mission, of the meaning, value, and purpose of your country called the United States.

This unitedness, this *union of states*, is a connection to this temple and a connection to the *source* within and of, dear ones. It is the reuniting of yourselves with such temples as the Temple of Sun located in New York City, which will allow this great configuration, transformation into unity, into oneness and allow you to open your hearts, to open your arms, to open your souls to all those north and south and east and west of you to come into this land called America. For each and every one of you who are presently here or yet to come are destined to be an essential part of this final golden age of the planet.

So who is humanity to set a law to prevent what is divine in the individual soul plan or to prevent the activation of the individual's soul plan, dear ones? This is a vital message for you at this time. All of the diversities of humanity through this Temple of Sun are expressed in New York City. Have you ever noticed? The cultural, the economic, the spiritual, all aspects of humanity have come together on a rather tiny piece of real estate to demonstrate the twelve star systems that seeded your planet.

Each of these, whether it is the arts, the sciences, education—all of these are factors in the diversification that represents these various star systems that seeded your planet and interact with the Temple of Sun. For what are these stars? These stars are suns, and they have come together in oneness to create this miraculous planet called planet Earth. What a divine endeavor! What a divine mission that has brought so many civilizations and frequencies together to create you, dear ones. So let us now open up to any questions or answers that you may have to further allow your integration of what has been spoken here now dear ones. How may we assist you?

Joel: Wow! That was such a profound message and a wonderful gift. The Temple of Sun, are you the consciousness of the Temple of Sun?

Temple of Sun: We are the Christ Consciousness, your God Power, dear ones. We are the awakening of your I Am Presence, your divine aspects, and your connection to *source*, dear one. We are nothing less.

Joel: You indicated that Manhattan is a representation of humanity from the twelve star systems. All you have to do is ride the subways of Manhattan to see the incredible diversity that is always represented there. I think of that a lot, and it's so obvious and powerful that Manhattan represents the diversity of the founding star systems.

Temple of Sun: Yes, dear one, your transportation systems allow you all to connect unlike any city on the planet. There are no modes of transportation to separate you. There are modes of transportation to join you. You see all races, all representations of your planet being human, being one.

Joel: Well, it is so evident every time that I go back to Manhattan. We're of course in South Florida right now, and I will be returning to the Manhattan area very shortly. One of the first observations I have when I arrive there is the incredible diversity I see there that I really see nowhere else.

Temple of Sun: Look at the channel's ring, as we shall lift his hand. It is pink and gold, the colors of God Power. The colors of pink and gold that envelop your Manhattan allowed ancient civilizations to come there before Atlantis, where this temple originated. Now it is in an etheric format. Surround yourselves in this pink and gold, connecting with your I Am presence, connecting with your Christ Consciousness whenever you wish to come to us and join the Goddess of Liberty, the Temple of Sun, the Archangelic Realms, Legions of Blue Ray Angels, and all of the star systems that bless and make this holy temple possible.

Joel: You said so many powerful things. I'm just going to refer to a few of the most important ones. You said, "America represents the 'heart space' of consciousness and oneness of the planet." That's a very powerful teaching.

Temple of Sun: It has to do with—long ago, long, long before your recorded history—your sister planet Venus, where you all were in another format, much lighter, much less dense than your present format, in preparation for your colonization of this planet, along with other civilizations, you seeded into the core of Earth unconditional love in what is now the heartland of the United States. That is in the process of being activated, that heart energy, that God Power. That unconditional love energy brought over from Venus. Venus is very actively involved in the Temple of Sun. These activations or rebooting's are assisting your country to be a way shower in this new paradigm of we-ness dear ones.

Joel: You talked about how the mission of the United States is to bring people together. You discussed the role of the Statue of Liberty and said that America is to be a refuge and sanctuary.

Temple of Sun: The Book of Law is held in her hands close to her heart, and within it, are the teachings from the master teachers and the ascended masters whom we speak of at this time.

Joel: You called it our divine mission and warned us that restrictive immigration laws might interfere with the mission of souls to come together here.

Temple of Sun: Indeed. Honor and embrace your destiny. For your shores have been the shores of refuge for all of those who sought sanctuary. Not one of you or your ancestors before you came here on other circumstances. They are the same circumstances of those who wish to enter now.

Open your hearts and understand that all who are led to be here or are presently here are a part of the golden age process. It is their divine right to be here. Do you understand?

Joel: You said the Temple of Sun encompasses the whole of Manhattan and spills over into New Jersey?

Temple of Sun: Yes, dear one. And the center altar, the main altar of our temple, is the Statue of Liberty.

Joel: For both residents and visitors to Manhattan, how can we engage consciously with the fact that we are essentially residing in the temple?

Temple of Sun: We will state again for clarity, connect with your Christ Consciousness energy, your I Am presence. Connect with the Blue Ray Angels. Connect with beloved Venus, the unconditional love being, and simply ask to join and to be with us.

Joel: We're going to be ending our conversation now. Is there anything additional you would like to tell us?

Temple of Sun: For those, for whom this is new information or a revelation, take these words within your hearts. Open your hearts and know the destiny of these United States, the location of this particular God-Power portal, the Temple of Sun, housing the Goddess of Liberty and many other beings.

Know you are all on a divine mission in this incarnational cycle to create a new paradigm of oneness, to lead the world, to "way show" the world through resonance—not through force or deceit or denial of the deceit but simply through your hearts that you are moving into oneness.

Joel: Thank you.

Chapter XXXVI

There once was the Land of Lemuria
That stood in grandeur for millennia.
Some say it was fable,
While others knew it was quite stable.
Believe it or not,
We are all from Lemuria's lot,
A land of light, which fathered divine thought.

CONVERSATIONS WITH ADAMA, HIGH PRIEST OF LEMURIA, FATHER OF HUMANITY

    This chapter is a recap of a conversation I had with Adama, Higher Priest of Lemuria, during a sacred journey to the spiritual vortex/portal Mount Shasta. See my book *Coming Home to Lemuria: An Ascension Adventure Story* for in-depth details. As our planet and humanity continue to shift into a higher-frequency / God-Power existence, this conversation becomes even more pertinent today...

Phillip: Thank you, Adama, for once again being an essential guide and teacher during this unique God Power–ascension process we are assuming. Your wisdom will greatly assist us for those who are ready to apply it by focusing on the content, not the source, if they cannot believe the source. Many know you brought your wisdom from another galaxy long ago to create what we call humanity.

Adama: You are most welcome, dear one. Let us once again speak truth, and through your enlightenment, we shall join as one. Your world continues to be filled with many erroneous belief systems imprinted in your souls that continue to produce much pain, lack, and limitation. But thanks to many light workers and way showers among you, that is beginning to change.

As stated above, this is a very special time for our planet and both our civilizations, we in the Inner-Earth within fifth-dimensional frequency and you on the surface.

All planets go through what is called an ascension process where they shift to a higher frequency in order to continue their growth and expansion. Look up at the night stars. Each one of those stars was once a planet that went through a process similar to what we are experiencing now, destined to return to a body of light. That God Power time has now come for Earth.

We Lemurians, who once walked upon the surface of this planet, through our love of you, wish to assist you in the process of ushering in a new, final golden age of equality, harmony, and balance—we consciousness / oneness / God Power. Your planet is in its final two-thousand-year cycle to achieve this. Your present world cannot stay the way it is and survive.

Mother Earth has already shifted her frequency, thus everything within and upon her body must do the same or move elsewhere. Billions of you have agreed to be here for this wonderful event. It is time to remember who you are and why you are here. *Man Power God Power* is filled with higher-realm teachings to support you.

The name of Lemuria's capital is Telos, which means "communication with spirit." And that is just what we are being/doing. We are being God Power through direct communication with *source*. All planets are hollow and inhabited by life forms of many vibrations, most often living inside a home (the planet), not on its roof (the surface). There is so much for you to learn that will thrill and delight you.

Phillip: So that's new information for many that planets have life forms within them. How many of you are there in our hollow Earth?

Adama: There are over 120 subterranean cities within the Earth's interior with millions of inhabitants. The interior structure of our planet is not exactly the way your science explains it. Beyond the known molten parts is a central interior where higher-frequency beings exist. This interior core can be reached through holes at either the North or South Pole.

The northern and southern lights in your skies are actually reflections of the Earth's interior central sun, which we created. We utilized technology from higher realms to create this other sun. Someday soon, you will have this ability as well.

There are many names for all the places and peoples inside our planet, but we do not wish to overload you with details now. Suffice to say it is well organized. And all this information can and will be made available to you.

Although Atlantis, Lemuria, and other "lost cultures" have become myths in your world, their peoples are living in higher frequencies in these underground cities.

Phillip: Why have most people not heard about all this before?

Adama: There are hidden forces that control your world and your world governments who know all about us and keep it from you in order to continue to control you. We have not come forward because your world has not been ready to receive us. We cannot interfere with your freedom of will and choice. If we come too early, there are many who will try to destroy us. But our being revealed is happening sooner rather than later, since many of you are now ready and creating a quantum shift.

Phillip: I do not wish to get into the drama of conspiracy theories, but there does seem to be a continuation of corruption in many governments on the surface. What is the core issue?

Adama: The governments you have on the surface reflect the Man Power consciousness of the people they govern. The people have largely given their God Power away because of a lack of interest or a feeling that nothing can be done. It's not your leaders; it's you. In Lemuria, we have highly evolved individuals as our governmental and spiritual leaders. Being immortal, the advantage of repeated lives adds greatly to our collective wisdom. Stand in your God Power now, and make another choice.

Phillip: Can you speak more about the "hidden force" of which you speak and their impact on religions and corporations? Again, I am going for truth here, not attachment to drama.

Adama: Religions were the first governments and became fairly corrupted early on by Man Power. Jesus, a.k.a. Lord Sananda, with whom we in Lemuria work closely, never intended the creation of what became humankind's (not so kind) version of Christianity. He wished his primary teaching (Love one another) to be purely made available to all. He wished you to know you are God Power.

Your corporations reflect the structure of your governments (and are now running them) and religions. These three—corporations, governments, and religions—control your world with deceit and denial of deceit. It's time for a new God Power world paradigm filled with truth, transparency, and authentic leaders to be created. If you so choose. This is not to say you do not have some good people in places of power; you do. But they are largely handicapped by the existing systems.

You the people can choose to change the system through God Power.

What do you choose?

Phillip: Can you explain what is happening with the planet during the many natural disasters and man-made events taking place?

Adama: Please know, dear people of the surface, that your mother Earth has had enough of your abuse. She is a living, conscious being who has been largely ignored and been patient long enough. The natural disasters are her way of clearing and cleansing herself and getting your attention, but they go ignored most of the time. Do you need entire continents to sink (it has happened before) to understand? The air, water, and minerals are her vital organs that make life possible for her and you. They are not a limitless supply to be bought and sold for profit.

All the elements on the planet (animals, plants, minerals, air, water, gas/oil) are interconnected and have a divine right to be here. They are made of the same atoms as you. They are not here for your exclusive use and abuse. Human-made disasters can show you the same consciousness needed as the natural ones. Be aware these events will increase until you shift your Man Power consciousness and behavior into God Power. How rough do you want it to get?

Phillip: Are the financial shifts taking place (quick up and downs) and huge debts being acquired reflecting a larger picture?

Adama: Yes, they are. The largely hidden Man Powers that control the world's finances (again without getting into drama or conspiracy theories) know that what they have been doing for a long time no longer will work in the future of the new world paradigm being created. They know God Powers are in place to replace greed, inequality, and duality with abundance and unity for all.

Know you will continue to see stops and starts of the old, as they attempt to hold on to Man Power, until the old collapses and a new economy is created based upon new definitions of abundance through God Power.

Phillip: What will this new economy look like?

Adama: It will be based on truth and reality, not myth and fiction. Most of the world's money supply is based on inflated credit. Most money is an IOU, not real money. An option will be to return to a precious-metal economy, based on free or cheap new technology fuel, based on principles reflecting Mother Earth, not human-made fiction. Economies that maintain and sustain the balance and structure of the Earth are essential. This means some of the resources and energy will go back to the Earth, not just to humankind. With the advance of new energy technologies, eventually you will become as we Lemurians, not needing money at all. You will be able to manifest everything you need through the mastery of energy. How does that make you feel?

Phillip: What was it like to have your entire civilization physically destroyed overnight?

Adama: We knew for many hundreds of years this would take place, that there would be an ending to our great continent and that we were not to interfere with the destruction. Out of the destruction would come creation. The spiritual leaders throughout the land prepared the people as best they could. They stayed with the people and went down with them. Most were sleeping when some 350 million of us perished. Many of you were there, including you.

As horrible as it was, we were allowed to save the jewels of wisdom of our civilization and bring them underground to our home beneath Mount Shasta. Our enlightenments are now available to you on the surface so you do not have to experience what we did. Gloriously, we can now advance together into our divine plans.

Phillip: What was the cause of the destruction?

Adama: It was two *Man-Powerful* civilizations not agreeing on how life should be and one trying to control the other. One was an assertive masculine energy, the Atlantean civilization, and the other a receptive feminine energy, the Lemurian civilization. In the end, both were destroyed because of their disconnection to *source* and their soul plans. You, too, are in the process of learning that war never works.

Phillip: Please explain some more the importance of our knowing one another.

Adama: In order for this planet and all upon it to continue to ascend in consciousness and create a higher frequency of existence, the entire planet must be united and join into one light from below (us) and one light from above (you) through God Power. That's why we are connecting with you at this time. Knowing us now will prepare you for what is to come. Books like *Man Power God Power* will assist greatly in revealing our purpose and your future, if you so choose.

Phillip: What is the purpose of being immortal?

Adama: All advanced, higher-frequency civilizations are immortal. Only lower-vibration civilizations continue to have life and death cycles like yours. When you live a very long time, you can apply your experiences to your civilizations. This is wisdom, not knowledge. When you have limited life cycles like yours, you forget from lifetime to lifetime what you learned. It is limiting. This limited cycle is coming to an end for you. You will be amazed how natural it will feel to live forever (you already do energetically; you just don't remember it physically). The best part of being immortal is your constant conscious connection to the creator, your God Power.

Phillip: We live in the third dimension, and you live in the fifth dimension. How many dimensions are there?

Adama: There are an infinite number of dimensions reaching toward the creator who is forever expanding. So the creator is always allowing us to rise to higher frequencies, as it does the same. For the moment, we all have enough to be/do to achieve unity on this planet by both civilizations achieving a higher frequency than the one you live in now.

Phillip: Why did you decide to live under Mount Shasta?

Adama: The atmosphere of the planet was largely interrupted by the advanced warfare between Atlantis and Lemuria. There were also other beings from outer space on the surface and within the Earth. We needed privacy and noninterference from others to complete our reason to be here. Mount Shasta allowed that privacy and protection to advance into who we are today. Mount Shasta is a mighty vortex of energy that continues to love and support our needs. It is a new concept to you, but most planets are lived from within. When our continent existed, Mount Shasta had always been a beacon of galactic communication and a remaining part of our homeland. So it felt very natural to go there.

Phillip: Can you further explain why you have not made your presence known before now?

Adama: As we explained, we went underground so we could evolve without any negative interference. We had enough war and destruction in our time on the surface. When will you?

If we had revealed ourselves sooner, your world would have seen us as an advanced enemy. Would most of your world today see us as someone to help? You were and still are not completely ready for us to come forward. By universal law, we were not allowed to interfere with your affairs, nor would we wish to. You have your own path to follow (divine plan), as we have ours. Now that we have advanced to the level we have, we can share with you. If we had not done what we did, you may not have a way back home to your divine destiny. So we did what we did for love, for both of us.

Phillip: We now know you are immortal. Are there any other major differences?

Adama: Even though we feel physically as you do, our bodies are much lighter because of our higher vibration; we experience many different sensations in our bodies, which you will experience when you shift. Our having sex is more of a connection with the creator experience than an orgasm.

We have eliminated disease and can repair and replace organs and body parts at will. We can become invisible by shifting our vibration. This allows us to travel to even higher frequencies. This is an ability you will develop when you further raise your consciousness. Can you imagine if your criminals could become invisible now?

Phillip: Can you explain how others and I are able to communicate with you?

Adama: It is part of an individual's divine soul plan to be able to do so. You usually spend many lifetimes to prepare to do so. Basically, they remove themselves from themselves, let go, and we come into their being speaking through the channel. There are conscious channels who stay partially awake and trance channels who have to be totally removed from their bodies to receive messages.

More and more of you are connecting to your telepathic and higher-frequency projection gifts and connecting with frequencies beyond your own. Humankind has done this from the beginning. Most of your advancements were a result of such connections. It's actually a very natural part of your God Power being. Simply trust you can...

Phillip: Why don't you need money in Lemuria?

Adama: We have no need for money. We create our own homes through the power of manifestation (alchemy) and all foods and commodities are free or bartered. There is no profit gained at the expense of another, for we are truly one (we know what effects one, affects another/all). We believe in the rights of all to live in equality, peace, and abundance, with justice for all. We do not need to own anything and share what we have. Your Man Power system of money has made you all slaves to your jobs, paying taxes, and making money for many things you do not need.

Philip: Please tell us about the teaching of the Sacred Flames and how they relate to our ascension process.

Adama: *The Sacred Flames* are a process one must go through to shift frequencies—for you from 3-D to 5-D; this is called ascension, Man Power to God Power, if you will. You ascend from one vibration to another.

The planets and the universe are in a constant state of ascension, shifting to higher and higher frequencies, ever toward the light. These so-called flames are a great gift to humanity. Without them, you would have no way to get back to your true God Power home/essence, directly connected to the creator. In Lemuria, we have temples dedicated to these flames with many ascended masters and other beings maintaining these unfed flames with their love and devotion. We have kept these flames for us and now for you. Remember, ascension is the main purpose of your many lifetimes on Earth. (See the book *The Seven Sacred Flames* for a complete study of these flames).

Phillip: How did you create a sun inside the Earth?

Adama: Our sun is not as big as yours. It reflects all the light we need. The light is a God-Powered crystal we brought from another planet, and it will burn brightly for millions of years. All light radiates life rays and creates life. Our crystals and our thoughts create all the light we need.

Phillip: Where do your water and air come from?

Adama: We have Inner-Earth oceans, which flow through the Earth creating streams and lakes, not unlike on the surface. We harness ocean and lake energy to create our atmosphere underground. Before the surface became so polluted we used to have openings to the surface for air. We now produce all our own pure air. Someday soon, we shall share our crystal technologies, which will clean your oceans and other bodies of water and air.

Phillip: How do you create perfect weather?

Adama: Your thoughts and emotions stored in the atmosphere and consciousness create all the negative weather on the surface. Our atmosphere is protected by the content of our emotions and thoughts, which are always in harmony with the planet and the creator. Thus, our weather is perfect. As you are experiencing more love and light on the surface, your weather will shift. Have you ever paid attention to where you have bad weather and connect that weather to the thoughts and emotions of that area? Begin to pay attention to this. Reliable weather has allowed us to evolve more quickly.

We can use our talents and gifts and inspirations and not have to wait for bad weather to pass (a waste of energy). How many opportunities do you think you have lost on the surface because of bad weather?

Phillip: Is it true you have living crystal libraries in Lemuria?

Adama: Yes, we have wonder-filled living libraries within crystalline platforms. You can go to any of them and experience firsthand any history or knowledge you wish. These libraries are filled with the truth of this planet's history, which no one on the surface knows. Much of your history is not true. True history is an effective way to learn and grow and expand. These crystalline platforms are one of the many technologies that we have that will amaze, delight, and empower you.

Phillip: Legion says there are spaceships coming and going out of Mount Shasta. Is this true?

Adama: Of course, we take many explorations into outer space and also monitor conditions on this planet from outer space. Once you know there is more to life than what you just see now, the entire universe will open for you. You will see the oneness and the beauty of the universe. We have the ability to make our spaceships invisible to keep your military away from them. Many beings from other worlds come in to Mount Shasta for reconnaissance. There are people in your world who know all about our space-faring abilities and us. Your governments have kept the reality of UFOs away from you in order to control you. Suppose you knew for a fact there were advanced civilizations all around you. How would you and your governments feel about that? Are you and they ready to accept this truth? And not see it as a threat?

Phillip: Tell us about your diet. What exactly do you eat?

Adama: You who are on the surface largely eat dead foods that contain little or no life force. No wonder you are sick so often and die so young. We only eat live food—vegetables, fruits, grains, and nuts. And we do not destroy the plants in the process. There is no eating meat, thus no killing of animals to eat them. The animals on this planet were not originally intended to be eaten.

We have special areas where our organic hydroponic gardens produce all we need. We don't freeze, can, or process our food. Our advanced technology allows us to produce large quantities in efficient areas. We use everything and discard nothing, never burying anything in our soil. The Earth and the soil are alive, and we honor and protect them. You vibrate according to the light-energy portion contained in what your body assimilates.

You maintain and sustain your body by the light-energy you consume in what you eat.

Phillip: Do you have sex the same way we do?

Adama: Not quite. Our bodies are less dense than yours, so we connect with our partner in a higher vibrational level. It is a complete union (body and soul) with each other through divine love and the creator. Our relationships and sexual expression reflects a more evolved understanding of divine love and sexuality.

Your relationships on the surface are often based upon duality, consciousness, and control. We have learned that our partner is a mirror of ourselves from whom to learn. We unite with a balance of the masculine and feminine energies.

When this balance is in place, the perfect relationship always shows up. Then a divine union with your twin soul or flame always appears, reflecting your higher selves. We have several levels of relationships that allow complete sexual freedom until a couple may choose commitment leading toward parenthood. We have the same sex organs and never dishonor them. It's revealing in your slang language on the surface you often use the names of your sexual organs as curse words.

Phillip: Do you have children the same way we do?

Adama: Not exactly. Much more responsibility and preparation comes into play before a couple can have a child. There are no children having children or unwanted pregnancies here. Since our bodies are less dense, our gestation period is one-third of yours.

A couple must be in a committed relationship (remember, we are immortal and bringing another soul into physical form is a well-thought-out, planned event). When the couple is ready to commit to a child, they have the spiritual training and support of their temple and community.

In fact, most of the pregnancy is spent in a temple where the couple and child to-come are in a loving and supportive environment. The child receives this level of divine love throughout his or her childhood and adulthood. The actual physical aspects of pregnancy are very similar to yours but in our case, reflecting a complete balance of the male and female energies.

Phillip: What do you wear down there?

Adama: Not much, since our weather is perfect. We have no shame associated with our physical bodies, so nudity is a nonissue. For eons, robes and loose-fitting clothing have been used.

Phillip: Light seems to be an important part of your world. Can you further explain the principles of light?

Adama: You are composed of many layers of light, the densest of which is your physical body. You have other bodies that are not physical (light bodies), which support your physical body. All this vibrating light (energy) is what you are. Everything is composed of energy and light. You came from light and will return to light. That's what *Man Power God Power* is all about. There's nowhere else to be, to go. You are an eternal light being having a human experience at this moment. And you've had many of these human experiences in preparation to return to the light as an immortal light being.

Phillip: Please explain the concept of always "now" in Lemuria.

Adama: Now is all there really is. Your mental body creates the past and future, which we no longer need. Universal law has taught us to always be in the moment of now. Now is your contact with your divinity. Life is meant to be lived in the present moment. Think about all the time you have wasted being concerned about what happened or is going to happen.

It takes away much of the joy of life. The now allows you to take full advantage of all the forces coming together to create growth and expansion.

Phillip: What is universal law?

Adama: The purpose of universal law is to maintain oneness throughout the universe. All advanced civilizations adhere to this law, which creates equity, harmony, and balance in all expressions of life. This law establishes divine order and maintains it. This law comes from the mind, love, and will of the creator.

Phillip: So, who or what is the creator?

Adama: The creator is God-Powered love, which creates, transforms, heals, and harmonizes all things. It is the highest consciousness, and through its ever-expanding wisdom, it creates the elements necessary to manifest seen and unseen reality everywhere. You are an individualized, unique, unlimited expression of the creator experiencing itself. Your religions have largely personified and misrepresented the creator.

Since it is love, it cannot judge, condemn, or punish you. That is control. The creator is an unconditionally loving force that knows you and it are one. The creator is trust that only exists in the heart, not the mind. The divine union of you and all that is being spoken of here is the creator.

Phillip: How do you transport yourselves inside the Earth?

Adama: Through our advanced technology (which, one day, you will have), we use crystal and electromagnetic energies. It's the same technology we used when we were on the surface. Nothing better has come along, and it does not abuse the planet. It's clean and free. We have a major tunnel system using this technology. We can also travel telepathically through our thoughts and astral-project anywhere on or off the planet. Thoughts are light, and light is energy. Energy manifests matter as it becomes denser. You will soon experience the unlimited freedom this creates...

Phillip: When do you come to the surface?

Adama: There are many openings that only Lemurians know about, which allow us to come and go often. These we have concealed, and humanity cannot find them. We are constantly checking conditions on the surface.

More and more, we are revealing ourselves to the light workers and way showers on the surface. The author of *Man Power God Power* is one of many with whom we are connected.

Phillip: What is the significance of the recent "natural" events taking place on Earth? They seem to be intensifying.

Adama: This is a very special time for your planet. It has changed frequencies in order to move forward in its evolution. Thus, everything within and upon the planet needs to shift as well. This is the ascension process. You are in your final two-thousand-year cycle to create the final, permanent Golden Age of Oneness.

So things are changing rapidly, and significant cataclysms are continuing to occur. This is the planet's clearing and cleansing process. Preparations and messages from higher realms, like us, are coming to you now...thus, the reason for *Man Power God Power*. If they resonate, allow them to connect you to your higher selves and the shift. We have been waiting many thousands of years for this ascension to take place. Mother Earth has sacrificed much for us below and you above. The end of that time has come. The time for transition into light is here. The time for Man Power to become God Power is here.

Phillip: Much of our new media has been revealing government cover-ups of chemical and biological warfare. Many think this is all conspiracy-theory thinking. Without going into the drama of it, what light can you shed on these matters?

Adama: First and foremost, hidden biological and chemical warfare is real and so are the cover-ups. Most of the people on the surface are completely unaware of, don't care, or don't believe this. We check these conditions regularly (chem-trails in your skies, land and ocean mines buried all over your planet). Many of your diseases (HIV) are Man-Powered and have been released on purpose to control humanity by unseen, powerful forces.

These same measures took place when the Atlanteans and we Lemurians were on the surface. We are saddened that this behavior is repeating itself...attempting to destroy the Earth and control her peoples again.

We ask you not to turn to fear but to choose ascension into another frequency where these 3-D dramas cannot harm you. We tell you these things not to upset you but to make you aware of the truth (which will set you free).

Phillip: It is really difficult for some people to believe or understand and accept what you are saying about cover-ups and controlling the people. Can you please explain further?

Adama: Throughout our planet's history, humans have been controlled by other beings from other galaxies (ETs) and advanced civilizations and by Man Power.

Your genes and DNA have been altered by them in an attempt to control you for their purposes, but they are being repaired and additional genes and chakras are being activated in order to directly connect you to the forces that created you. We know this sounds far out for many. But for those of you who can resonate with this truth, we ask that you begin to make other choices in empowering yourselves.

We had these same things happen with our time on the surface. The assertive masculine energy, the Atlanteans, and others often tried to control us with gene manipulations and enslavement. This was the major reason for our destructive wars with them.

What is happening to you is not new. Your wars and additional events to get you into war are examples of Man-Powered governments creating situations to control the population for the benefit of a hidden few controlling the many (call them what you may). Dear ones, the "terrorist" is within yourselves, not outside of you. The dark forces that are creating these events are ancient. But their time of control is coming to an end and they know it. They are putting up a fight to the finish. They have been in Man Power for a long time and do not wish to give it up. But give up power, they will, for we are all destined now to return to the light.

Phillip: Why was I led to facilitate sacred journeys to Mount Shasta? (See *Coming Home to Lemuria: An Ascension Adventure Story*, by this author.)

Adama: It was in your divine soul plan to do so in this lifetime. You were once an important part of our civilization in Lemuria.

You still are. Along with many others, you chose and were chosen to assist in revealing to the surface world that we exist and for what purpose. The actual physical trip to our home, Mount Shasta, is to open an energetic gateway between our world below and your world above and beyond and to assist in balancing the masculine and the feminine energies (to balance giving and receiving). You also opened additional vortices and performed specific rituals, as guided by Archangel Michael, who was instrumental in the creation of Lemuria.

The creation of these new vortices and the opening of the Lemurian Gateway allowed the rebooting and activation of certain crystalline technology within the mountain. The energy from these activations will allow Mount Shasta to become an even stronger beacon in assisting the planet and its inhabitants to make a shift into a higher frequency of existence. Each member of your expedition was very different from the other because you represented proxies for humankind.

Phillip: What prevents us from coming to Lemuria now?

Adama: Your consciousness and frequency prevents you from coming to Lemuria now. When you reach a critical mass of God-Powered consciousness concerning immortality, that's when we shall join in balance and harmony. If you came down now, it would interfere with our higher frequency. When more of you accept us in your consciousness, we shall more and more come forward.

Phillip: What do you consider to be one of the most important missions of your civilization?

Adama: It is an essential part of Lemuria's divine soul plan to care for this planet until you on the surface can. We shall join together and bring the light of ascension into the entire Mother Earth, to assist in moving the planet and all her inhabitants into a higher, more-evolved frequency of existence (which is your destiny as much as hers).

Everyone who ever lived on Earth has returned for this amazing event of Earth's transition into the light. That's why there are billions of you on Earth now. Our light has never stopped being sent to the surface, this is the main mission of our remaining here. When this is complete, some Lemurians and some of you will return to the galaxies from which you originally came and many will stay. As below, so above.

Phillip: Who are the light workers (and way showers, those taking the light en masse into the world), and what do they do?

Adama: The light workers are individuals and groups committed to assisting the Earth in transitioning back into light, moving into a higher frequency of existence through their God Power. These people receive large volumes of light from below and from above, which supports the planet and increases the people's consciousness, mirroring universal consciousness. And this consciousness travels at the speed of light, consuming lower frequencies all over the planet. Light workers are being born at increasingly faster rates. Children (indigos, rainbow, and crystalline children) are coming into the earthly plane fully equipped for the task at hand, which is to bring humankind into oneness.

Phillip: What is your intention for humankind beyond what has been spoken?

Adama: Our intention and mission for humankind is for you to live as God-Powered immortal beings (like us) and to grow and expand in consciousness in an ever-expanding universe always toward the creator within each of you. For you are the creator experiencing itself.

Phillip: From your perspective, what is love?

Adama: Love is the highest God-Powered vibration and frequency (energy) in the universe. Thus, it is the building block of everything. Everything is maintained and sustained by love. Without love, there is no creation, only destruction. Love will always bring our thoughts and emotions into oneness. The organ of love is our heart. Your heart knows that love is all there is. Everything else is the absence of love. We are all here to learn to be love, first with self.

Phillip: Some people are going to have difficulty with the source of the information given here. Can I believe the message if I cannot accept the source of it? Can you discuss the difference between belief and truth?

Adama: At one time, you believed the Earth was flat and that the sun revolved around the Earth. And those who said otherwise were punished or killed.

At one time, you believed (or in many cases were forced to believe) that religion was the only true path to God.

Beliefs come from your Man-Powered mental body, often representing control, and they can change. Knowing comes from the God-Powered heart, and truth does not change or wish to control. Your acceptance of truth can change. You may now believe that Lemuria inside the Earth, within another frequency, does not exist. Because you cannot see it, your mind cannot believe it...like the flat Earth and revolving sun. You have not arrived at the truth yet.

There is actually very little truth you do know about your world. And new truths are soon to be revealed that will amaze, delight, and free you. Through acceptance of not knowing, you can arrive at the possibility and probability of truth. For the moment, focus on the message if you cannot accept the messenger. Use your resonance and discernment to guide you. You have killed or not believed many important messengers throughout your Earth's history. Killing them did not make them untrue.

Phillip: Can your further explain the importance of crystals in advanced civilization?

Adama: Within most advanced civilizations crystals are the main God Powered source of energy and are used in every aspect of our lives (transportation, healing, communication, building, information storage, etc.). What you are aware of in your world about crystals is rather limited. Crystals, like animals and plants and you, are conscious, living beings. They are a fundamental part of the structure of the universe. The core of this planet is a crystalline grid that is the heart (central sun) of the Earth and has received ascension activation from *source*.

So, in effect, the crystalline heart of the planet is God Powering all the shifts that are taking place now. Crystalline technologies are powering your advanced computer / cyber-communications, as well. The first radios were called crystals because the crystals inside the radios were the receiver.

There is an important difference between your crystalline structure and ours. Since we live in a higher frequency, our crystals are lighter, clearer, more luminous, and more able to absorb and store light. We can create crystals through our thoughts, and they can take unlimited shapes and frequencies to meet our needs. The use of crystalline energy is limitless.

Your world is changing dramatically and quickly as the result of crystalline technology. When we introduce you to our level, our crystalline ability, all things will become possible.

Phillip: In conclusion, consciousness appears to be such an important part of ascension and advanced civilization. What are the basics of consciousness?

Adama: The teachings of consciousness have filled entire libraries and continue to do so. So in a limited amount of space (and we refer the readers to the other consciousness teachings throughout *Man Power God Power*) let me say, consciousness is a unique choice and path for each individual who chooses it. Consciousness is a heightened awareness and understanding of yourself (self-mastery), which reflects beyond you as a total understanding of life and the universe, and you being God Power. It is an ever-expanding process that unfolds according to the level of readiness and commitment you are willing to put into it. It is about knowing through your heart your purpose (your divine soul plan), which is to be expressed through your talents and gifts, by choosing to give these to the world (service). Developing higher consciousness involves moving from the unhealed me into the healed we consciousness of oneness. Consciousness is your travel ticket to your divine destiny of God-Powered freedom and connection to *all there is*.

Phillip: Thank you, Adama, for this time together and bringing humanity in our world. Let us affirm your answers to my questions will give our readers more insight into Lemuria and themselves while expanding us into their God Power.

Chapter XXXVII

To call higher beings
Let us first think upon them, and in our mind's eye,
Let our seeing become their being.
The higher being
Gives of itself unconditionally,
In all conditions, unceasingly.

UPLOADING ARCHANGEL URIEL

Uriel Message #1: My First Invitation to Channel via Trance Channel Jeff Fasano

We come to you as your creator to speak to you at this time. We are a vortex of energy created for you moving into the depth and breadth of your heart chakra.

We are Uriel to speak to you part and parcel upon your divine plan, divine plan ever emerging into you. It is time to open to the depth and breadth of that divine plan. And now to begin to build the fences around the divine plan. Fully immerse yourself in the dedication, the commitment, the intention of that work. Now is not the time to differentiate between that divine plan and what is outside of yourself.

For the next fifty days, mark on your calendar, for this day forward, the time where you will specifically pay attention by building the fence around that divine plan. And now begin to study your divine plan within this next fifty days; devote your studying to this divine plan. To uncover all the aspects and ingredients in that divine plan. Now make this your priority, if you chose to.

Let go of the extraneous energies outside of yourself. And only focus on what you need to do in your day-to-day activities outside of yourself. And your main focus, if you chose, in the next fifty days will be dedicated to your practice.

The practice of developing, refining, and defining your divine plan—defining the meaning, value, and purpose of you and the meaning, value, and purpose of the divine plan. Allow this to come to you, dear one. You should be spending an inordinate amount of time in your practice now.

It is now time to release any extraneous energies outside of yourself that do not directly coordinate to the revelation of your divine plan. It is now time to connect with these energies directly. These are specific energies of the Uriel archangelic realm because messages are coming to you at this time.

You can feel the messages, you can see the messages, and you know the messages.

We have knocked at your door often. It is time now to listen. It is now time, dear one, to listen to these messages and these energies that are moving through you and coming through you. Now, to impart these messages upon the world, which is why, dear one, we ask you to build the fence...around your divine plan. Not a place of setting barriers or lines of demarcation but a time where you can now build the fence and hang a sign outside that fence where it says, "men at work." Because what you are doing, dear one, you are at work.

You are now at work to improve the depth of where you are moving into the depth and breadth of your heart space to bring to the world, the depth of the message. You see, dear one, in many ways, you get the message, you know the message, but you don't know the depth of the message.

You know what the message is. "I know what the message is; don't worry. I know what the message is." But we have knocked at your door once too often, dear one. And we are now opening that door for you. Because we see, dear one, that you have been quite reluctant to open that door for yourself where these messages are concerned.

So what we asked you to do, dear one, what we suggest that you do, dear one, at this time, is now opening the depth and breadth of your soul space, your heart space. And open up to the depth and breadth of the Uriel message.

The Uriel message moves in conjunction with the Michael message that you receive, that you receive quite often. What will come to you through another source, if this divine soul choses, will be the Rafael message. That is not of your concern. What is of your concern right now, dear one? Because you do have the source of the Gabriel and Michael messages. *Now to be the source, dear one, of the Uriel message. Now be the source of the Uriel message.* It is now time for you, dear one, to choose this.

If, in fact, you find yourself, dear one, so inclined to remove yourself from it, to remove yourself from it, to remove yourself from yourself, to fully move to a depth and level within, to remove yourself from yourself, to hang that sign on the doorway around that gate that says, "men at work"...

I am now at work on my divine plan. I now sit at my desk from two to three hours each and every day to work on my divine plan, to receive the messages, to import the messages that allow myself and others to eradicate the follies of the mental body, the intellectual mind. The folly that holds them and myself in place in the pursuit of the spiritual journey.

What, dear one, are the follies that hold you in place? Because you see the follies outside, dear one. It is now time, dear one, to build that fence around the depth and breadth of your heart space in direct relation to the divine plan and begin to focus your attention and set your intention and commit to this. It is now time to see the folly of the pursuit. What is the folly that you still pursue, dear one? Because when you see this, you will see the folly that others pursue. And you will know this. You will know at this time most pursue the folly. The folly of validation and gratification for which they are. Many, dear ones, have ceased to pursue the depth and breadth of truth.

Archangel Uriel

Uriel Message #2: Uriel, Yes, We Are Working Together

Oh Happy Days! We are delighted with your choice to work with us, dear one. Welcome. There is much work to be done at this most dramatic time of change upon your planet. Much is being revealed to humanity of the many levels of assistance you are receiving, if you choose it. There has never been in the history of your planet such a "concert" of effort from the angelic and star realms. But remember, dear ones, we can only do so much, you have a freedom of will and choice. We cannot and must not interfere. But forces like never before are coming into your world to assist you, at last, to join into oneness, to stop the few controlling the many, if you so choose. Your summer will be a most powerful time. We shall see those who choose to move forward and those who do not. Those who do not will no longer receive the assistance of the past times. Our focus is upon the portion of your beautiful planet that chooses to move forward into oneness—the Club of Love, Acceptance, Peace, Unity, Oneness. How does that make you feel in contrast to your planet's past and present history of separation and war? By the end of your hot summer months, we'll have all the forces connected to assist in allowing the greatest truth to come forth for you all, to know that you are spiritual beings having a human experience. We have watched lovingly throughout your history as you chose not to love one another, as a collective whole. Now you can see that you are all unique expressions of that whole.

There are many institutions and governments and their leaders who will facilitate this shift. Pay attention to who you put into office. Know their true intentions. Check their background. Reform your "professional" political career structure. Remember, it was the private common man who was to go into public office and then return to his private life after servicing his fellow man, not professional politicians, who through generational greed have created your corrupt system. You can change that now, dear ones.

The feminine energies coming in will assist in balancing the masculine that has created much of your cause and effect. There must be a balance of male and female energies; this has nothing to do with either gender or sex. These energies are here to assure that love stays in place. For when the male and female balance, it equals love. Then you think with your hearts, which is your true mind, not your brain.

Set aside all fear and resistance as the changes take place. Remember, fear is just an absence of the love you've needed all along. And love is the glue that holds the universe together, the highest vibration that allows great, creative, loving things to manifest into your third dimensional world.

Don't worry about how all this will happen. Surrender to the unknown; in the void lies creation and all possibility. In the not knowing, the knowing will surely come. There is no need to strive for anything. The divine plan of your planet is unfolding through your individual divine plans. It's all perfect, dear ones. Fear not. Love is on the way to save the day!

Now rest and know the truth of who you are and why you are here. It is all being revealed. Relax. Love. Rest. And listen to that quiet voice within you. It is we speaking to you, guiding many of you. Use your solitude to know the quiet and truth coming forth. You will not find it outside in your world. It lies deep with you. It's been there all along.

Now you know for sure.

Love and Light,

Uriel

P.S. Many of you use forming groups to facilitate the work that needs to be done. State the intention/mission of the group and allow those souls who resonate within it to appear. Remember, change is all there is. Allow your fellow man an opportunity to change or not. Through holding the focus/mission of your groups, you will know who the light workers are. Allow all to become so. The history of your planet has excluded most by the few. Don't fall into that trap again, dear ones. The portion of your planet that is there to be and do the work will just appear. They will reveal themselves soon enough. Know this present truth, and be free of your past history.

Uriel Message #3: Our Planet's Soul Plan

Greetings once again from the vortex you call Uriel. For far too long, your planet has gone without knowing your divine plan, or should we say, remembering the divine plan. Quite simply, but not so simply for you, the divine plan of your planet is to find the unity, non-separation through all the diversity you find in your world. Have you ever wondered why there are so many different peoples, languages, nations, and religions on your planet? Or do you simply just say that's the way it is and not really know why or ever ask why? It all has to do with how your planet started. It began with many influences from many worlds, many star worlds (not star wars). In fact, there is no other planet just like yours, with so many different influences (seeding's) in its beginning. Most just take it for granted that's the way it is. But, in fact, it's quite unique within the universe for a world such as yours to exist. It's sort of an experiment, an experiment that has not worked very well, very often. But all of that is about to change for your world. There are messengers and messages coming in via our angelic realm and the star worlds that "seeded" your planet that are going to allow a portion of your humanity to know the truth and set you free from your past separation from each other.

You are all unique expressions from the same source. Even the different worlds that seeded your planet are from that same *source*...there's nowhere else for anything to come from except that *source*. The creation of your planet was set in force by an energetic intention that would allow you to find the unity via all your diversity.

You all represent the many expressions/versions of *source*. Your agreement was to find the oneness in spite of your differences. You've been struggling with your "agreement" for many eons. That time is coming to an end. The struggle is almost over. Many realize if you don't accept your differences in order to be one, you won't survive. You've made this mistake before, and it's not necessary to make it again. You've advanced to a stage where you are ready to accept all of you, include all of you, love all of you. The only thing standing in the way in the past and present has been you (your relationship with you) not loving yourself enough to love others. It all begins with how you feel about yourself. Someone once said, the only relationship you're having is the one with yourself. And all other relationships are a "mirror" of you.

The special powerful energies coming into your world now are going to allow enough of you to know the truth of your being to effect the change necessary to move into a world of self-love and oneness. We know this sounds impossible to most of you. But there are worlds, more advanced than yours, where this possibility is a reality. In fact, some of those worlds are assisting you all now. Many know you are divine spiritual beings having this human experience. And that experience is about to become more accepting and loving than ever before. There is no further need for a few of you to control many of you through lies and deceit. Most of you have simply given your power away and allowed it to happen. The walls of power and deceit are about to crumble, dear ones. The few have controlled the many long enough. There is enough for everyone to share and have plenty left over. No need for further greed.

Your divine plan includes knowing this truth and creating a world where these things mentioned are normal. We are being and doing our part. Are you yours? Together, we can change your world where you know how to be and act to create a loving, safe world for all. This is your world's true divine plan. And it all starts with each one of you knowing who you are and why you are here—questions never asked in school. But we ask it of you now. There are many messengers and messages that will allow you to answer these questions now. Listen. Be ready to find you and your place in your world.

Uriel

Uriel Message #4: Who Are You? Why Are You Here?

Greeting from the energy, the vibration, the consciousness you call Uriel.

Who are we? Why are we here? All archangelic realms are "bands" of high vibratory forces of energy, thus consciousness. For consciousness is merely concentrated energy and intention, dear ones. Why are we here? To serve mankind as the "keeper of your planet" through the wisdoms, energy, and purpose of love. For through love, the highest vibration and energy in the universe, you can create the most glorious and joyous world possible.

Only through a lack of love and purpose have you not done this in the past, dear ones.

So as the energy moves from the core of your planet (during your fall season) out into the universe, moving through your physical, mental, and emotional bodies, feel our love and intention to remind you who you are and why you are here, to know you are eternal energetic beings having this physical experience in order to learn love of purpose, dear ones.

Today is the birth of one ascended soul who once walked your Earth and knew and understood the power of love of self and purpose. You called him Gandhi. Through love, not resistance and separation, he allowed the greatest military power on Earth to experience love and allow his country to continue their own destiny without interference from outside. This focused energy in the physical called Gandhi knew his purpose to set his country free through love of self and others.

You can begin to set yourself free also, to know and see yourself worthy to be loved by yourself first, accepted by you just the way you are, and to attract the love of others through your love. That's the formula, dear ones. The basis is always love or, often in your case, an absence of love.

So today fill your hearts with love and acceptance of self and begin to know your purpose, meaning, and value in physical life to fully love yourself in order to love and serve others. By giving, you receive. By receiving, you give. And the circle of energy is complete, and so are you.

Know and remember that beginning to think with your hearts can refocus you into a world of love. For love is the most powerful force in the universe, and everything else is merely an absence of it.

So fill yourself with love, dear ones. And watch others drink from that full glass and change your world forever.

Keeper of your planet, through your hearts and love,

Uriel

Uriel Message #5: Truth and Hope

Greetings, beloved people of Earth, from the loving, heartfelt force and realm of Uriel.

When all seems lost, it is an opportunity to find hope and solution, dear ones.

Your world is filled with so much hopelessness now, so much conflict and separation from yourselves. This is all due to a lack of love within your world. We must remind you at this time that the purpose, the divine plan of your planet, is to experience love...the highest force in the universe, and that your planet is a supreme experiment in diversity to find that love, thus oneness toward yourself and others.

Each day, the forces of love are coming into your world, and each day, many of you deny these loving forces because you do not love yourselves enough to accept and receive them. It's as simple and as complex as that, dear ones.

Why is it taking so long to know this truth? Because you have been taught otherwise.

You have been taught from generation to generation that you are not good enough to receive this love. And why is this so? By experiencing what is not true, you shall experience what is true. This is one of the ways you have chosen to learn. You often choose to learn how to be by how not to be. Within the contrast and untruth, you reveal the truth to yourself. You discover and know light by the contrast of darkness. You come to know love by the absence of it. For since love is all there is, it cannot not exist, only your experience of the absence of it for whatever the reason. And the absence does not make it true.

So it's all about the truth, the truth of who you are, and then you can know why you are here, if you so choose, to know you are creations of the highest vibratory, loving force in the universe. You are a unique portion of that force, experiencing itself in the moment of now in your Earth realm.

And why are you here? To grow and expand into the value, meaning, and purpose of your being here. And you cannot have value, meaning, and purpose outside yourself until you know it within yourself. And how do you do this?

By not worrying about the "how," know who you are, and the why and how will be revealed to you without much effort on your part. This lives within your hearts, not your minds. Your heart knows you are here to express love. And only you are preventing this through a lack of self-love.

Learning "what is" by experiencing "what is not" allows you to choose what is. Focus on what is in each moment of the now, and see how your world changes.

Your hearts await you, dear ones. To fully move into your heart space, allow yourself to know what love would do now in each and every moment. And your awareness and actions will be a direct reflection of your love of you.

Just imagine that love is the building block of everything in the universe. Within love lies everything you need to know, be, or do. You just need to tap into it. It's always been there. It's you who have not been aware of it in order to receive it.

Open your hearts now, dear world, and allow the deepest mysteries of your world to be revealed—the interconnection of everything. You all need your love of self and one another and all things for the cycle of life to be complete. Everyone and everything on/in your planet is connected by the force of love (or not). The vehicle for knowing this is to feel it from within your hearts. Once the feeling becomes a knowing, you will remember who you are and rediscover why you are here.

Uriel

Uriel Message #6: Your Planet and Love

Greetings beloved Earth beings, from the consciousness realm that always focuses upon your planet and all things upon and within it.

Your Earth is a living being just like you, dear ones. Made up of all the same parts from the same materials. Your planet has organs, body parts, and feelings not separate from your own. You've treated your planet like a lifeless, non-feeling thing for many of your Earth years. You've forgotten that it's your home in the universe, to be loved, honored, and protected. But just like yourselves, your treatment of your planet reflects your lack of self-love.

And now, you're beginning to realize and know what effects your planet has on you and vice versa. It's all interconnected. And only through loving yourselves can you save your planet from your destruction of it. How you treat your planet is a mirror of how you treat yourself and each other. That's why the processing of the "me" to get to the "we" is so vital now. Only till you truly love yourselves can you love your world and all things upon it.

This is an excellent example of how love is the glue that holds everything in the universe together. For without love, all things collapse and fall apart. It's the key ingredient in the recipe of life.

Through the possible destruction of your planet and home, the truth of who you are and why you are here can come to you, if you so choose.

You are here to learn to love, support, and serve one another. And this relationship with the self has stood in the way of this.

So we remind you again at this most important time in your world to know the importance of love. It ain't just a lyric in a pop song. It can mean survival or not.

Awaken your hearts and souls to the importance of love now. Stop and ask, "What would love do now?" in each moment of the now. And follow your heart in saving your world and all things upon and within it, dear ones.

Love, love, love can create a relationship with yourself that will spread out into your world, creating harmony and equality and sharing for all.

So once again, we remind you: it all begins with you and the "mirror" of you out there...

Love,

Uriel

Uriel Message #7: Higher Realm Messages and Support

Greetings, beloved channel of the realm of Uriel. Today, we would like to speak about commitment to the task at hand of being a conscious channel for we of Uriel.

It is our plan for our messages and teachers to be revealed into your world at this time. We are aware of your Angel News Network website and know that our messages will be sent out into your world at that time. That is all preparation for that glorious moment for a collection of angelic messages to be sent at the same time, revealing the abilities to experience other realms at the same time in your realm. This is necessary at this moment in the evolution of your species. You shall come to know that you are not all there is, that there are forces of creation beyond your physical world that create and support your limited view of the universe. This limited view must be expanded in order for you to understand yourselves more fully. Knowing there are other beings will assist you in better understanding yourselves. For far too long, you have believed you are all there is. At one time, you believed you were the center of the universe, that your sun revolved around your planet.

Dear ones, you are a tiny, yet important part of the universe. You are an especially important experiment in diversity and unity. Your planet is teeming with life forms, many you have not even known yet. And yet your ego minds wish to keep yourselves separated and a part from yourselves and others. Through knowing what is not true, you shall now know what is true, dear ones. It's the way you have chosen to learn. Not always an easy way, but your own way.

You are now collectively beginning to realize that everything and everyone on your planet is interconnected. All things affect the others. By knowing and loving yourself, you know and love others.

You are gathering a "white army" of light workers to know, to share, to be the truth of who you are and why you are here.

You are divine spiritual beings having a physical experience within diversity to find unity from the same source, dear ones. This one sentence is your reason to be or not to be. And through this being, you can create wonderful "doing nesses." A lot of your doing is just "do-do" right now.

To know the unseen portions of you that create the seen portions of you is essential now. You've lived in matter exclusively long enough. And it doesn't matter anymore. It always only matters in matter.

So, dear channel and others reading, as we come together again at this time, remember your commitment to us, to yourself, and to your world service. For as our beloved Michael has said, there is no other true path but world service. For staying trapped within yourself will not allow growth and expansion, only greed and imbalance.

Some of you have come to realize it's the distribution of abundance, not the accumulation of it, which matters in matter. And as those give, they shall receive beyond untold measure.

Uriel

Uriel Message #8: Children of the Awakened Heart

Greetings, beloved Earth beings, once again, we come to you from the light-being-ness, you know as Uriel, a realm of consciousness and awakening to the truth of who you are and why you are here.

You are indeed children of our light, your light that is moving from your minds into your hearts. For only through your heart can the light fully enter and awaken you all from a deep, long sleep: To become *children of the awakened heart* from a sleep that now has come to an end. It is an awakening that must come in order for you to fully know who you are and why you are here.

We have recently spoken about the illusion of time and the star realms' seeding's that began your planet. These truths and wisdoms are a further preparation of you knowing and loving yourselves, to begin to know firsthand the "mechanics" of how the universe operates.

Since you are a micro of the macro of the universe, everything must begin with you loving and knowing yourself; then that awareness can spread out into your world and even beyond it, dear ones.

For far too long, you have not been aware that you are the universe, in effect, that the universe would be incomplete without each and every one of your unique nesses. Once you begin to comprehend that you are the forces of the universe expressing itself, you will begin to know your power and purpose. You are God experiencing itself, dear ones.

Your God Power is that you are fully creating your reality in each moment of the now through your thoughts. That's how powerful you are! Your purpose is to fully express your greatness through love of self and others.

You are now becoming awake and aware of this reality. This is necessary at this time in order for mankind to move further toward its divine plan. And what is that plan?

Through all of your diversity, find the connection to the single source you are all created from. Once you fully know this source and your connection to it, you move deeply toward it, into its vibratory influence. At that moment, you become one with everything, and you know and feel the interconnection of everything, where separation is no longer possible, only love and unity.

Can you image what a world of love and unity would be like, where the interest of the self no longer rules supreme, where the equation of giving equals receiving is in full balance, where you know the connection of everything? There are worlds like this that exist in the universe. And they, too, went through their evolutionary path to achieve consciousness and their greatness.

There have been civilizations on your planet that almost achieved this. And when they knew their power, they abused it and destroyed themselves. That was why it has taken many epochs to again get your species ready to know your power and purpose again. Then the choice arises again, to abuse it or use it for all mankind.

We raise these issues at this time to remind you that as the wisdoms of the universe are revealed, they can be misused, if enough of you are not fully conscious to prevent it.

It is not about the individual but all. Think with your hearts, dear ones, not your minds. True power is love, not greed. But you must love and understand yourself fully to prevent power from becoming greed.

The foundation of yourselves is being laid. The cement is drying. Let's see what you build upon it. You have a freedom of choice and will. Know we are guiding and supporting each step of your way, dear ones. And the final choice is always yours.

Lightheartedly, Uriel.

Uriel Message #9: Moment of Now

Greetings from the beloved consciousness and en-"light"-en-ment of the realm referred to as Uriel, in your Earth realm.

At this time, we would like to talk to you about "time"—or, we should say, the *illusion* of time. Time is a "creation" of your physical, third dimension, so you may experience yourselves more fully. But the creation of time is a myth, a fiction, a non-reality. For within your time, there is a "past" and a "future," when in reality, there is only now (containing all time).

And it is humans focusing upon the past and future and their inability to focus upon the reality of now that creates much of the imbalances, separation, and foolishness within your world.

Much of your existence is focused upon the past, worrying about what could have been, what should have been, or on the future, projecting what might happen, what will happen. Neither is reality, dear ones. For in each moment of the "now" you are given (it is your divine right to receive) exactly what you need (not always what you want).

Stop and think about it. You've always received in each moment of the now of your life what you need. You always have; you always will. It's most often your thoughts about your fictitious past and future that get in the way of experiencing the now, the only true reality there is.

So how can you better enable yourselves to focus upon the now and not the past and future? By truly experiencing the now fully. Stop, breathe, see what you are seeing, taste what you are tasting, know what you are thinking and feeling...become conscious and now know the now!

Fill your heart with gratitude for the now. For in each moment of it, you are fully loved and supported always. Only your nonbelief in this prevents it.

Only your lack of self-love prevents the now from existing.

No
Other = N-O-W (no other way)
Way

In reality, there is "no other way" (now) than now. Know this truth, and you'll set yourselves free from the prisons of the past and future, prisons that have kept you behind bars long enough, dear ones. The doors to that prison have always been open in the moment of now.

Begin living *now* and know the only reality there really is by stepping outside that prison door and acknowledging each moment of the now bringing you all you've ever needed or will need.

Trust in yourself. It requires trust to fully know that you don't need anything else but the now. The rest of your "time thinking" is not serving you, dear ones.

As more of you begin to experience multidimensional realms directly, and you remember/realize that everything is happening at the same time, the now will make more sense.

The ability to be vessels and messengers of other realms allows you to fully experience the now. That's why it's happening now. Get it?

Through other realms, you'll realize they are all happening at once and that the past and future are an illusion.

Uriel

Uriel Message #10: Ready and Prepared

Good day from the angelic energy and realm of our consciousness known as Uriel in your Earth plane.

These are exciting days for your planet, beloved humans. We and many of you have been preparing for this moment in your Earth time for quite some time.

It has taken a great deal of readiness and preparation, you might say. You have had to "advance" to a certain vibration of consciousness for what is about to unfold to happen. It has been a "concerted" effort on our and your parts to see these necessary changes happen in your world.

You first had to be reminded who you are and why you are here in order to effect the change. You are multidimensional beings (spirit and physical) believing you are living in a third-dimensional realm. But, in fact, you've been living in several realms at the same time all along. You just most often were not aware of it. You've had a hint of it when you sleep and go into the fourth astral dimension or when you have a near-death experience and come back, remembering some of what you experienced.

You are now being prepared to experience, in an awakened state, other realms. It is these realms that created you and maintain and sustain you now. They are working very hard to assist you in moving into your full divine plan of love and oneness. You've had to experience a lot of separation from yourself and others to know this oneness now. It's how you chose to learn. The most important lesson has been love of self in order to love others. This has been the major imbalance upon your planet. It has created your greed and wars and separation from one another.

Now you are realizing you are all divine, diversified expressions of the same *source*. And you are becoming "super mutts," as Archangel Gabriel has told you. As your races complete their genetic mix through interracial unions, you truly and literally are producing the oneness you need to achieve in order to advance.

Once this consciousness is fully in place, you will be able to know and experience directly the forces that have created you. But up until now, you have not been able to experience us fully because of your low vibration of consciousness/awareness. You cannot know what you cannot conceive.

Now that you are ready and beginning to experience us, things will and can happen at a faster pace. You'll be able to manifest change more quickly in order to unite and prevent the destruction of yourselves.

These are indeed "good days" as we began in this message. You now know the goodness in yourself and others and the connection of the two. You are not alone, and you now know this truth. And this truth will set you free from yourselves to know the truth of your being, which is about to change your world in order to incorporate its divine plan of love and oneness. Stay tuned...

Uriel

Uriel Message #11: Beloved Channel

Greetings to our "beloved" channel of the vortex, the energy, the realm of God's light known as Uriel.

You have had many Earth lifetimes to prepare for the work you are about to do. We are "delighted" that you have chosen "to be," in all aspects of your life, a messenger of our wisdom and love for your planet and mankind.

This next year will be an important one for you, dear one. You will move into maximum speed and intention in your work with others and us. Your foundation has been the messages of Gabriel. That is true for most of us. You have opened your heart to receive the lessons and wisdom of Michael. You are now beginning to be exposed to Brother Rafael, as well as the energies of many others and several star realms.

The purpose of all this is so that you fully become into knowing and experiencing whom you are and why you are here. We pose questions constantly until you all fully know the answers.

You are now a teacher of our wisdoms so that others will more fully be able to answer these two critical questions. You have completed enough of your "me" focus to now make the "we" more important than the old addictions that no longer serve you or others.

The Angel News Network new group order is a proxy for the world service to be done. You three cofounders will create a foundation of all of the lessons and wisdoms you have chosen to receive to be given to mankind. Can there be any more important work for you, dear ones?

It is time to move yourself and others forward into the truth of your existence. Much is being revealed. Much more is to come. Few of the many will accept the task at hand and take our love of you into themselves and their world.

But change is all there is and it doesn't take too many to reach the critical mass and effect the necessary changes to save you from yourselves.

Never before in the history of your planet have you received so much assistance from the angelic and star realms. You have the best chance ever to make a go of it, dear ones...to return love of self and others into your world so you may achieve your full individual and planetary divine plans (all connected to God Power's divine plan).

So as you focus on the day you came into this world, two days after the close of World War II, you can commit and intend that there shall never be that type of separation again; that was created through lies and deceit, creating fear in the masses in order to control them for the benefit of the few.

At a time when most humans choose aging and disease, you have chosen truth and love. We welcome you to the realm of truth and love, you child of the awakened heart, you child of light, you child of God Power.

Now choose the use of your energies left upon your world wisely in order to be the master teacher you chose to be.

Uriel

Uriel Message #12: If Not Now, When?

Greetings from the "beloved" vortex and energy and consciousness of Uriel. Today, we would like to speak about "If not now, when?" There is only now, dear ones. You have had your illusionary past and future affect you long enough. They have not served you well into moving into your purpose for being here. The past and future, that is. It is necessary now for you to become aware of multidimensional realms in order to know that your time is an illusion that no longer serves you fully. There is a fluid in your spine that is being activated; it allows those who choose it to experience and know now-ness by experiencing other dimensions rather than the only one you thought existed.

Once you are better able to move into now-ness, you can better be able to effect the necessary changes in your world to allow you to move into your divine plan as humans, a plan so glorious, motivated by love. This plan is allowing you to more fully love yourself, thus others and begin to end the separation in your world, the separation from your authentic self, thus others.

In the now is the true you, dear ones. You can no longer blame the past and future on what is not. The now is what is. And that is that you are a divine spiritual being having this human experience learning to truly embrace your divinity. Divinity does not include killing one another through your wars and having a few of you controlling the wealth and resources of your planet while so many go without. When you learn to go within, you will learn you do not have to go without. For within is now. And in the moment of now it is your divine right to receive all you need. Only the not giving to others has created your not receiving and you accepting you are worth enough to receive.

Right now, dear ones, you can chose to balance the equation of giving and receiving and allow the eternal abundance of the universe to unfold within each of you.

Now is now, dear ones. The word *consciousness* contains the letters "I-O-U" (consc "I-O-U" ness). The "I" is "U." This means *you owe you* awareness, the consciousness to be present, to be now.

And within this *nowness* and awareness, you will discover/remember you are the creator of your life, your world, your universe, dear ones!

"K-*now*-ingly" yours,

Uriel

Uriel Message #13: Commitment

Greetings from the loving consciousness of Uriel, at this most glorious time in your Earth's history. Presently, we would like to speak to you about commitment—commitment to yourself and others.

Without commitment to yourself, you cannot have a commitment toward/with others, dear ones.

The first commitment is to love yourself, as you would others. But in order to fully love yourself, you must know who you are and why you are here. Familiar questions that we constantly ask you, dear ones. And ask you, dear ones. Questions you are quite tired of hearing. But are you truly hearing them? Are you truly listening, dear ones?

Through your work with our beloved Michael, we are assisting you to learn who you are and why you are here. There are working tools and lessons being given to you that will facilitate you "remembering" whom you are and why you are here.

These are not easy questions to answer. On the surface, they seem obvious, simple, and silly questions to ask. But once you go deep within yourselves and truly ask these questions, many will realize they do not know the answers.

And not knowing is OK! Dear ones. It's a beginning to learning and being teachable, to not know.

Many have picked up some metaphysical sound bites on who they are and why they are here, but this is mostly mental masturbation.

So we encourage the investigation of you. Look at yourself like you have never done so before. Determine what is old and no longer working for you that you can release. Begin to understand and know your tools, talents, and gifts and how they can better serve you now, in preparation, for better serving others.

For deep within the commitment to yourself lies the commitment to others. The truth of who you are and why you are here will allow you to transcend yourself through the balancing of giving=receiving.

You are learning (again) many of the mysteries of how the universe and life works. Equations that create and give meaning, value, and purpose to this thing called life. These mysteries and teaching are being revealed again so you can remember how magnificent you are! *We are breaking the energetic vortex of the shame of self,* dear ones. It has been passed on and served its purpose long enough.

Once each of you come to know who you truly are and why you are here, most of your current world problems will disappear. Unity and non-separation can become the mantra of the day.

You will begin to experience your spiritual aspects *directly*, so you *know* you are a spiritual being having this human experience. You will begin to experience the balancing of the physical and spiritual. And know you cannot have the seen world without the unseen world (without dogma and control behind this wisdom, dear ones!) Truth, truth, truth, will set you all free from all the untruths you have experienced through most of your planet's history.

Since your planet is a priority for Uriel, we have a keen interest in its survival and success. We are assisting in every way we can.

Now we ask for your commitment to yourself, others, and your planet. And see the connection of these three.

So again, we ask you to explain to yourself:

1. Who are you?
2. Why are you here?

Don't use your mind to answer. Just be still, go into your heart space and allow the first words you feel, hear, or see to be written down. This will be your soul "dictating" to you who you really are and why you are here. The truth of your commitment lives deep within each one of you, dear ones. And when you feel and know these truths about yourself, there is no going back to the old you. It's a new day. A new, true you arises into the world, if you so choose.

Love and Light,

Uriel

Uriel Message #14: Choice

Greetings from the beloved realm of Uriel, the light of your world.

We once again come to you at this most important time in your planet's history. It's about *choice, dear ones.* What do you now? Choose? Move forward with changes in you that are necessary for your planet's survival, or resist these changes, stay in the old, and die. Harsh words, dear ones, but necessary words. For your world must realize you are at a crossroads of choosing truth or untruth. Knowing the truth of who you are and why you are here or not.

Many of you are awakening to the light and energies coming into your world assisting the necessary changes. Many shall resist it and stay stuck in the old. But in fact there is no staying in the old. The shift has already begun for humanity. And there are communication systems (cyberspace) in place that, for the first time, allow the truth to be revealed instantly, if you so choose to see the truth and act upon it. Percentage-wise, it won't take a large number of you to effect the change, a quantum shift, as they say, a shift that allows love of self to move into love of your fellow man as yourself.

Your governments and leaders must reflect this shift. You must see that they do, dear ones. The time of giving your power away is at an end. Only you can prevent or create the necessary shift of love becoming the new exchange. True abundance is manifested through love, dear ones. Now it is time for all to share in the abundance of your planet, not just the few. There's plenty for all.

So what do you chose right now, dear ones? Love of self and others that makes heaven on Earth possible, or continuation of the old selfish behaviors that mean your destruction? It's about choosing life or death, isn't it? Either way, the shift will happen. For it is your planet's divine plan, and it's time has come, dear ones. Even the ones who die (unseen humanity) will work in the etheric to effect the change. It could be as many as two-thirds of you (seen and unseen), if you chose it. Now that's a shift!

Be joyous this day has at long last come. You've all had many lifetimes preparing for it. There are combined forces, like never before, at play assisting you. You have the best opportunity ever to pull it off, as they say. So pull away, my dear humans. Pull yourself into your full spiritual potential of love. For the reason, the divine plan of your planet, is to learn to love. And you've hit the central core of this divine plan at this time. So connect your individual divine plan with your planet's divine plan, which is connected to source's divine plan. You're all part of the plans, dear ones.

Now you remember you are not alone in this effect; you've never been alone. We've always been there. You are just now ready to know of our existence by experiencing your physical and spiritual aspects at the same time. It is time to know who you are and why you are here, dear ones—to truly know it!

Uriel

Uriel Message #15: Peace

Greetings from a high from the vortex of energy you call Uriel. Peace be with you. Today, we wish to talk about the lack of peace upon your (our) planet. This unrest comes from within each human being; a being that is not capable of fully loving itself. It is time for mankind to continue the processing of the "me" in order to uncover its self-love. To fully discover the truth of who and what you truly are—spiritual beings having a human, physical experience—and know the truth of who and what you are and why you are here, to love one another (first and foremost yourself).

What has prevented you all from loving yourselves? It has been taught and passed on from generation to generation through the "shame of self." You've all been carefully taught there are things about yourself that make you "not good enough" in the eyes of yourself.

Too tall, too thin, too fat, wrong gender, wrong religion, wrong race, too ugly, wrong sexual preference—how many countless ways have you created to keep yourselves separate from yourself and others? This epoch is coming to an end for those who choose it. Many have awakened to the truth of who and what they are. They are remembering they are here to service mankind through honoring all the diversity upon your planet. And to remember it all comes from the same *source*—a *source* that created you to more fully know and experience it now.

You are all in the process of being able to experience the physical reality, along with the nonphysical at the same time, to know and experience that you are multidimensional beings. This will be your salvation from yourselves, not some religion that attempts to control you through partial truths. You must come to experience it all directly through yourselves, not outside yourselves. All you need to know is within you. You merely need to slow things down, get quiet, go within, find the peace there, and take that peace and love outside yourselves to your world by first honoring yourself and thus others around you who are from the same source as you, dear ones.

You are all unique expressions of the same *source*. Here to learn to love yourself first and foremost and spread that love outside yourself by accepting who you and others are—and creating a peaceful place to be just that!

When will you begin to create peace within and outside yourselves? What is preventing it now—anger, depression, fear? Love is all there really is. Your many song lyrics got that part right. Now when will you deeply apply it to yourself and others? And not allow unexpressed feelings (trapped in your body) to prevent that love?

It is time to shine a great, bright light upon yourself and your world. Let that light bathe you in the truth of who you are. Take a bath in that light each day. Wash away the untruth about you and your world...which you have passed along for far too many generations now. It is time to stop the madness. The insanity of a lack of self-love prevents peace from spreading throughout your world.

This "light bath" we are speaking of has already exposed many of the hidden Man Powers that have kept you all in the untruth of yourselves in separation and non-peace. It has been to some's advantage to keep you in non-peace. They have profited from it for thousands of years. This must come to an end. The way to end it lies within each of you through self-awareness, God Power, and love of self. You have given your power and love away far too long. When will you stop it? Why not now! Let there be peace on Earth, and let it begin with me (as the song says).

You are the light.

Uriel

Uriel Message #16: Chose Truth

Dearly beloved, we once again send greetings and love from the vortex of Uriel: your planet's chief guardian angels. Throughout the ages, we have guided you humans to the truth of who you are and why you are here. This is an especially God-Powerful time for your planet and you upon it. It is a time to choose truth or stay in denial. Few of you accept the truth of who you are. And by not knowing that you cannot fully know/understand why you are here. Most of you have been here many times before. And now is an accumulation, if you will, of all those lifetimes, a time to put all the pieces together, to know the whole (of you). You are God experiencing/expressing itself. If God is *all there is*, then you are God because you are part of the "is." You are the "is-ness" of it all. Know this truth, and set yourselves free from the entire untruth about yourself and others. You are diversified, unique expressions of the same *source*. We have continued to repeat this many times, so you will one day come to fully know it.

Right now, many of you just hear the words and do not believe them. But truly hearing the words is a beginning to knowing them. Only by listening can you begin to know. Your world is full of sounds and words, most of which you shut out, because of overload. There is too much sound that has become noise and become meaningless. Life has become meaningless for many because people have shut out the truth. The truth is not outside yourselves in sound or noise, it is found within you through silence. You must learn to stop and listen to what's inside each of you. It's all in there, you know. All you've ever needed to know is deep within each of you. You merely need to stop and listen. And our promise has always been in each moment of the now; you'll receive exactly what you need (not necessarily what you want). It's your divine right, your birthright; to have your needs met.

Your planet contains air, fire, water, and light—all you need for life. Most of you shut off the air by shutting down your breathing (because of a shame of self, which has been taught). Most of you choose not to drink enough water to hydrate your body.

There is a God Power born into each of you, which is your fire/desire for life. And most of you fear living fully with this force, more than dying.

And finally, you are light—eternal light that never dies, merely changes form. You are light-beings having a human experience in the third dimension of the physical. All that you need is here in these elements, which make life possible upon your planet. Embrace them; use them by accepting them as your divine right.

Dear ones, if you could imagine for one moment how much we love you. Only a lack of self-love prevents you from fully receiving our love and gifts. Open your hearts today to our love, your love and begin fully living a loving life. Once you love and accept yourself, you will see the expression of love in everything and everyone upon your planet. Remember the mission of your planet is to learn how to love.

How are you learning to more deeply love and accept yourself today? To dissolve the untruths about yourself that have been carefully taught and now can be untaught by you? By knowing the truth of who you are and why you are here.

You are a divine spiritual being having a human experience. Through your humanity, you learn who you are (through your mind/thoughts, emotions/body). It's the only way you can experience life here. But once you fully come to know life here, you come to know it's not about just you but all of you. For you are all expressions from the same *source* remembering this together, again.

Blessings, Uriel.

Uriel Message #17: Where Did You Come From?

Greetings, divine beings of Earth from the archangelic realm you call Uriel.

At this moment, we would like to discuss where you came from before your earthly experience. We have spoken a great deal about "light" in past sessions with this channel. Light is the grand creator of all. When what you might call God thought "his" thoughts, "he" used light as the tool to manifest another reality (sometimes) in physical form.

As you think about the universe, you are aware there are millions of other worlds within it. You "seeded" your present world from out there. It did not completely begin upon your planet. It began elsewhere. You are also aware there are many planets circling many stars within a vast universe. You are one of many.

Each of you originated from various star systems with worlds revolving around them. Some of you know that most planets are influenced by one star system only. And it "appears" that way with your planet and star, the sun. But this is not the case.

Your planet was founded by the influences of some twelve star systems, while the other planets in your solar system were influenced/founded by one star each.

This actually makes your planet a "divine experiment" in the cosmos (to have so many star influences).

What was the purpose of all these star systems influencing your planet? It was to create a vast diversity unlike any other world! A divine experiment: through all the diversity these stars would create upon your planet to find the oneness. For even all these stars are from the same source:

one universal consciousness, the highest vibratory force in all creation: the creator.

The diversity of these different star worlds on your planet formed the many races, languages, genders (and there are more than two), nationalities, religions, and sexual preferences that have kept you separated from yourself and each other throughout your history.

So the purpose of the "multi-creation" in your world is to find the oneness through all the diversity. You haven't done a very good job so far. So far, the experiment is largely a failure.

So now these truths and wisdoms about your existence are being imparted to you so you may know the truth of who you are (multi-star beings) and why you are here (to find your oneness through diversity).

You are at a critical point in your evolutionary path, dear ones: choosing love or non-love. It is time to begin celebrating the diversity among you all in order to find the common "*one-source*" connection to your creator.

How can you best achieve this at this time after so much failure in the past and present? By loving and accepting yourself fully and knowing you are a part of a divine plan to know love. Love is the force that holds all things together, dear ones. Without it, things fall apart, and that's what's happening in your world now.

We have come to you at this most precious time to remind you where you came from and your purpose for being here. Remember you are diverse beings of light, unique individuals; the universe is made up of each of you...not one more special, nor important than the other.

It is time for you beings of light to God-empower yourselves with love, embrace your diversity, honor your oneness from the same source, and move into your greatness.

Once you truly know this truth, you can end the separation, greed, wars, and disease within your world. You can get on with creating a world where you know what you cause others to experience you experience yourself, that you all have the desire to be loved.

The only thing that has prevented that is a lack of self-love.

Energies and wisdom are coming into your planet from your originating star systems. This light can assist you in changing your world if you take it into your heart and allow love to be the new currency of exchange. To honor yourself, thus others. To share all things. To support each other.

And when this is in full force, you will become the light and your world will become a star. This is the cycle and secret of the universe revealed.

You are the light,

Uriel

Uriel Message #18: Seasonal Shift

Greetings, beloved Earth beings from the realm called Uriel, "you are the light" consciousness.

As your season of summer begins to shift and the light becomes more acute and clear, you are becoming more acute and clear as to who you are and why you are here.

As the energy within the core of your Earth begins to reach outward now, it also passes through you, dear ones. As it passes through you, it "magnetizes" you with its energy. As you are magnetized, you thus attract the energy/forces coming into your planet (joining the physical and the spiritual/energy). This "season shift" is a micro of the macro of what is happening during this period of your planet's evolution.

Your entire world is joining the physical (the seen world) with the spiritual/energy (the unseen world that creates the seen world). As these forces form an "energetic cross" (the physical, the horizontal, the spiritual, the vertical), the truth of who and why you are here is being revealed, for those who's choose it.

Only by experiencing your spiritual aspects directly can you now save your physical being. That is why many of you are beginning to experience multidimensional realms beyond the third dimension of the physical into the fourth, fifth, and sixth dimensions. Only through directly experiencing these other realms can you now prevent your continued duality, separation, and destruction.

Many will resist experiencing these other realms (or their messages), holding on to the "old" like a drug addict to his/her drug. For others, it will become too intense, and they will choose to leave their bodies and continue working in the spiritual. The remainder will stay in their physical bodies and effect the necessary change by combining/experiencing the physical and the spiritual at the same time, if they so choose.

This is a most exciting time for your planet's history. Never before have so many been given the choice to directly effect the change so needed in your world.

Many teachers and tools, in addition to the energetic shifts / assistance from outside your world, are arising in your world to facilitate the change, for those who choose to receive it.

You are loved and supported beyond your comprehension at this time, dear ones. We know who you are and why you are here and see some of you are aware of this also.

It's all a choice, through your freedom of will, to choose change...knowing that change is all there is, dear ones. What you resist will persist until change becomes necessarily clear in order to survive.

You are the light,

Uriel

Uriel Message #19: Lack of Self-Love

Greetings from the vortex, the realm of the consciousness of Uriel.

Do you know why you are here in this Earth plane? To love one another. Someone, long ago, attempted to teach you this. But what has been preventing this is the lack of self-love. Some of you mentally know the only relationship you are having is the one with yourself. Take a look at that relationship now. Is it a loving, accepting relationship? Or are you constantly passing judgments upon yourself, thus others? If you accepted you, if you loved you, you would love another. If everyone instantly realized they were spiritual beings having a human experience and chose love of self, what a different world you would have—one without war, without separation from each other. It's the separation of you from you that has caused the separation from others throughout your history. It's time for this separation to end, if you so choose. But it must begin with you, dear ones. A terrorist blows himself and others up because he sees no purpose, meaning, or value in his life. Suppose this terrorist remembered he is God expressing/experiencing itself, that he is a divine being. Would that change things? We think so. It's what's missing in most of you. Not remembering/knowing your divinity. Why do you think we put so much effort into you? Because we know who and what you are, dear ones. We are all from the same *source*—at different levels of consciousness to our reality. It is time for mankind to wake up and remember the truth of his being. The truth of why you are here. Why are you here, dear ones? To love yourself, thus others. To receive and accept the talents and gifts given to you to serve others, not just you, but including you, yes. What talents and gifts are you not using right now that could make a difference in your life and that of others? You all have them. Some have chosen to receive them more fully than others. These talents and gifts that you can choose to receive, or not, can move your world into a world with war, strife, separation. You've done this long enough. It does not work. When will you stop it? If you continue, you'll destroy yourselves, again. You've done it before, dear ones. Why not learn the lessons now? Those lessons of self-love lead to love of others and serving the whole of humanity. Why not right now?

Receiving and giving the gift of love, Uriel

Uriel Message #20: You Are Limitless Light

Greetings from the energy and light of Uriel. Dearly beloved, once again, we are gathered to know the truth of who you are and why you are here…a very familiar message that is not always easy to assimilate into your reality. There are many distractions within your physical, mental, and emotional world that prevent you from remembering the truth of your being. You are all star light, which can never die—light that travels for eternity from world to world. You started from one *source* and shall return to that source, always. But where you travel in between is up to you…your journey, your path, as they say. You can do whatever you wish with the light. Be sad, be happy, be rich, be poor. The power of that light is within you all, always. If you could remember how powerful you are in creating your world, your reality, most would not believe it. But you are that powerful. You can create anything, at any time. A child knows this, but you humans lose this truth as you approach adulthood. You believe the untruth about yourselves that you were taught by others. It is now time to reteach yourself that you are a light with limitless possibilities. Know this truth, and you will set yourselves free from the limitations of your physical, mental, and emotional world. Only your thoughts about yourself prevent you from reaching any goal. Most of your thoughts creating your reality are not the truth. They were learned falsehoods from others that you can now reprogram, if you choose, dear ones. If you choose to truly know who you are, you will discover this light and power within you. There are many energetic activities happening in your world to assist you all in discovering the true you, a you who can learn to love yourself, thus allowing the love of others. Through this improved relationship with you and others, you can more fully give and receive love. You can use your light to first shine upon yourself and then others, knowing this light is all from the same source. You are merely the diversified expressing of it, learning to love yourselves and each other through giving and receiving. What are you allowing yourself to receive from your world that will more fully allow you to give?

Dearly beloved, we are now speaking about taking charge of yourself.

There is a "charge" within you all to take charge of, a divine God Power that is your birthright to receive, if you chose it. Only separation from your true self has kept you separate from yourself, thus others in turn, learned thoughts and behavior that do not truly reflect who the human species is. You are divine spiritual beings in human "space suits" for a few Earth decades at best. And this "space suit" has served as a true disguise for many. It is time to see through the masquerade, the disguise, and know the eternal spiritual beings you are. There are energies and wisdoms coming into your planet that will better allow many to know, to see the truth of who they are and apply it to why they are here. Take charge of yourselves and each other, dear ones. You can no longer live in separation from the truth of your being and survive as a planet, as a species. Your planet has destroyed advanced civilizations before and can do it again; it's your choice: life, which is growth and expansion, or destruction and starting over again. Why not get on with it, dear ones? Choose life. Choose love of self and others. And achieve it joyfully without pain that becomes suffering. It all begins with you taking "charge of the charge" and charging ahead into the truth, dear ones, the truth of who you really are, and why you are here. How many of you truly know the answer to these two key questions? Being able to ask the questions is the beginning to the answers.

Love and Light,

Uriel

Uriel Message #21: Talk about Love

Greetings from the realm, the energy, the consciousness of Uriel. Today, we would like to speak about *love*.

Love is the foundation of the universe. It's the highest energy force that creates worlds and holds them together.

It creates worlds by allowing matter to be manifested into physical form and holds that matter together.

Many of you are remembering how your *thoughts*/intentions/energy creates your reality. Most of you have received exactly what you asked. You just weren't aware of it.

If you have a high vibration of self-love and love of others, in place, things can manifest almost instantly. In fact, much of the new energies coming in make manifestations happen even faster. So *be careful what you wish for or ask for.*

Be impeccable with your thoughts and words, they are creation. The level of love that you demonstrate and intend allows manifestation. That's the importance of love. That is why throughout your history, many of us have attempted to teach you *love*—to love another by loving yourself.

Each and every energy/emotion is merely an expression or absence of love. The absence can allow us to know love by not having it, as darkness allows knowledge of light. But we need to always return to the foundation of love in our lives. For without it, worlds can fall into confusion.

You've seen this in many portions of your world now; the Middle East, Africa, and Asia are filled with a lack of self-love and love of others (your country is not without it either!). Without this love, people give their power away to others whose focus is not love but control and greed.

Many of you are being reminded who and what you are so you can recapture love and the control and power of yourself, your life. Once you have a full expression of love in your life, your life becomes service to others, for you know you are all connected through love. You see a new meaning, value, and purpose to your life through love.

You are indeed reborn into love of self and thus others.

Lack of love is the main issue with your world now. You cannot have peace and sharing of resources without it. We in the angelic and star realms are assisting you in clearing out many of the past obstacles, which have prevented love. Feminine energies are balancing the masculine ones, as you enter a new cycle of choices, as you pass through the photon belt and soon begin a new twenty-six thousand year calendar, your true calendar.

As you learned, 2012 was not the physical end of your world; it is the possible beginning of a new spiritual world that blends the physical and the spiritual so that love can be the focus of your world, so wars can end and your new consciousness can begin to create constructive weather systems rather than destructive ones. You will see the entire planet as a beautiful diversification of the whole (the same source). Instead of trying to eliminate your differences, you can begin to celebrate them, if you so choose.

A day of awakening is upon mankind, a new day of choosing to love or not.

Those who do not choose love (of self and others) would no longer receive our support. The focus from this point on is on those who choose love in order to effect the necessary change in your world to create a world of order, "harmony," through love. Love will be the new exchange of values, meaning, and purpose to you and your world.

So today begin the love affair of your life with yourself. Realize your gifts and talents that have been given to you by us...Use them for mankind through giving, and watch what you receive.

Love and Light, Uriel.

Uriel Message #22: Truth

We are here to speak the truth to the world. The truth of who and what people are and why they are here. You are here to learn to love yourself and others. It all begins and ends with the relationship of the self. Since you are God experiencing itself, know that you are a powerful being of love. And only your thoughts and actions are preventing love flowing fully throughout your world.

The purpose of this planet is to know and experience love through all the diversity there, as a result of your multi-stars influences—a unique and challenging experiment you all signed on to. But we above, at this time in your Earth history, are sending forces of energy that can maintain and sustain you into your next planetary stage of acceptance of self and others.

Many teachers and masters are among you, and more are coming to assist in this evolution of your planet.

You have choices possible now that have never been available before, choices that can create a world without separation and conflict. And it all must start with a love of self. Once you remember how to love yourself fully, you will better be able to begin honoring those around you and your home planet Earth. Your planet will not allow any further assault without dire consequences to you humans. Know this truth. And it will set you free from future destructive behavior to yourselves and your planet.

There are many books, courses, and masters available now to further your personal growth. Say, "yes," to them and you say yes to your survival, a survival that can ensure an advanced culture beyond your present imagination, a world where laws and restrictions and wars will become obsolete, a world where you will see yourselves achieving self-mastery through unity.

We are Uriel.

Uriel Message #23: Self-Empowerment

Greetings from on high. This is the day of our creator, a day of *Thanksgiving* and receiving.

Dearly beloved, we are gathered here to remind you who you are and why you are here. Today is the beginning of the rest of your life. Know this truth, and this truth will set you free, free from the imprisonment of the self. You have all been imprisoned long enough. It is now time to break out. Set yourself free from yourself and thus others who have kept you in their control far too long. Many of you have given your power away to those very willing to take control of your thoughts and lives. That time has come to an end. The few will no longer control the many. The powerful will no longer control the weak, the rich the poor, if you choose not. Only through love of self can you prevent others from not loving you. It is time to heal the inner wounded child in each of you and thus humanity at large. The strength to do this is coming from above and below, below deep in the core of your Earth and above from the angelic realm and your creator. Mankind is being given a choice now like never before to choose love of self in order to achieve love of others. You are all here merely to learn to love, dear ones. And it must begin with the individual. The God Power of one, dear ones. That oneness will heal your entire world if you let it. Only you can prevent it, no other truly has that power over you; you have simply given that power away to others. It is time to stop that, to stop the further destruction of you and your world, dear ones. Simply chose love. Start with self-love. Archangels Gabriel and Michael have set forth many tools to allow the investigation of the self. It is now time for those tools to go firmly out into your world. Teacher souls are being prepared each and every day. Babies are being born fully equipped for this task, the task of saving you from yourselves. You have a freedom of choice, you know, dear ones. We can only do so much. And we are doing a lot. More events are taking place in your world than ever before to assist you in your abilities to survive yourselves, transcend yourselves, and find yourselves and your place in your world—a place of world service, beginning with you...through you into the "we" from the "me."

Each of you has been given a unique contribution to make, if you choose it. The universe would be incomplete without each and every one of you, dear ones. There's a reason each of you is here. You are God Power experiencing itself, the body, emotions, and thoughts of God expressing itself. God fully knows itself through each of you. Know this truth. And you will be free of all the shame that has been passed down upon you throughout the ages. It is time for this shame of self to stop. It no longer serves any purpose. The shame was created so you could find/discover your greatness by knowing smallness. Shame is the other side of God—the dark Man Power side. And we must know the darkness to know the light.

The light is coming into your world like never before. Allow it to enter your heart spaces. Many of your star systems, along with the feminine energies are assisting you now to balance the dominant male power. The male must come to know the feminine within it. As the feminine comes to know the maleness within herself. You see this in your aging process as human. Men become more feminine as they age and women more masculine. These are all aspects of the same thing, male = female, dark = light, solution = problem, shame = love. They are all here to show you your true self: a spiritual being, once again, having a human experience.

It is time to know, to remember, why you are here, where you came from, and where you return to when you leave the physical. You are merely remembering that now. Love is the glue that holds everything together. You fall apart and lose your way without it. The foundation is the self-love. That is what is absent in your world now. Love of self. People are crying to be heard, to be loved, to be accepted just the way they are, not the way someone judges them to be. There is little of the foundation of the self in your world, dear ones.

The divine plan of your planet is through all the diversity to find the unity, the oneness, the non-separation from self and others.

Archangel Gabriel has explained your twelve star systems that seeded your planet. This diversity has created many nations, languages, religions, and gender issues that have kept you in separation. It is now time to stop that separation and remember the truth of the commitment each of you made in coming here...through all the diversity to find, to celebrate the diversity, knowing it's all from the same *source*. Many of you have heard this many times before and have chosen to do nothing. It's time to step up to the plate, speak your truth, and set yourself and your world free from itself, dear ones.

We have assisted you in creating cyberspace, which can break down old patterns of control and allow new thoughts to come forward. It is accessible to many, overriding the few who seek to continue to control you in separation. This epoch is coming to a close. You can choose or not to be a portion of humanity to move your species forward in its greatness, to allow your planet's unique divine plan to shift the entire universe further into the light of consciousness. Will you accept the challenge, dear ones? Become the part of humanity that stays in human form and begins the shift today (in you).

You Are the Light, Uriel.

Uriel Message #24: Keepers of the Earth

Greetings from the archangelic realm of Uriel. We are indeed the keepers of your Earth and all things upon it, all things large and small, seen and unseen.

Your planet is a unique experiment within the universe. So much diversity has fueled so much separation for far too long. As a force supporting the interrelationship of all things upon your planet, we feel it necessary to again to state the purpose of your planet. It is through all your diversity to find and celebrate your unity from the same source—a God Power that we in the archangelic realm are very connected to. We wish to support and guide you to that connection also.

The path to that connection is through love found in your hearts. For only through love can your species find and remember its value, meaning, and purpose, to know who you are and why you are here.

And it all begins, as we have stated many times before, with the God Power of one: you! For if each of you truly filled your hearts with self-love and allowed it to radiate out into your world, you would create a very different experience from the one you are having. For love is the most powerful source in the universe and can only create your greatness.

For far too long, through a lack of love, you have celebrated your smallness time and time again.

Your so-called religions speak of love, to love your neighbor as yourself. Where is this truly taking place?

Where are your spiritual leaders leading the way to the truth? Why are most of your wars and separation a result of your misinterpretation of God? Because they do not love themselves enough to love others. You can only love others to the degree you love and honor yourself, dear ones.

What has prevented this lack of self-love? It is a "misteaching" passed on from generation to generation. That's the bad part. The good part is that if something has been taught, it can be untaught. So now, as keepers of all things upon and within your Earth, we urge you humans to begin teaching the truth of who you are and why you are here.

Release the shame and blame of the past. You are here to love yourselves in order to love others, to celebrate your diversity by finding your unity through it.

You are indeed at a crossroad, beloved humans: continue old patterns of behavior that can lead to destruction, or embrace your true loving selves and create a world of harmony, balancing giving and receiving. Which do you choose?

It's always about choice, through your freedom of will created by your thoughts, dear ones.

So choose love, choose love, choose love of yourself and others by creating a new world based upon love, and eliminate the separation and lack of love that permeates your world today.

And if you don't know how to love yourself and others, seek out a teacher who can remind and teach you. Put that intention forward into the universe and watch what happens.

Open your hearts to love, and await the miracles. Become teachable. There are those ready to teach you throughout your Earth.

Keepers of the Earth, provider of love.

We of Uriel.

Chapter XXXVIII

Discourse with the ignorant and the wise,
For in reality, we are all simply teaching
What we need to learn and prize.

ANNA, GRANDMOTHER OF JESUS

Interviewed by Joel D. Anastasi

My beloved children:

What a blessed time it is in your evolutionary path; we come to you as the energies and the frequencies known to you as Anna, the mother of Mary, *the mother of all mothers*, whom I am the mother of, dear ones.

There are more of you on the surface of this beloved planet Earth than have ever been here before, dear souls. The time to join the feminine energy with the masculine energy, the mother with the father, the brother with the sister, the child with the adult, dear ones, has come.

We of higher realms, who have also walked upon the body of your Earth and know your feelings, your physical sensations, and your mental thoughts, dear ones, join you at this blessed time.

We have gone through a process that you know as ascended mastership, where we actually go through a transformation and transition into a higher light body of existence, master *ascendership*, if you will, in order to be who we have become.

It was a process that combined our incarnational cycles on planet Earth. We are now in full fruition of this expression of higher self again, as you know, as ascended mastership and the work that we are doing with and for God Power/ *all there is*. Whatever you choose to call this entity of creation, it has been quite a journey, hasn't it? Quite a path for you to return to the *source* from whence you came.

You tried most recently in six beloved attempts, what you might call six past golden ages. They were miraculous and marvelous; we worked with you then, as we work with you now, as we worked with you when we walked on the surface of beloved Earth.

It was the separation from *source*, from *all there is*, from God, who created the end, the demolition, if you will, of those golden-age civilizations. For the mental body came into play, largely through the assertive masculine energy, and said, "We have a better way. We can do it. We no longer trust that we will be provided for through *source*." And you lost the connection to the *source* that we of the ascendant master realms are in service to now and that you are in the process of returning to, dear ones.

We come to you most actively at this particular time for you are in the process of healing this *divine reconnection* with *source* through the balancing of the feminine and masculine energies, dear children. It is through the balancing of these often misunderstood, misplaced energies called masculine and feminine that you shall have your return ticket, if you will, into the higher realms that we provide and reside in at this time... your ticket to your God-Power re-connection.

My incarnational cycles when *I* walked on the planet, which seem miraculous to you now in your present state of consciousness in three-dimensional reality, were the result of *my* being able to return to *my* fine light body on a regular basis in order to extend my incarnational physical cycle into what you would call hundreds of years.

I've now even transcended that ability and gone into a complete state of immortality, eternalness, if you will, which you are being prepared to do as well, dear ones. But *I*, as a way shower, was in a transitional process, as many teachers were at the time of my walking on planet Earth, and *I* extended *my* incarnational physical being through hundreds of years in order to complete *my* divine soul plan and allow *me* to go into a final, immortal, eternal state of being, which *we* are in now.

It is a marvelous time to be able to share these messages that have been sent to you throughout the eons and millennia. You've often denied what we've had to say.

You've often killed the messengers who have brought the truth forward. So we ask you, are you ready now to fully embrace this extraordinary final golden age of your planet?

As you've been taught, your planet goes through cycles, and this will be the completed final cycle of your world, as you have known it. It will increase in velocity and vibrational frequencies ever more—ever more as portals, vortices of energy, are opened and activated upon the surface of your planet and within the interior of your planet that will assist you in this process called ascension.

We wish not to get into the signs and the complexities of it, but it is basically learning how, through the healing of your thoughts and emotional bodies, to manipulate, if you will, matter—the electrons, the atoms, the electromagnetic fields of God-Power creation—which have allowed you, through your divine service to *all there is*, to manifest whatever is necessary to that service, only if it is for the highest service of all with no intention to harm anyone. It is the key ingredient, the key formula of the process, dear ones.

We are now becoming more and more known to humanity—all the players who have laid the foundation as a part of our divine soul plan to make this divine moment, this new paradigm, what some have called we consciousness into oneness, possible. You all chose to be here at this particular moment. Most of the souls who have ever reincarnated on this planet are presently on the planet at this time. Some will stay for the transition. Some will leave. Some will be lost in the middle, dividing into a third, a third, a third, which many of you are aware of.

So we ask you, which do you choose to be? Do you choose to be a part of humanity who knows and participates in the process or who chooses not to? It is your choice through freedom of choice and freedom of will, which has been a gift of this planet, which many do not have. Many planets, many solar systems, many galaxies are in the state of, if you will, serving directly in the now divine *source*. And freedom of choice and freedom of will are not necessary.

Since this is a part of your process of reawakening and eliminating the veil between its *source* and its veil once again, freedom of choice has been a component of your process, dear ones.

We are sensing that you may have some questions that will help the integration of this process called ascension, our involvement and the involvement of many other realms, for many of you have become aware that it is a multidimensional process of Inner-Earth activities, which many are not aware of, of archangelic processes, of ascended mastership processes, of Intergalactic Federation processes, and, certainly, the processes of the star realms that seeded this particular planet, this solar system, and this galaxy, which are all interconnected, for all things are. So how may we assist you with any questions that might give you more integration and revelation?

Joel: Let me first say that I'm *thrilled* to talk with you.

Anna: We, as well, dear one.

Joel: I've been reading, *Anna, Grandmother of Jesus*, about your wonderful time on Earth. It's a powerful book with very moving descriptions of many of your experiences over six hundred years of our Earth time.

Anna: Which seems only a moment to us where we are now, dear one, where we are eternally and immortally in the now, where there is no time. But we fondly remember that time as well.

Joel: You were such a nurturing source of support for so many generations, including, of course, your daughter Mary and Jesus, her wonderful Christ child. You say in the book that we, essentially, are birthing the Christ in our own lives as Christ was born two thousand years ago. Would that be an accurate statement of what you said?

Anna: Yes, the Christ Consciousness energy, not only through the genealogy and chronology of *my* incarnational cycles (soul plan), preceded those as well and came through many embodiments throughout humanity, most recently in your (last) two-thousand-year cycle, which was the most recent inspiration.

The energy that *I* was supported by was a combination of the archangelic and the ascended masterships. *I* was chosen and chose, as part of my divine soul plan, to bring this lineage into place. *I'm* presently in the now in all of your hearts, dear ones.

Joel: You may have already partially addressed this by what you just said, but you were such a vibrant force two thousand years ago, and you say you are also that today. What would you say about the role you could play in our lives today for those of us who would turn to you? How are you assisting us now?

Anna: Through inspiration, through a knowing in your mental bodies and your emotional bodies that we actually existed in a format very similar to yours, bringing that story to life during this era where visual communication is so important, in your digital ages, where you're beginning to really personify and see who we were, what our lineage was, how our experiences were very similar to yours. Begin to trust and surrender, dear ones, to our experiences and our processes, which were very similar to what each and every one of you travels through in your own individuated personal process.

Joel: We have entered a new twenty-six-thousand-year cycle in the evolution of consciousness. The date, 12/21/12, received a great deal of attention as the end of the last cycle. Many people expected some major event to occur that they could see and perceive in the third dimension. Since that did not happen, some are disappointed and believe nothing happened. What can you tell us about what, in fact, has happened energetically as we transit from one age to the next?

Anna: Let us reiterate that this is the last two-thousand-year cycle of the planet, as you have known it. Those who were disappointed were looking outside of themselves for something to happen, for something to shift and change.

The process is an interior one, from the inside out. Your bodies are being reconfigured and transformed from your carbon-based reality into the light bodies, into the crystalline bodies that you have been taught.

This process is monumental. There are processes and shifts and changes taking place in your mental and emotional bodies as well, which affect your physical body.

Look around your soul family as you love and support one another. There's chaos outside every major format of your governments, your religions, your corporations, your financial institutions, your education. All are crumbling in preparation, from the ashes of the old, to create the new.

To say that nothing is happening is simply not being aware and conscious. There are tremendous shifts happening in your world in every moment within your leadership and in all of the endeavors that appear to be and think that they are in control of your reality.

Joel: So much of the wisdom in this book is wisdom of the heart. I just asked you a question that relates to the wisdom of the head. Let me end this by inviting you to speak to us from the heart. I see us as your children, so what, Mother, would you say to us?

Anna: That mind that you were speaking of has now finally gone back into service to your heart, dear ones. Your heart that knows every aspect of yourself, the experience that you've had, and how it has been a learning tool for yourselves. A heart that can think. You are learning to connect with and to think with your heart and allow the ancient wisdom and knowledge within that heart to guide you, to protect you, to lead you, to love you, in order to surrender to source, to surrender to the entities that maintain and sustain every aspect of your being, and, most important, this heart is connected, beat by beat, pulse by pulse, moment by moment, to Mother Earth, dear ones.

Joel: I would like to call you "Grandmother" and say, thank you, Grandmother. We love you.

Anna: We love you, too, dear ones, beyond your comprehension and your ability to love yourself. And until you are fully able to embrace the love, the unconditional love that we hold for each and every one of you, we shall hold our love in the higher realms until that day we unite in oneness and embrace that love together as one.

Chapter XXXIX

Look above or below,
Whether high or low
Things are the same.
It's all part of the oneness game.

BOUNTIFUL BLOGS

From the Angel News Network Blog
From a Diversity of God-Power Realms

Bountiful Blogs #1: Understanding Oneness

We are just beginning to understand the mystery of Oneness whereby a thread of contact between each life and its source serves to connect all on this planet, in this solar system, in the galaxy, in this universe...

Bountiful Blogs #2: One with All There Is

When humanity becomes one with all there is / source / God, we shall realize that we are truly all there is / source / God. This is not blasphemy but the fruit of total surrender to truth. Then we shall finally be free to be we!

Bountiful Blogs #3: Mother Love

True unconditional mother love is a direct connection and reflection of the cosmic love higher realms and the source has for humanity. A love without control neither wounds nor needs. It is this permanent reconnection with unconditional love that will allow our destined ascension into higher-self existence. As our wounds and defenses now arise for healing, let us allow the balancing of the masculine and feminine energies, which is vital within our ascension process. Celebrate today this cosmic love reflection within mother love and know it is a pathway to our truth and oneness.

Bountiful Blogs #4: Most Important Part of You

The most important part of you is your eternal connection to higher realms, the will / wisdom of source / all there is. We can no longer go it alone. The reconnection to our higher self and source will power us into our intended immortal beingness and service to oneness. The rest of us are a bundle of impulses/wounds crowded with bits of human knowledge, which contains very little truth. Let us now know the reality of our higher selves and source and be free, at long last.

Bountiful Blogs #5: True Alchemy Defined

The holiest and highest form of true alchemy is when humanity shifts into knowing they are God Power experiencing self. Know right here, right now, we are indeed destined to become co-creators with God, fulfilling the purity and destiny of the creator's loving intent. True alchemy is not a secret formula to change base metal to gold; it is a spiritual, all-loving science of changing the illusionary image of humanity into the pure gold of the true being, being who you are. Then you will be ready to have the empowered compassionate dominion over self and Earth.

Bountiful Blogs #6: University of the Spirit (US)

Beloved Saint Germain and other ascended masters conduct courses at the etheric Royal Teton Retreat (Jackson Hole, Wyoming) for those pursuing a path of soul mastery (a key mission of the Angel News Network). At this university of the spirit, souls are also tutored in divine illumination and the practical application of universal ideals and laws. If you resonate with this and wish to be tutored at your soul level at this etheric retreat, you can ask your higher self, angel guides, or us to escort you there in your light/finer body while you sleep...

Bountiful Blogs #7: Master Teachers

Masters and master teachers do not identify themselves; they recreate themselves in silence. Use your discernment with anyone who calls him-or herself a master teacher or master otherwise.

Bountiful Blogs #8: Ownership

Give to us within higher realms your problems, and we shall give you your victory, but we shall not take your responsibility from you. That we cannot do. Everyone's problems are in his or her world because his or her own creation built those problems. And we urge you not to blame somebody else for what's in your world. Face your I Am presence honestly and say, "It's my creation. Either I built it, or I opened the door and let it in. If I created it, I can un-create it." That's how powerful you are! Through ownership, you will set yourself free.

Bountiful Blogs #9: Source of All Life

Whatever and whoever denies all there is: the source of all life and light... they can only exist as long as the energy they have already received can sustain them; because the moment an individual, group, or nation or civilization denies the very source of life, that instant, the inflowing stream of life energy is cut off, and it can only continue to function until the force that has already been accumulated becomes exhausted. The collapse and self-annihilation of these are inevitable. This is the reason for the destruction of all past golden ages: the disconnect from source. We are now being given the teachings and tools to maintain and sustain a permanent connection to source during the creation of our next and final golden age.

Bountiful Blogs #10: Divine Love

Divine love contains perfect activity
In every sacred second of the God-within.
When we enter the conscious path
To self-mastery, we understand and know,
We declare, we demonstrate
Divine love from now on...

For divine love contains
Wonder-filled wisdom and perfect power.
It is composed of wondrous wisdom

And all-ready power of the God hour.
When we manifest enough divine love,
And send it out,
We demand and command the love,
All around.

So love your divine love,
Immensely and then,
Nothing else can enter mentally, but love.

Bountiful Blogs #11: Consciousness=Creation

Remember what your consciousness is held firmly upon, you bring into existence in yourself. It is impossible for your life to contain anything that is not your present or past accumulation of consciousness. Whatever you are conscious of in thought and feeling stamps itself upon the universal substance in and around you and brings forth after its kind, always. This is a mighty cosmic law from which there is no variation or escape.

Bountiful Blogs #12: The Light of Source Never Fails

There are higher realms and frequencies ever present and continuing to bless humanity in marvelous, silent ways and through their unconquerable power and intelligence forever fulfilling the law of the eternal: the light of source never fails.

Bountiful Blogs #13: Gratitude

It is because humanity has forgotten to be grateful to life for all the blessings upon this Earth (focus on what is rather than what is not) that it has shut the door to peace and become bound by the chains of its own selfishness. The mass of mankind seeks the possession and holding of things, which is an inversion of the law of life. Life forever says to the individual, "Expand, and ever let source pour greater and greater perfection through you forever." As you receive from source, the law of life is to balance giving of oneself to further expand…giving = receiving = giving = receiving…

Bountiful Blogs #14: Purpose of Life

If thoughts and feelings of anger, hate, selfishness, condemnation, and doubt of the I Am presence are permitted to remain in the consciousness of any human being, the door to perfection closes and his or her existence becomes but a process of sleeping and eating until the energy drawn by the outer consciousness spends itself and the body is left to dissolution. It is because of the desire to avoid such continual re-embodiment into limitation that it is so imperative for the individual to have conscious understanding of the purpose of life, because the knowledge of how to release love, wisdom, and power enables you to fulfill that purpose perfectly.

Bountiful Blogs #15: To Know…

Each individual knows a thing only when he or she attains the consciousness of it by the expenditure of his or her own energy, for then he or she feels it.

Bountiful Blogs #16: Life as Perfection

Life is perfection, and it contains all perfect manifestation within itself. The only duty of the personality is to be a "cup" that carries and reveals the perfection of life. Until one obtains obedience from the outer senses and maintains a feeling of peace within him or herself, there is an imbalance of the purity and perfection of the life that is flowing through.

Bountiful Blogs #17: Discernment

The lack of discernment in distinguishing the true from the false is the thing that makes mankind fail most often in the outer world. The one who determines to attain perfection can choose to train the outer activity of his or her mind to listen to no voice but that of his or her inner "mighty I Am presence." If you so choose, accept only its inner wisdom and obey its direction: hear the light, see the light, feel the light, and be the light of the infinite I Am.

Bountiful Blogs #18: Harmony and Peace

The average person's thoughts and feelings are nothing but a mass of chaotic pictures and negative suggestions, which he or she has accepted from the world about him or herself and keeps repeating and consuming by his or her own energy through his or her attention. Order is heaven's first law… Harmony and peace are the cohesive power of the universe. These come from one source only, and that is the mighty I Am presence of the universe, your God-Power self.

Bountiful Blogs #19: Permanent Perfection

Love, wisdom, and power are the primal attributes life uses to build permanent creation, and when mankind ceases its self-created discord, all life around it and in nature will express permanent perfection.

Bountiful Blogs #20: Human Monsters

The great monster, doubt, and its nefarious associates, ignorance, pride, ridicule, skepticism, fear, and many other useless barnacles, have so fastened themselves upon the mentality and feeling of humanity, they have become like fungi hanging from a tree and rotting its trunk. If it were not for these vampires, mankind would see and know, within the very light that animates the physical body exists an intelligence and power that can and will carry out perfectly whatever the mind directs, when harmony is maintained and all direction is constructive.

Bountiful Blogs #21: At This Time

During the present expansion of light throughout the Earth, it is absolutely imperative for the individual to keep an iron control over his or her own thoughts, feelings, and spoken word—compelling them to be constructive and giving recognition to nothing else...if you are to avoid continual distress and countless losses to yourself and your world.

At no time in the history of the planet has this been as important as it is at this present moment." The Earth is passing through the throes of a tremendous new birth. The hour strikes in the evolution of every planet and its humanity when they must express the full peace, harmony, perfection, and the divine plan of the system to which they belong.

Bountiful Blogs #22: Reincarnation

The experience called death is a constant reproof to mankind and a reminder to the personal self of its disobedience to the original God Power plan and its soul plan. If the student really wants to know the truth about re-embodiment/reincarnation and life, he or she must go to the source of life—the mighty I Am presence. For this presence is what maintains and sustains your life.

Bountiful Blogs #23: I Am Presence

Humanity is using a small fragment of its individualized I Am presence in its physical experience. This glorious presence is ever urging you to arise and receive your freedom forever from every limitation. This I Am presence is your own real master, the Pure Christ Consciousness self. It is all majesty and mastery over all worlds, over all created things.

Bountiful Blogs #24: A Real Master

Of one thing, you can be absolutely and eternally certain: that no one who is a real master will ever say so, and an ascended master never accepts payment of any kind for the help he or she gives...Because the first qualification of true mastership is to do all as a glad, free gift of one's service of love to the world. The real master uses only the all-knowing mind of God Power.

Bountiful Blogs #25: Desire to Commit

No one can ever attain self-mastery and ascension without the desire and commitment to do so; without desire of attainment, attainment is not possible. All constructive desire is your "god-in-action" within you. The desire activity is the forward-moving, ever-expanding motion of life itself.

Bountiful Blogs #26: Uncontrolled Feelings

Man Power does not like to hear this truth, but the waste of the life energy through uncontrolled feelings is the cause of the disintegration of all physical bodies outside of violence.

Bountiful Blogs #27: Being God

When Man Power becomes one with God Power, he/she realizes that he/she truly is God. This is not blasphemy, but the fruit of total surrender—the return gift of life's own identity.

Bountiful Blogs #28: The Time Has Come

The time has come when great numbers among the mass of humanity will awaken to the truth within them and realize they have a God Power within themselves...The magic presence of the mighty I Am. There are many who, from an inner standpoint, are far along the path of enlightenment because of previous self-effort and attainment. Yet, in this present embodiment, they are outwardly unaware of it. It is time to give such souls the freedom they crave and for which they are ready. These shall have help, and to this end, do we work here to give it.

Bountiful Blogs #29: Student of Life

If one is a real student of life, one will dig deep into the thoughts and feelings of those beings who express the superhuman conditions, qualities, and transcendent ideals. These, the ordinary personality considers impossible because of the greatness of the power required to bring them into outer expression. The effort needed to attain and express these divine qualities is more than the ordinary person cares to make. The effort this kind of attainment requires is a sincere, strict discipline of the human sense-consciousness until it learns obedience to the pattern of perfection instead of its own selfish temporary whims and appetites. The real student of life knows that whatever God Power quality the consciousness of the individual can think about, he or she can bring into existence through the creative power of his or her own thoughts and feelings of divine love.

Bountiful Blogs #30: Equality, Harmony, Balance

In order for your species and world to move forward into your next golden age, there needs to be equality, harmony, and balance in all aspects of your world. This includes governments, religions, corporations, and relations with self and others. You can no longer have the few controlling the many. As soon as you wake up to this truth, the most amazing world of abundance and freedom awaits you all. Set your fear aside, and surrender to knowing this truth. The God Power that created you maintains and sustains you always: the I Am presence.

Bountiful Blogs #31: Relationship of Death and We Consciousness

We humans are beginning to understand the relationship between our imbalances, unhealed ego defenses, negative thoughts and emotions, and our physical deaths. This Man Power within us actually results in our disintegration, which is another name for death. We are in the process of learning to love self and others and have this reflect out in all aspects of our life in order to reclaim our immortal state of being. In effect, mankind is learning to live its life by the eternal law of love. We are beginning to fully understand the God Power and essence of this thing called love. And when we learn how to fully integrate this love law into civilization and ourselves, we can and will be released from the cosmic wheel of birth and rebirth. Repeated Earth lives will no longer be necessary, and the imbalances/problems we experience now will disappear. We simply will no longer need to learn the way we have in the past (often through what is not). Rather than lack and limitation, duality, separation, and confrontation, in their place will come joy and abundance in ever-expanding perfection, which forever manifests within love. Then our most powerful enemy, other than our old selves, death, will simply vanish into the new world.

When our human wounds, defenses, and discord dissolves, not by so-called death, but by constantly raising our consciousness through the activity of the I Am presence (your connection to source), its power will be released into the outer world service through the individual first and foremost by complete life / self-mastery. This consciousness embracing the I Am aspects is being called we consciousness. And the relationship between consciousness and the I Am energies is vital in order for humanity to move into its final golden age. Through we consciousness, every human being can release the limitless power of the mighty I Am presence within each of us. And each of us has an equal, God-given supply that can be embodied to build communities of equality, harmony, and balance worldwide.

We can use these terrific tools of we consciousness and the I Am presence just like the all-powerful ascended masters who once walked this Earth and continue to support us now. This is the Cosmic Christ within us all! Throughout the universe, we consciousness is the only consciousness than can say I Am. And when we choose to say I Am, we are being and using the God Power, you.

Bountiful Blogs #32: University of Spirit

Saint Germain and other ascended masters conduct courses at the Royal Teton Retreat for those pursuing a path of soul mastery. At the University of the Spirit (US), souls are also tutored in divine illumination and the practical application of its ideals. This is one of the oldest learning centers on our planet. If you would like to be tutored at the soul level at this etheric retreat, you can ask the angels to escort you there in your light body while you sleep. Now the veil between your world and higher realms will be thinner than ever before. There will be much contact and teachings coming forth in this year of manifestation of we consciousness.

Bountiful Blogs #33: 2013 Soul Plan

Many higher realms have proclaimed this the year of the ending of our duality, separation, and confrontation with self and others. This does mean there will be more clearing and cleansing of planet and humanity, but rest assured, we are moving into we consciousness. It is our divine blueprint. Let us review how the year breaks out into three main portions:

Part I: The Continued Breakdown—the extremes of duality will surface in relationships, government, finances, and religions. All past habits and patterns will surface to be cleared and cleansed.

Part II: The Breakthrough—After part I, we shall further awaken to our divine soul plans, who we are, why we are here, and how to move into world service.

Part III: We shall restructure the new paradigm as new revelations, inspirations, and truths come into existence. This will allow full we consciousness / unity / God Power to manifest.

Bountiful Blogs #34: This Year of We Consciousness

By star realms that seeded this planet, inner-Earth forces, archangelic energies, and the Intergalactic Federation, it has been foretold that this year will be the epoch when humanity moves into we consciousness. We shall continue to receive teachings and tools to further heal the me and relationship with self in order to move into a oneness/we of world service.

Bountiful Blogs #35: Portal Opening

Today, 12/25, a five-pointed star portal has opened with the combined energies of Arcturus, Pleiades, Orion, Lemurian, and the Intergalactic Federation. These God Powers will assist us in evolving into we consciousness now. This new portal opening is the grandest Christ Consciousness gift we can receive today.

Bountiful Blogs #36: Personal Oath

I now take the oath of communion in we consciousness. I now release all that no longer serves the highest good and the purity of we consciousness. I now release all that no longer serves my brethren and me. I now take the solemn oath to move into we consciousness with my brethren and with those who resonate and vibrate as I and those who have a similar purpose and mission as I. I now move in we consciousness in resonance, harmony, community, and equality with those who share my vision in world service.

Bountiful Blogs #37: We Oath

We now come together in the here and now in we consciousness. We have fully revealed ourselves to ourselves. We have revealed to ourselves what is no longer appropriate in we consciousness. I now release what is no longer appropriate for my endeavors, mission, and my purpose as I come together with like-minded individuals in we consciousness. We join together and celebrate the uniqueness of the individual as we now join in similar endeavors. We now join this endeavor in we consciousness.

Bountiful Blogs #38: 12/12/12 through 12/21/12

Between 12/12/12 and 12/21/12 is an extraordinary nine-day period where you can best connect with the unique and powerful transforming energies from the universe. This is the highest frequency of Christ Light's gift the human form can sustain. You are being aligned with the forces that created the universe and you! You will now decide what path your life will take: this is a mass migration from the me to the we consciousness, if you so choose. Please accept with compassion and forgive the clearing and cleansing that needs to take place in the world and you. Here is a mantra to support you:

I live and move and have my being within the invincible strength and power of the sacred fire mastery in me.

Bountiful Blogs #39: 12/12/12

You have waited thousands of lifetimes upon my body for this moment in your time. Beginning today, 12/12/12, precious portals of energy are reawakening to support your ascension into your true being. You are receiving transforming energies unlike never before… all that your human form can sustain and maintain. Rejoice, dear children, your graduation is at hand—karma and cause and effect cycles are ending. It is time to step into your divinity and full mastership and connection to the forces that created you (and never lose that connection again). The next nine days will continue your clearing and cleansing of the old that has stood in your way to higher realms. The new paradigm of unity and oneness is at hand; joyously accept the fullness of the mighty I Am presence, the Christ Consciousness within you. Feel it intensify through your heart to every molecule of your being. You are the light and are protected by it. December 21 will be your final portal opening for this year.

Bountiful Blogs #40: Ascended Master Defined

The ascended master is an individual who by self-conscious effort has generated enough love and power within him- or herself to snap the chains of all human limitation, and so he or she stands free and worthy to be trusted with the use of forces beyond those of human experience. These masters feel the oneness of omnipresent God Power. Hence all forces and things obey their commands, because they are a self-conscious being of free will controlling all by the manipulation of the light within themselves.

Bountiful Blogs #41: Love

Without trust and faith in love, it is impossible for us to be pleased with ourselves or with any of our relationships.

Bountiful Blogs #42: Love toward Source

I marvel at the number of spiritual seekers who desire power over themselves, self-mastery, while not expressing love and gratitude toward the source and self and brother and sister, so they can possess the wisdom and power of the very God Powers that gave birth to your world and you.

Bountiful Blogs #43: Importance of Love

Every past ancient civilization and golden age on this planet or any other world that died did so because of the withdrawal of universal love from within. Are you ready to choose love of self and one another, dear ones?

Bountiful Blogs #44: Divine Truth

Divine truth reveals that love, wisdom, and power are in reality the one indivisible/undivided whole, which can never be divided or divisive... Their atoms sing as they chorus throughout the universe: "We are one. We are one. We are one. Thank God Almighty, we are one." When humanity knows and applies this truth, we shall move into we consciousness and never experience lack and limitation again.

Bountiful Blogs #45: Cosmic/Universal Law

Humanity's unknowing of and disobedience to Cosmic/Universal Law, its hesitancy in matters of higher God-Power realms, its gathering momentum of Man Power destructivity toward self, others, and Earth...these have kept you in lack and limitation. Now is the time, if you so choose, to free yourselves and join the God Powers that are here to support your ascension into a perfected reality.

Bountiful Blogs #46: Cosmic Colonic

December 12 and 21, 2012, were powerful energetic portal openings for our planet and humanity. It is a great time of clearing, cleansing, and releasing old patterns that no longer serve our highest good. Let us accept with compassion and thus forgive through gratitude what needs to take place. December will continue to be a time of a transformation process.

We shall begin to see how our coming together in we consciousness of thoughts and feelings will unite us. It is the time of knowing whom you are and why you are here to move into your purpose through your actions.

Bountiful Blogs #47: Spiritual Alchemy

Remember that the goal of true spiritual alchemy is to create nobility in the soul and virtue everywhere, particularly in the realm of the self.

Bountiful Blogs #48: Reincarnation

How great has been humanity's suffering from eliminating the truth that we have many lifetimes on this planet. To deny the truth of the continuity of your own being, its span of previous existence, and its future glorious destiny is to cut yourself off from the basic premise of life itself. Know you are eternal beings of light that can never die. And all the lifetimes you have had are pathways to your truth: a being without end. Removing this truth from your reality was a grave distortion of life's purpose that has challenged society to this day.

Bountiful Blogs #49: Christ Consciousness

As we approach the Christ Consciousness season (having nothing to do with any particular religion), let us further examine this energy: Ascended Masters Jesus Christ and Saint Germain have passed the torch of the Christ Consciousness and the I Am That I Am presence (the god within me sees the god within you) from the Piscean to the now Aquarian dispensation. Our reunion with these ascension energies is the way shower for our next and final Golden Age of Oneness. This will be the salvation through the resurrection of our divine souls (plans). Are you ready?

Bountiful Blogs #50: Atmosphere of Earth

Within the atmosphere of Earth is held all the creations of humanity that keep alive all the emotions and thoughts as a powerful force with our emotional and mental bodies. Through awakening and self-empowerment, we are in the process of freeing ourselves from the mass accumulation in this atmosphere. When this happens, we shall be surprised how fast our world improves.

Bountiful Blogs #51: Man: The Divine Alchemy

The Lord is your shepherd. You shall not want—if you will only understand that he longs to guide you correctly, if you will only understand that whereas evil has no real existence, its shadow veil has been the means through the centuries of binding man to the Earth. And you shall see that by cutting the bonds of evil and by acknowledging the God Power of Good, you will no longer strain at a gnat and swallow a camel, but you will enter straightaway into the City of God, into the consciousness that transcends the world and its options by recognizing the spiritual options that lie as gifts in your hand. Man is the divine alchemist in physical form. In his right hand, the gift of life lies beating. It is the pulsation of cosmic effort. Without acknowledging the gift, man fades away as a vapor upon the glass. By acknowledging it, the cosmic breath strengthens the manifestation of self until death is swallowed up in victory and life stands forth transcendent and splendid to every eye. Onward, we move progressively toward freedom and God Power in action.

Bountiful Blogs #52: Heart of the World

America is the Heart of the World and destined to lead your planet into its final golden age. Your founding fathers were given all the tools they needed to create a new paradise on Earth. For many reasons, that never happened... until now. By employing and embodying your mighty I Am presence, you can and will create a new paradigm of equality, balance, and harmony. Many higher realms are assisting in this: Archangel Michael, Mother Mary, and Mother Earth, just to name a few. You are at a crossroad through your freedom of choice and will to choose we consciousness over me consciousness. Your Lady Liberty standing in New York Harbor is here to remind you that true freedom comes from freedom from yourselves. No matter how things appear in your outside world, all we speak of here is true and ready to take place. But it requires your awareness and cooperation in your emotions and thoughts to manifest your destiny to create the final golden age. What do you choose, dear ones? All the wisdom and teachings you need are before you now (again). But soon, if you so choose, all will change and you will be truly free from the forces that have kept you in bondage for eons—you!

RESOURCES

Phillip Elton Collins

The Angel News Network
www.theangelnewsnetwork.com

Coming Home to Lemuria: An Ascension Adventure Story
https://www.facebook.com/ComingHometoLemuria
Order via: http://www.theangelnewsnetwork.com/page22/book-comingHome.html

Happiness Handbook: Being Present Is The Present (Phrases of Presence to Set Us Free To Be...Happy.
https://www.facebook.com/TheHappinessHandbookBeingPresentisthePresent
Order via: http://theangelnewsnetwork.com/page4/books.html

Man Power God Power
https://www.facebook.com/ManpowerGodpower
Order via: http://theangelnewsnetwork.com/book_man-power-god-power.html

Sacred Poetry & Mystical Messages
https://www.facebook.com/SacredPoetryMysticalMessages

Order via: http://www.theangelnewsnetwork.com/book-sacred-poetry.html

Joel Dennis Anastasi

The Ascension Handbook: A Guide To Your Ecstatic Union With God
https://www.facebook.com/TheAscensionHandbook
CreateYourEcstaticUnionWithGod
Order via: http://www.theangelnewsnetwork.com/ascension-handbook.html

Life Mastery: Creating the Life You Want and the Courage to Live it
https://www.facebook.com/TheLifeMasteryProgram
Order via: http://www.theangelnewsnetwork.com/book-life-mastery.html

The Second Coming: The Archangel Gabriel Proclaims a New Age
www.gabrielsecondcoming.com
https://www.facebook.com/GabrielTheSecondComing
Order via: http://www.theangelnewsnetwork.com/book-second-coming.html

Jeff Fasano

Journey of the Awakened Heart
www.journeyoftheawakenedheart.net
https://www.facebook.com/JourneyOfTheAwakenedHeart
Order via: http://www.theangelnewsnetwork.com/page23/book-journey.html

ABOUT THE AUTHOR

A Sense of Self, A Short Story

For over three decades, I had been in the advertising and commercial film production industry, working with some very talented, prosperous individuals. At the end of this, I thought I could morph into quiet. I began my Madison Avenue advertising career in the heady days of Man Power / Mad Ave / mad men days of advertising in the early 1970s, last century (depicted in films and TV) at the pyramid top of the ad game, Young & Rubicam, 285 Madison Avenue, New York City. Y&R had the prestigious accounts, creativity, and billing. It was a great place to work if your family could initially afford to send you there (their starting salaries reflected their competitive entry value). Beyond the three-martini lunches and the cigarette-smoking haze lunches, I would find my sense of self...

After a few restless years of changing departments four times (media to sales promotion to account management to creative departments), we both (Y&R and I) finally realized corporate America was not in my divine soul plan. I then enrolled in the New York University film school and jumped to the other side of the advertising business: commercial film production. The ad agencies became my clients. My soul plan now linked me with some of the most gifted commercial and feature-film directors in the world—the likes of Ridley and Tony Scott and George Lucas.

The Scott brothers and I, along with many multitalented people, founded Fairbanks Films, and that company took over the commercial film production advertising world in short order, producing for Apple founder, Steve Jobs, such famous TV commercials as the 1984 Apple computer spot that launched personal cyber-technology into the world. Today, this commercial is still considered the most famous and successful spot ever made. Mr. Jobs, I know you are still proud wherever you are, since you put your job on the line for this production. Then the George Lucasfilm people decided they wanted to get into the advertising game and came knocking. And why not? After the motion film industry, the advertising business was one of the most influential and lucrative forms of communication.

So over to Lucasfilm I went, with all their inventive, digital technology at hand. It's fair to say, Industrial Light & Magic taught the advertising world digital wizardry, even though others jumped on quickly. It was great fun being the director of marketing of the commercial division, teaching the ad world how they could bring any image to the screen (without killing anyone) if only they had enough money and time. We changed the look and abilities of commercial film forever, producing thousands of spots worldwide. Many of these short films became household icons.

During my three decades in advertising and commercial film production, I got to know the planet up close and personal. It was more than anyone could ask out of a career!

About The Author

So I thought when it came time to leave it...I surely would be ready for a more peaceful and quieter lifestyle—wrong!

If you are in the film production business, you get to know California really well. Or at least I thought I did. The weather, locations, studios, and crews made California an alternative on any production schedule. Only strikes and clients with low budgets would prevent you from shooting in California. Fairbanks Films was my finishing school in Southern California, and the Lucasfilm organization completed my Northern California training. George Lucas preferred Northern California to the south, not resonating with the values and needs of Hollywood.

While commuting to Northern California from my New York City base, my entire time with Industrial Light & Magic Commercials / Lucasfilm, I often took advantage of the natural wonders that part of the world has to offer. One of my most memorable trips was driving to the top of Mount Shasta, just south of the Oregon border. Mount Shasta is part of a dramatic volcanic mountain range that snakes its way north. The size and grandeur of this mother of mountains was amazing; you could see it from a hundred miles away. We had nothing like it on the East Coast. And I thought enjoying its wondrous size and beauty was enough at the time. I would later learn otherwise...Ten years later, I would return "awakened" for another purpose entirely...

Some say, as we grow older and get closer to leaving this world, some of us become more spiritually conscious, closer to God Power; women become more masculine and men more feminine, or something like that. Well, anyway, after some medical mishaps and "enough is enough" syndrome,

I did leave the film and advertising business. I mean, what else was I going to do, produce another commercial? The last spot we did was the biggest commercial ever created for Ford motor company (ninety days of shooting all over the world, the largest budget ever, aired in a "roadblock" all over the world); this was my perfect swan song. Did I need another cue to exit? No! And there was this curious notion that something inside of me was yearning to express a new sense of self. Something else was next, but I had no idea what it was. And surrendering to the unknown really challenged my mind, which always had to know.

My mother was of American Indian descent and my father Irish. My father's Celtic grandmother, my great-grandmother, was a backwoods Alabama healer. I call it my "I" and "I" links (Irish and Indian, both known for native healing). I remember sitting by my great-grandmother's bedside as a young child, listening to her stories of her healing potions and how people would walk for days to get to her for "a healing."

She knew how to pick herbs from the forest floor and turn pine-tree sap into a soothing medicine. So I imagined this ability was also in my DNA. And it was.

Filmmakers are often multifaceted people, and while I was working with one of my film directors on a project, I developed a cold and shared my family's healing background. My film director friend immediately suggested that I see his alternative medical doctor named Dr. Herbert Fill. This particular film director knew I was at the end of my film career and there was more to cure than a cold. Dr. Fill was a rare mix of psychiatrist, acupuncturist, homeopath, and commissioner of mental health in the city administration, all this in a Park Avenue office that he ran by himself. It was not long before the patient became the student of alternative medicine under Dr. Fill. This was my transition from advertising into the "healing arts."

Once my transition—or should I say, my transformation—began, it went fairly quickly. After a couple of years of studying under Dr. Fill, I easily moved into energy therapy training called Reiki and light ascension and became certified in these. These new alternative medical worlds introduced me to an entirely new community of people not associated with advertising or film. I began to know this was not going to be the beginning of a quiet retirement but a reinvention of my sense of self through the use of all past and present talents and gifts.

The next transition of my life took me into other higher-realm multi-dimensions, not unlike the worlds George Lucas brought to the silver screen...Maybe that's the reason my career included Lucas...to better prepare me for what was about to come. Anyhow, what transpired next felt organic, extraordinary, and natural at the same time. And I directly realized many of George Lucas's stories were real.

The next destination/stop on my transformation-train took me on a sacred journey to Egypt, where I connected with higher beings in the King's Chamber of the Great Pyramid, considered working with *New York Times* bestselling author Neale Donald Walsch of the *Conversations with God* books, and began to connect with higher beings myself. If George Lucas could imagine other worlds that gave us hope and people like Neale Donald Walsh could connect with God, why wasn't it possible for you or me to be/do something similar?

As I was often enthralled by the messengers (God, archangels, galaxy and star beings), could I listen to the message, apply it, and see if it could improve my life or the lives of others? Yes, I could! Today, there are the millions of people worldwide who connect multi-dimensionally through cyberspace, reading books, or directly experiencing messages from other dimensions or through films or workshops. Can we accept and support wisdom from areas other than the human mind? That is the question of the day for some. The number of people connecting beyond the human mind seems to be increasing daily. Something is shifting, not only in me but in the world. We are beginning to realize that we are not the only ones here, that our planet, our galaxy, and the universe are more diverse than we ever imagined and there is a plan in it all. And we need their help to move forward.

Through several years of personal processing work and working with others who were already "connecting," I began to trust and know this was not the only frequency/dimension of existence (Einstein and string theory physicists had already proven this). Now I would begin to connect with these higher frequencies myself, along with many others. OK, I want to be the first to acknowledge this is the tricky part for some. I, too, come from a world that says, "If you cannot show me, it does not exist." Some people's minds simply will not be able to accept or believe this story from this point on. For those who know the truth, that's cool, that's a gift. But let's accept those who cannot without judgment. For those who cannot accept what is being said or see it simply as fiction or non-truth, that's OK. The mind believes; the heart knows. But try to apply the message, if it resonates.

Ten years after my first journey to Mount Shasta, I returned this transformed guy, with a lot of hard-core business experience behind me. I have not been a monk living in a cave, for sure. I've now joined with other like-minded/spirited people on a sacred journey, back to Mt. Shasta, which is now considered one of the most powerful spiritual portals on Earth—little did I know ten years ago. We were there to serve as proxies for humanity to perform specific rituals on the mountain to assist the planet and all of us to move into higher levels of awareness through a unique opportunity called ascension.

We would heal some wounded aspects within ourselves, which allowed us to connect with a higher dimensional civilization inside the planet that coexists with us and intends for us to join together in the future. Where was George Lucas now?

Later I would cofound a website, www.theangelnewsnetwork.com, and a metaphysical school to teach and share what I had learned. I began connecting with more like-minded/spiritual people, writing more and connecting more with various higher realms. Each day, I sense I am always at the beginning of an ever-expanding process of a sense of self and expanding universe.

So when you get ready for a life change, watch out! You never know what destiny (your soul plan) has in store for you. You just may be talking to angels and all sorts of higher-realm beings changing you and your world. *Man Power God Power* is a testament to that truth.

Note: Phillip Elton Collins is a teacher, healing arts therapist, conscious channel, ex-journalist and ad man, and author/poet and cofounder of the Angel News Network in Fort Lauderdale, New York City, and Los Angeles, and The Modern Day Mystery School. His other books *Coming Home to Lemuria: An Ascension Adventure Story* (being adapted into stage and screen plays) and *Sacred Poetry & Mystical Messages, To Change the World* (116 original poems and 20 Inner Earth messages), and the HAPPINESS HANDBOOK: *Being Present Is The Present (Phrases of Presence To Set Us Free To Be... Happy* continues this story...

www.ingramcontent.com/pod-product-compliance
Lightning Source LLC
Chambersburg PA
CBHW020845090426
42736CB00008B/243